# THE CITY DOWN THE SHORE

ANTHONY
JOSEPH
MONTEDORO

authorHOUSE®

*AuthorHouse™*
*1663 Liberty Drive, Suite 200*
*Bloomington, IN 47403*
*www.authorhouse.com*
*Phone: 1-800-839-8640*

*First published by AuthorHouse 1/15/2008*

*ISBN: 978-1-4343-5534-8 (sc)*
*ISBN: 978-1-4343-5961-2 (hc)*

*Printed in the United States of America*
*Bloomington, Indiana*

*This book is printed on acid-free paper.*

Special Thanks to Professor Belinski

T.J. My favorite Editor

Nikki, and Lish


This book is dedicated to the CJPAMA

SUE

ROSE RITA

AND

JANET CEO-OIC

# TABLE OF CONTENTS

# PROLOGUE

## The Burglary

*The fifties and sixties were a time of great change in this great country. In the late sixties when the Viet Nam war was at its peak and people were protesting everything, there was turmoil in the cities all through the country. The civil rights movement was growing and there were race riots all through the United States in major cities as well as the city down the shore. By the nineteen seventies the smoldering city was beefing up its police department in an attempt to rebuild itself. Technology was developing, sirens and lollypop lights were changing to high intensity "Vis_Bar Light Sets". Saps and night sticks were changing to Taser electric stun guns and chemical mace. Officers no longer needed a ring of callbox keys as the call boxes were being replaced by portable two way radios. Here are some tales of the police officers in a shore city over the next fifteen hectic years.*

Tony walked to the big, green, cast iron box on the telephone pole; picked out a large brass skeleton key on his heavy key ring, and opened the bulky cast iron door. He picked up the phone to police headquarters and waited. The desk officer, Sergeant Harriman answered "Ya!", and Tony said," This is post 1; I will be out at Kimmouth Alley making a check." The desk sergeant said," Okay Kid." Tony hung up and closed the call box door. The men on the department had taken to calling Tony kid because he was the youngest member of the department and there were five other Tony's on the job.

The rookie officer walked up the alley, and out to the corner of Lake Avenue and Main Street. Something did not look right at the Sinclair gas station. As he checked the rear of the gas station, he noticed a crescent shaped hole in the back window, and that the window was ajar. Tony went to the front, and the iron gate was down and locked .The front was secure.

He walked over to the pay phone on the side of the gas station, and dialed "O". When the operator answered he said," This is badge number 161 please connect me to police headquarters." When Sergeant Harriman answered Tony told him what he had, and asked for backup. The sergeant said,"Listen Kid all the units are tied up at the Orchid Lounge, there's a big fight, but I will send you Bolton."

Harry Bolton was an ex marine He fought with the Fifth Marines at Iwo Jima during World War II and people said he held a strip of land on the beach for two days until his unit could form a beach head. Tony had never met him. Bolton worked burglar squad.

The young officer went back to the rear of the building and waited. Bolton came out of the night like a ghost. Tony looked, and he was just there! He said "What'cha got Kid?" Tony showed him the hole in the window; and Bolton shook his head and muttered," Sam Blackstalk." Bolton told the rookie to climb in through the window and open the back door so they could check the inside of the building.

Kid scrambled through the opened window and into the gas station. He made his way to the back door and unlocked it. Bolton was in like a cat. He was six and a half feet tall and about two hundred fifty pounds, but he walked like a leopard. He was almost fifty but was very spry and agile. The pair of officers checked the ground floor. There was no one there.

They found a burlap sack in the corner by the rear door. In the sack were some cash, and an assortment of tools from the tool boxes. Bolton looked at the goods, he shook his head. He put his hands to his mouth to form a funnel. He barked in a booming voice, "Okay Sam, I know you are here so come out and make it easy on yourself."

The officers waited a few minutes in the silence, then Bolton said," All right Kid, climb up into that loft and see what you can see." Tony went up an old rusted steel ladder and threw himself over the ledge into the loft, then he walked the area and shined his flashlight into the corners, it was very dark. All of a sudden the loft lit up. Bolton had two large car batteries with spotlights on them on the work bench aimed at the loft. This was much better, but there were stacks of old tires blocking most of the light. The back of the loft was still very dark. Bolton said. "Hey Kid, kick down some of the tire stacks so we can get some light to the back of the loft." The stacks were about five feet high and the tires were chained together. There were hand written signs on the stacks,"$2.00, $4.00 and $10.00".Tony pushed over the first stack. It fell to the concrete floor with a thud. Then he kicked over the second stack, and as it fell the officers heard a shrill scream, then a low moan. To their amazement out of the roll of tires crawled Sam Blackstalk. Bolton looked at him and said," You should have come out when I called you Sam, you could get hurt falling out of lofts like that". Then he said," Now get over there and hug the wall." Sam leaned against the wall with his hands reaching for the sky as Bolton frisked him and cuffed him. The two officers walked poor Sam to the door. Just as they got there a marked unit pulled up. Bolton stuffed Sam into the rear of the patrol car.

He came over to Tony and said, "Stay here Kid and wait for the owner. Then come to police headquarters and do the report. Leave a copy for me in my box." He then went back to the police car. He got in the front on the passenger side, and as they pulled away he opened the window and said, "Good work Kid."

When Tony got to police headquarters he began the report. It was his first investigation report. Sam had been booked, processed, and a complaint for Breaking and Entering was awaiting Tony's signature. Sam and Tony would appear before the judge in the morning, a bail would be set, and Sam would be a guest of the county at the Grey Bar Hotel until he could make bail, or go to trial.

This was the beginning of Tony's police career that lasted almost 30 years. This story will tell the tales of many police officers. Tony and how they called him "Kid" because there were so many Tony's, and he was the youngest person on the department as well as many of the officers that worked with him during this troubled time. Kid was a name of convenience that lasted Tony for many years. Over these years he worked Homicide, Street Crimes, Sex Crimes and Vice. He was a patrol supervisor, a squad leader, and a shift commander, and handled thousands more calls and witnessed many adventures.

Tony was to work fifteen years with Harry Bolton. They worked together quite often after this. Bolton died on the job just before he was to retire. He will always be remembered by those he worked with. He showed many how to live, how to be a cop and how to do police work. He was a true friend. He was a Marine. He was a "Good Cop."

Here are some of the adventures of Tony and his fellow officers during the next fifteen years.

It was about this time Richard Bergerwasser was getting out of Prison after spending twenty-five of his thirty-eight years in some sort of correctional institution.

At ten years old he had had no friends. He was being raised by his grandmother, who he thought was his mother until he was first arrested. She raised him as her son; he even called her mom. She loved him as a son and tried to give him everything she thought he needed.

Richard would skulk around the neighborhood killing bugs, pulling off their legs as they died. He tortured and killed small animals when he could get them. He set small fires anytime he had the chance and thought he could get away with it. When he was caught first committing these antisocial acts, he was ten years old. He was put away for six months in a youth correctional institution in an attempt to correct his behavior. At the reform school he was treated for psychological disorders and re-educated. When the doctors were convinced he would mend his ways, Richard was released back to his grandmother.

She was so glad to have him back she gave him a party to celebrate his return. She invited all the children in the neighborhood. No one came. Richard got so mad he ran out of the house. The first thing he did outside was kill his grandmother's cat. He hit it in the head with a hammer, then tied it to a tree and tortured it until it died. He really enjoyed the torture. It made him feel much better. He dug a hole, burned the ripped corpse, then he covered it with dirt and rocks. Over the next five years he continually got into more trouble with the violence of his acts increasing, until finally he was arrested at fifteen for burglary, and attempted rape. He received fifteen years. He was sent to a state correctional prison to serve his time. He threatened the judge and prosecutor at his sentencing. He promised to kill them and their families when he was released.

He was released in eighteen months, after he was deemed to no longer be a threat to society. The first thing he did was track down the prosecutor and kill him.

Richard broke into his home, shot him as he came home from work, then he captured his eighteen year old daughter when she came home from school. He tied her up and tortured her until she died. He found that he really loved torturing people. After she was dead, he sexually assaulted her corpse. He then waited for the prosecutor's wife to come home; he did not know she was away at her dying mother's bedside in California. This saved her life. After a long wait night fell and Richard decided to leave. He dragged the two bodies to the center of the house, soaked both with gasoline and burned the house down around them. He left with the prosecutor's gun.

He was caught quickly in just a few days, and after a short trial he was given life in prison. He was just eighteen years of age when he entered the maximum security penitentiary.

Twenty years later he was deemed safe and no longer a threat to society and so he was released from prison. At last he was free at thirty – eight years old, he vowed to himself to make up for lost time, and never return to prison.

He had decided to move to the City Down the Shore. He felt he deserved it. His mother had a house there, and he had had the best times of his life when they were there.

He had learned very much in prison. Prison can be a great school for the eager young man. He had been transformed into the perfect criminal. He would prowl the city for over eleven years and do horrible things. He would take the young lives of many runaway girls. He would select them carefully, but he would always wait until the time was right for him. There was no need to hurry, and there were more than enough girls. He would pounce on them like a catamount when the opportunity presented itself, he was merciless. He would operate silently in the night. No young girl trying to make it on her own was safe. He would love having the power of life and death over these girls. This was his passion, to injure, brutalize, and cause pain. He thought of himself as godlike, in the end he even began to believe he was a god.

# CHAPTER ONE

## The Boardwalk

The ocean water turned blood red as the Morning star rose over the eastern shore of the city. The boardwalk seemed to glow. Mike and Tony were just finishing their last check, and were waiting for a pick up to go to police headquarters to do their reports and sign out. The fight at the Jay's bar took its toll on the two young officers. They were bruised, battered, and totally spent. The hectic night was typical in the heat of July.

It had started as a normal Friday evening. Crowds pouring into the city to see the shows at the fifty some bars on the beachfront. There was a name group playing at the hall in the center of the boardwalk. People were lining up for the last show hoping to get a seat. Parents putting their children on the rides for the last time, and then they would return to their motel rooms until the next day. The usual calls to the bars for, kids complaining because they did not have enough identification to get in a bar to see a show, and for drunks fighting weakly to keep their keys as their friends tried to keep them from driving were coming in to police headquarters. Young kids were racing their hot rods on the circuit with their hopped up engines. It was rampant now. This would slow as the night got older.

Most of the early night was spent by the officers moving the crowds of kids from the corners of the intersections, and the parking

1

islands. On a given weekend night in July, as many as 100,000 people would crowd into the mile and a half strip of beachfront to walk the boardwalk, go on the amusement rides, play the games of chance, and visit the bars. The city really was hopping. The Carterette Hotel called every half hour with complaints about the kids outside who were revving their motors and laying patches of rubber showing off the power of their hot rods, and bating others into a drag race.

The young officers worked the 2200/0600 shift, and walked post 4 which consisted of the Boardwalk and amusement areas up to two blocks west. This was a long walk and the officers were backed up by two marked police cars with two men in each unit. Six officers were stationed in the area to monitor the beachfront area. The real fireworks would usually happen between 0200 and 0400 hours. The bars closed at 0300 hours and all the neighboring towns closed at 0200 hrs so all the drunks from all around would migrate if they could into town to get one last drink. They merged with the drunks already in the bars. It was rarely a smooth transition.

This night in particular was a dangerous night. A national biker gang, Devils Angels, was in town at Jays bar and had taken control of the place There were over two hundred bikers and their women in the bar. Ten members of a rival gang Bad Breed had walked into the bar, and a tense truce was in place, but it did not look like it could last as both sides kept drinking and bragging.

When Mike and Tony made their first bar check, all was quiet at Jays, but the officers hit a call box, and they let the desk sergeant know what was in the bar. This could and would become an explosive situation. Because of this, the shift commanders chose to hold the 1600/2400 shift over until 0400 and called in the 2400/0800 shift in at 2000hrs. This would give them about fifty officers on duty to handle whatever would come up.

The heavy action started around midnight with a fight at Joe Martino's Bar on Main Street. There was a knock down drag um out fight between Sanders Ervin, a local bully and Richie "Green Giant" Mack. Both fled when they heard the police cars arrive each threatening the other on their departure. The officers quickly broke up the crowd, and no arrests were made, a marked car with two officers was left at the scene just to keep it quiet, and it worked. This cut the available manpower by two.

The next incident was a blowup at Sonny's Orchid Club. This was the hottest spot on the Avenue. Everyone who was anyone was there on Friday Night. Matty Greene had caught her man at the bar with a young girl. He had told her he was too sick to go out. When he failed to answer her calls to his apartment, she went looking for him. Where better to look on Friday night than Sonny's Orchid Club.

Matty had cut the young girls breasts with a straight razor. They got the young girl to the hospital, but she was in bad shape. It took four men to subdue Matty, and pull her off the bleeding girl. Matty was taken into custody. This further reduced the available units by four much needed officers, as they were tied up to cover the situation at the Orchid Club. The officers had to clear the bar, preserve the scene for the detectives, and one officer had to go to the hospital with the slashed girl.

A fight broke out behind the Carterette Hotel between hot rod groups, but they dispersed as they heard the sirens of the police cars rushing to the scene. The sound of sirens from the responding police units can be a great weapon for the police if used properly. Another police car with two officers was left here, but they did remain available if needed. Manpower was thinning out and the bikers who monitored the police calls knew it.

By the time Jays Bar made the last call, the bikers knew that half the police were tied up, so the Devils Angels made their move. Boot Man, a particularly nasty brute, about six and half feet tall and four hundred pounds hit one of the Bad Breed members in the face with a beer mug and the bar exploded. It was like watching a scene from a Wild West movie.

The first thing to go was the mirror behind the bartender. A table was thrown into the mirror, bringing seven years of bad luck to the man who threw it. The bartender hit a panic button which sent an alarm to police headquarters and pulled a short baseball bat from under the bar. He locked the register, and backed into a corner. He hit anything that came near him. The patrons and barmaids ran out onto the sidewalk, as the two biker gangs fought it out.

When the first two police cars arrived, car 4 and car 5, they were greeted by the sight of a Bad Breed member flying through the front plate glass window and landing on the hood of car five in a shower of glass. The hood of the white police car turned red with the injured man's blood. They called for backup, went to their trunks, and began to put on their riot gear. As Officer Fred Cook bent to get out his gear a brick flew out of the bar and hit him in the head knocking him out. His partner Big Geno put up his shield and guarded his partner as the other cars and posts arrived. As Fred was coming to, Big Geno sat him in the police car and told him to wait for first aid. He formed a wedge with six other officers, and the phalanx of police officers entered the bar to stop the fight.

Then, Sergeant Bolton arrived. He gave shotguns to the next four officers responding to the fight; he ordered them to form a line. As they lined up, Sergeant Bolton called for the bikers to stop over a loud speaker and was met with a shower of beer bottles and chairs.

Sergeant Bolton ordered his officers to fire a volley from the shotguns into the line of parked bikes outside the bar, and at the explosion all the bikers froze with horror. As the mangled bikes toppled over and gasoline oozed out around them, Sergeant Bolton shouted a second order, "Stop this now or we will light up your bikes and clean up the mess after the fire department is done with the burning mess!" It was unbelievable, but the several hundred or so bikers stopped what they were doing and ran to their bikes. Sergeant Bolton and the fifteen officers watched as the bikers climbed on their bikes and sped away, most giving the finger to the cops as they fled the beachfront. The officers smiled as they watch the bikers put a half dozen mangled bikes in trunks of cars and the backs of trucks and take them away.

There was no way the few cops could stop and arrest anybody. There was far too many bikers to single out any of them. The police just picked up those who were hurt too bad to escape, and sent them to the hospital. Their names would be picked up by the detectives the next morning, and the proper complaints would be signed in the Municipal Court. It took an hour and one half, but the police finally got it sorted out. The area was finally cleared, and order restored. Jays bar was trashed. Luckily the bartender escaped unhurt. He said to the officers, "I'm quitting this place tomorrow." After boarding up the broken windows and doors he locked the door and walked to his car and headed home.

As Mike and Tony walked to their ride, they joked about the night. Mike said to Tony, "Did you see the look on those bikers faces when the Sarge ordered us to shoot their bikes." Tony laughed, "Yea, it was like we shot their mothers." Both officers chuckled, but poor Fred Cook received sixteen stitches from the brick, and he was admitted for the night because of concussion syndrome. Although most of the other officers were cut and bruised, no one else had any serious injuries.

As they were leaving Mike said, "I thought Johanna was going to meet us for breakfast." Tony replied, "I guess she left because of the fight." "Yea, but I thought she had no home." Mike responded. "Maybe she isn't a runaway" Tony answered. "Well, we'll see her tomorrow and find out." Mike said. The two young officers got into Car three and headed to police headquarters. They did not know it then, but they would never see Johanna again.

Johanna was a runaway. She was sixteen and was missing from her home in Pennsylvania for two years. Her real name was Mary Woods. She had phony identification saying that she was Johanna Stevens. It showed her to be twenty-one so she could work in the bars. She had a Social Security card she obtained with a birth certificate she got in town. Johanna Stevens was the name of a dead girl Mary had gotten off a tomb stone in the local cemetery. She had read the name in the obituary column and tracked it down in the local cemetery to make sure. The dead girl was the age she wanted to be, so she waited almost a year then she went to the local Borough Hall, and obtained a copy of the girl's birth certificate to use to get her new identification. The identification had served her well for two years. She had a driver's license too.

She was on the boardwalk when the raucous brawl started. She was sitting on a bench watching the action when Richard approached her. He offered her a beer. "Is it always like this?" Richard asked the girl. She shook her head yes as she took a beer from him. She suggested they should go on to the beach to drink them because there were so many police here. Richard agreed; she led him under the boardwalk.

It was here that Richard killed the young girl. First he punched her hard in the face stunning her. Then, he shoved a small towel into her mouth as he taped her hands behind her back. He sexually assaulted her several times for the next few hours battering and slicing her with a pocket knife as the mood struck him. Finally, when he became bored, he ended her pain and terror by slitting her throat. He pulled the gag out of her mouth so he could hear the gurgle as her life drained from her body. He had loved the sounds of death.

After the young girl had been dead for some time, Richard removed her head and put it in the plastic bag that had held the six pack of beer, and saved it for later. He took all her clothes jewelry and possessions balled them up, and put them in the bag with the head. Next he dug a shallow trough in the soft sand, and pushed the headless corpse into it. He covered it with a mound of sand. He put the plastic bag into a paper bag replacing the now empty beer bottles, and buried the bottles in the sand. Satisfied with his work, Richard turned and walked out from under the boardwalk. He started for his new home. He found he was humming a tune. He was happy when he arrived at his house.

He cleaned the head in the kitchen sink and combed the hair. He left the eyes open, he thought it was a nice touch. He wrapped it in butchers paper and then in heavy plastic wrap. He carefully put it in the freezer. Richard went upstairs to the bedroom. He bounced into bed and lay down. Yes, he thought this was the place for him. He would fix up the old house and stay here. He shut his eyes and relived the night. He saw the tears and terror in the young girls face and became aroused. After he satisfied himself, he fell off into a dreamless sleep.

# CHAPTER TWO

## The Flasher

As the outline of the black moon faded into the west side projects it was replaced by a glowing globe in the eastern sky. The 2400/0800 shift was preparing to go off and the 0800/1600 shift was finishing its briefing. The week had been a breeze so far a very quiet one indeed and the officers have had a very uneventful tour.

Dr Henry Quigly was a Psychologist. He had been working on a drug to help autistic children. He was on the brink of stabilizing the dose when the children started to exhibit unwanted complications, and when one child died, his work was halted. It was a crushing defeat that had destroyed his work for the last twenty years. He fell apart, and had a nervous breakdown. For the next ten years, he was hospitalized with acute depression. He was living with his daughter in a fine, wealthy area just next to the city. He enjoyed his daily walks, and seemed on the road to recovery. He was doing very well.

Sergeant Bolton told his men at briefing that the town next to the city had been experiencing a flasher for at least a week, and he fit the description of a suspicious man wearing a grey raincoat and a fedora hat that had been spotted in various locations of the city the day before. He said it is today's priority to locate this person, check him out, and bring him in to Detective Fowler for questioning. It would be a day to remember for the officers working the day shift.

8

Queen Bee McQuade was a small woman in stature; at less than five feet, and only seventy-five pounds, she was tiny, but she was all dynamite. Queeny, as she was called by her friends, could never be thought of as small. She certainly was no small woman when it came to her family. She had eleven children and made all of them finish high school. They all had good jobs and none of them were ever in any trouble with the police. Her man was Big Jim Jones. He was a mason and worked very hard for the local construction company. He had one flaw. It was the reason Queeny had never married him. He was a drunk. He had stopped drinking everyday ten years ago but occasionally he fell off the wagon.

Bonzoni and Big Geno were in car four and patrolling the west side. They were just preparing to go to Sonny's Honey Diner for breakfast, when a call came in to see a woman on Borden Street. When the officers arrived at the location, they were flagged down by Freeny Jackson. She told the officers she saw a suspicious looking man with a fedora hat and a long rain coat walking down the block. He had disappeared by Griffith's Laundry. Freeny said, "He would stop look around, then look up and down. He would continue for a few steps then go through the routine again." She said she had never seen him in the area before. The officers checked the area to no avail. They reported to headquarters that he was G.O.A., area checked negative, and headed back to breakfast.

Queen Bee arrived at Sonny's Honey just as Bonzoni and Big Geno were sitting back down to finish breakfast. She asked as she walked in, "Sonny did you see my worthless man Jones anywhere this morning?" Sonny replied, "No." And Queeny squinted her eyes and said, "I hope you see him before I do. You tell him to take his good for nothing ass somewhere else from now on, and that if I see him I'm gonna skin his hide!" Queen Bee turned and walked out but stopped at the officer's table, smiled sweetly and said, "Good morning gentlemen." to Big Geno and Bonzoni as she stormed out of the diner. Bonzoni looked at Big Geno and said, "I wouldn't want to be in Jones' shoes when Queeny gets a hold of him." Bonzoni nodded and smiled at the thought; the two officers finished there breakfast.

Pete and Tony were in car five and were patrolling the north section. They were told to meet Lupe Gonzales on Drummond Road.

Lupe reported a strange man in a fedora hat and a long grey raincoat standing on the corner of Drummond Road and Third Street for quite a while. Lupe said, "This guy just kept looking all around, even up in the sky and down on the ground. She added she thought he was humming or singing softly." She never saw him around this area before. The officers checked the area and they reported that the subject was G.O.A. area checked negative, and resumed patrol.

Frank and Davy were in car two in the east section. They were told to see Rose Rita Perrella. She had seen something suspicious at the bus stop. When the officers arrived, Rose reported seeing a man in a fedora hat and long grey rain coat standing across from the bus stop on Emory Avenue, and he was spinning in circles and singing. The officers checked the area for the strange man, and reported the area was checked negative, subject G.O.A.

When the call came in from the business district from Guido Fafalardi that a man in a fedora hat and long grey raincoat was standing across the street from his news stand dancing, car three was sent. Sara and Vill called in that the area was checked negative, and the subject was again G.O.A.

As the officers turned the next corner, they were looking right at the man. He was going the other way. Vill shouted, "Stop!" and the man turned around opened his coat and flashed the officers with his naked body. He stuck out his tongue and closed the long coat, as he slid around the corner and disappeared.

Vill got out of the police car and gave chase, but when he got to the corner he could not see the man anywhere. Sara called in to headquarters that they spotted the subject, but he had eluded then on Cook's Avenue; he reported that they checked the area to no avail; they would resume patrol, but stay in the area and keep an eye out for him.

Big Geno and Bonzoni were heading towards Cook's Avenue to help check the area when they got a call to go to Building Five of the City Village projects, report of a man throwing furniture off a balcony. When the officers arrived, there was Big Jim Jones throwing an armchair off the second story balcony. As they exited there police car they heard a scream and saw Big Jim fly through the air and land in a thorny bush under the balcony. They looked up to see Queeny peering over the balcony with tears in her eyes, She said, "I hope I didn't kill him I only wanted to teach him a lesson; sometimes I don't know my own strength."

What happened was two nights ago Big Jim had left after an argument and gone out on a binge. He spent the money they had saved for their youngest daughter's birthday party. When Big Jim came home he was greeted by Queeny and a rolling pin. He would never hurt Queen Bee, she was the woman he loved, but he went into a rage. He took his anger out on the furniture. He started throwing the furniture around the apartment, and as his anger increased he began throwing it out of the patio door. As he threw the new leather arm chair, Queeny decided she had had enough of this, and she had hit him in the butt with the rolling pin as he lifted the chair to throw it over the railing. It was just enough to send Big Jim over the edge of the balcony right after the chair.

Luckily he was just scratched and bruised. The bush had broken his fall. Queeny ran down and hugged the big man, and wiped a trickle of blood from his face. The two kissed and made up. Queeny turned to the officers and said, "We were just remodeling and Big Jim got a little carried away. We will clean this all up and you can just go on your way." Big Geno and Bonzoni looked at each other and returned to the police car. They radioed, "Car Four to Eight Three Seven all parties advised matter settled, and there is no cause for police action at this time."

May Bailey was having a very hard day. Her six year old son Jason had been sent home from first grade for hitting Reenie Johnson. Jason really liked Reenie, but she was talking to a boy he hated, and the boy was older and bigger than him so he hit her.

May dragged him into their house and sent him to his room. "You are grounded for the next week, boy." she shouted through the closed door, "That means no television either." Jason was asleep in his room before May could finish her threat. She smiled as she looked in and saw her angel lying there so peaceful. He was such a good boy, but what a devil he could be when he was bad, she thought as she walked outside to finish hanging out the laundry.

While May was hanging the clothes she heard singing from the alley that bordered her back yard. She looked toward the singing and saw a man in a grey raincoat and fedora hat just a few feet away staring at her singing. This startled her, she grabbed the nearest thing, which was a garden shovel for protection, and when the man opened his coat and flashed her it startled her. Reflexively she swung the shovel and hit him hard on the side of the head. He fell to the ground like a pole axed steer. May ran into the house and called the police.

Frank and Davy arrived in the alley way, and May met them there waiting near the unconscious man. She asked, "Did I kill him?" As she spoke she pointed to the man lying on the grass under the clothesline. The naked man moaned and tried to get up, but collapsed down to his knees and shook his head.

First aid arrived and looked after the man. In a few minutes he was fine, but he had received a good size bump on the side of his head. They suggested he be taken to the hospital for a checkup just in case. Davy rode with the man and Frank followed in the police car. Detective Fowler was waiting at the hospital when the ambulance arrived.

"We got the flasher." Frank radioed as he drove to the hospital. "I'll give you a 10-2 when I get to the hospital with the particulars." He finished.

Detective Fowler was waiting in the emergency room when the ambulance arrived. The head nurse recognized the man as Doctor Quigly. The doctor had been treated at the hospital before. His family was notified by Detective Fowler after a brief interrogation. No charges were brought against the doctor and he was admitted to the psychiatric ward. His medication was increased and he was stabilized. His family agreed to keep a closer eye on the doctor and they took him home. So ended the career of the flasher of the city down the shore, Dr. Quigly was never a problem again.

Richard had come to the city and settled into the summer house he and his mother shared in the good days when he was very young. It was owned by her, and she was glad to have Richard living in it. It had been vacant for twenty years. She had no use for it while Richard was in prison. She could not drive and her only way to the city down the shore was by train, and this was an unbearable trip for her without Richard. She really loved him.

Mrs. Bergerwasser had worked hard in a small office near her home in Staten Island and had saved a small trust for her adopted son Richard. She never missed a payment since his birth. Now the trust had grown into a considerable sum and Richard would receive over one thousand dollars a month from it to live on. This was a small fortune for a man in the early seventies.

Richard was not a handy person, but he could paint and clean, and within the week he had an area in the house in livable condition. The first and second floor were now fine. His next move was to check out the area. He hated people so he decided this could be done best at night.

He had found this spot on his first night on the beachfront; it was on the south side of the boardwalk. It was a perfect spot. He had met his first lover there. Below in the sand was an opening to a glorious place under the boardwalk. On the boardwalk, there was a bench, and the street light over it was out. He sat down and looked out to sea. He began to dream. He saw himself walking on the water. When he looked closer he saw he was walking on the heads of young faceless girls. Richard continued his vision. He was brought back to reality by the call of a young girl asking if he had a light for her cigarette.

Richard said, "No!" and the girl walked away, turning back to glance at him as she disappeared into the night. Richard was approached by four more girls this night, and he realized this was the spot for his new avocation. To take one of these girls would be easy. The city was filled with nameless faceless young girls from all over the rural United State. They came to this shore town to find fame and fortune, or mostly to start a new life. The runaways used phony names and had fake identification. Most of the time they moved on to a new town after a short stay and no one knew who they really were, or even that they had been there. Usually they just left and were never seen again. It was as if they never existed. These girls were the perfect victims for a crafty predator like Richard. His first girl the one he killed last week was easy. The lure of a free beer was all he needed to get her into his trap. She showed him this wonderful spot, and she became his first lover. The girls tonight were practically begging him to make them his lovers.

Richard would go home, think about this, and be ready in a few nights to continue what would turn out to be eleven years of carnage on the young runaway girls who would come to the city to find a new life. They would find only a gruesome death at Richard's hand.

At home in bed he was thinking of the head in the freezer and how rewarding it was to find his first lover. He knew that the skin would not last but he would keep the skull even if the skin rotted away, after all it was his first. He shut his eyes and saw the girl's face and savored his pleasure again as he relived her fear and dismay and the expression of hopelessness as it crossed it, and then the glory of the final release as he made her his first lover. This was true love he thought. I made her an angel. She must be an angel because she had her hell here with me he said to himself.

Only God and I can make angels he thought as he passed into a deep sleep.

# CHAPTER THREE

## The Good Son

A s the sun set over the projects in the west of the city Millie O'Mally wondered where her son Sean was. He was a good boy she thought and he never failed to come home after work without calling. She called the police department and asked for her neighbor Detective Arnold Fowler. The detective was tied up, but he told the desk officer to tell Mrs. O'Mally he would stop by in an hour on his way home. She was satisfied and went into the living room, sat down in her favorite easy chair and began to say the rosary. As she started the fifth group of ten Hail Mary's, the doorbell rang, and the kind old woman knew it would be her neighbor Detective Fowler.

She ushered the detective to the best chair in the sparsely furnished parlor and offered him something to drink. She brought out a pot of tea and some soda crackers. As Detective Fowler listened, Mrs. O'Mally began her tale. She said her son must have left for work at the High School early this morning because he did not kiss her good bye. "That is not like my Sean." the old woman told the detective. "He always kisses me good bye even if I am asleep. He comes quietly into my room and kisses me on the cheek, I always know he is there but I always pretend to be asleep . It bothers him if he thinks he has awakened me." "Did you call his job?" the detective asked. The concerned mother just shook her head no. "He does not like it when

15

I check up on him; he says it embarrasses him, and people think of him as a "Momma's Boy" when I do that."

Detective Fowler nodded as he pulled himself up from the chair. He told the worried woman that he would go to the High School in the morning and try to find out what he could about Sean. The detective said, "If Sean comes home before then, don't confront him, let him alone and just call me at work. I will come by tomorrow and see Sean and we can talk this out together."

The concerned mother smiled at the detective, thanked him for his time and courtesy, and escorted him to the door. As she watched him walk to his house next door and go inside, a small tear rolled down her cheek. Something bad had happened to her boy, she just knew it. She thought to herself that a mother could always sense when her child is in trouble, and she had that feeling now. She walked back to her chair and began another rosary, praying to God that Sean was safe. It gave her comfort. The Lord must watch over her boy when she could not she thought. She fell into an uneasy sleep praying for Sean's safe return.

Detective Fowler walked to his empty home. It was lonely since his sister had married and moved out. He missed her and her scatter brained running about. They had lived together since their mother had died seven years ago. She had been gone three months, and it seemed like three years. He opened the sandwich he had brought home for supper, took a can of beer from the fridge and sat down in front of the TV with his dinner and turned on the news. This matter puzzled him because he had known Sean all his life and knew he was totally devoted to his mother. Mrs. O'Mally had raised him alone from an infant after his father died in the war. The old woman had often worked two jobs to be able to give Sean anything he wanted. Sean often stayed with Arnold and his family when his mother was working. Arnold knew Sean would never just leave his mother without a word.

The next day was slow so Detective Fowler drove over to the school hoping to speak to Sean O'Mally or someone who had seen him. The detective went to the principal's office and there he saw Mary Beeman the school's vice principal. He always looked forward to seeing her; she was his first girlfriend back when he was in high school. She still looked as good now as she did then over fifteen years ago. "Hello Mary!" the detective roared as he walked into the room. Mary smiled and walked over to him and offered her hand as she asked, "What can I do for you today Arnold?"

"Can I speak to Sean O'Mally?" Arnold asked as he kissed her on the cheek and leaned against the counter that divided the office. She frowned as she said, "Sean has not been to work for several days. He has not called. I was going to stop by his house after work today. I did not want to call and upset his mother. The dear woman worries so about Sean as it is. Why do you ask?"

"He hasn't been home either, and his mother is worried. This is not like Sean. He is usually a very reliable and caring person, especially when his mother is involved. He would never hurt her or cause her concern." "You are right." Mary said. "This is just not like the Sean I know." Mary said with great concern, "Something must be wrong."

"If you find something out, or find Sean, please call me right away, or have Sean call me at police headquarters." the detective said as he turned to leave. He stopped and said to Mary, "You still look just as good as the day I met you Babe, I think I let a great one get away." He smiled and left the office. Mary stared after him and watched him until she lost sight of the big detective down the long corridor.

As he drove back to police headquarters Arnold thought that he might see if Mary was free for a date sometime this weekend. That would be good, he could use a night out, and Mary would be a great person to spend that night with, he always had a great time when they were dating. He climbed the stairs to the second floor of police headquarters where his office was, sat down and thought about Sean and where he could be.

The next morning he left work soon after he arrived and he went to the High School and into Mary's office. He put a bag on her desk as he shut the door and sat in the chair across from her. They both looked concerned.

"Have you seen or heard from Sean?" the detective said as he opened the bag. He took out a container of coffee, and an Italian pastry, then he pushed the bag towards Mary. He said, "Help

17

yourself." Arnold took a sip of coffee and looked down at the floor as Mary took a container of coffee out of the bag.

He looked up at Mary and said to her,"I am worried about Sean, this is not good. If something has happened to him, it will kill his poor old mother and it would be a tragedy for the community. He is so involved here with the kids." Mary nodded as she sipped her coffee and stared over the detective's head. She dropped into thought, then looked at Arnold and said, "We have to talk to his mother and find out when the last time she saw him was and start from there. I agree that something has happened to Sean, and if he needs help, we must be there to help him." Arnold smiled. He said, "I will pick you up after work and we can go talk to talk to his mother together. You may pick up on something I miss. Afterwards, we can have dinner if it's alright with you? Maybe we can get to the bottom of this tonight." "That will be fine." Mary answered.

Arnold got up, picked up his coffee, and walked out of the office. He was smiling; he was looking forward to having dinner with Mary. Mary stared after him as he left. She wondered why they had broken up after High School. She could not remember the reason. She went back to work.

Arnold left work a little early, went home showered and shaved, then he dressed in his best jacket and slacks; he left to meet Mary. The detective picked her up at the school, and the pair left together in his car. They drove to see Mrs. O'Mally. Mary had walked to work as she often did when the weather was this nice; she lived only three blocks from the school. Arnold was glad of this because he enjoyed having Mary with him.

It was eerily quiet as they waited on the porch for Mrs. O'Mally to answer the doorbell. She looked haggard as she ushered the pair into her home. She forced a brave smile and asked them to sit down and make themselves comfortable. She directed them to the parlor with a sweeping motion. They sat in two armchairs on the sides of an oval coffee table; Mrs. O'Mally sat down on the divan across from them.

The detective hated this part of his job. He was not good at delivering bad news. He looked in Mrs. O'Mally's eyes and said, "Sean has not been to school all week. When was the last time you saw him?" The anxious mother put her chin in her chest and sadly murmured, "He had lunch with me here at home Sunday after church. Then later, we went out for a movie, and Sean took me out to dinner that night. After we ate we came home. I was tired and went right to bed. Sean stayed downstairs reading. When I woke up Monday morning he was gone, I assumed to work. I haven't seen him since then and it is Wednesday evening already. A tear rolled down the worried mother's cheek.

Arnold began to gently ask Mrs. O'Mally about her son and his habits, checking on all possible places he could be. After an hour of gentile questioning the puzzled detective could get very little information that would help him find Mrs. O'Mally's missing son. He got up and shook the old woman's hand. He assured her he would fill out a missing person's report at work tomorrow, and that Sean would be found soon. He could tell his false promise did little to comfort the concerned woman. Mary got up and hugged the worried old woman and she whispered in the worried old woman's ear, "God will protect him, Sean is a good man." As the two women released their embrace, Mrs. O'Mally seemed comforted by Mary's words. She escorted the couple out the door and returned to the parlor, she sat in her favorite chair, put her head in her hands and sobbed .

Mary and Arnold quietly returned to Arnold's car, and drove away. It was several minutes before Mary asked, "What do you think?" Arnold just shrugged his shoulders. In a few minutes he offered, "It certainly is not good. When somebody goes missing the first forty-eight hours are critical. After two days, there is usually little hope of finding them, let alone finding them alive. Something bad has happened, every bone in my body feels it, but what can it be, and where is Sean? I just don't know." "Do you have any thoughts on what Mrs. O'Mally told us tonight?" Mary just shook her head no.

The two went to Dinner at the Marine Grill and had a wonderful meal. Afterwards they went for a walk on the boardwalk. When they finished the slow stroll down the boardwalk they returned to the car and Arnold took Mary home. At the door, they kissed and Mary said, "We haven't done that since the prom." Arnold smiled and replied, "It was as good now as it was then." Mary offered, "Why don't you come in? We could have a night cap or a cup of coffee and butt our heads together and see if we can solve this mystery, it's still early?" Arnold nodded and the couple walked into Mary's living room.

Mary went into the kitchen and returned with a board of assorted cheeses and some toast and roasted peppers in a pretty glass bowl. She said, "I'll be right back, I am wrestling with a cork and a bottle of wine. I am not a good wrestler." Arnold followed her into the kitchen and said, "Here let me do that." In a few minutes the couple was back in the living room sipping wine, nibbling the snacks, and discussing the problem at hand.

The next morning Arnold awoke to the smell of fresh roasted coffee. He was in a bed with pink sheets, and the smell of lilacs filled the room. It made him sneeze. He heard Mary call, and he got up and realized he was naked. He wrapped the bed sheet around his waist and looked for his underclothes. They were neatly folded on the chair in the corner of the room. He pulled them on and picked up the rest of his garments which were neatly draped over the chair, and slipped into the bathroom.

Arnold heard footsteps and turned; Mary pushed against him and kissed him full on the lips. "Good morning Arnold." she said as she prepared to kiss him again. "Good morning." Arnold mumbled through the second kiss. Mary stepped back and smiled. Arnold blushed and smiled and tried to look like he belonged here. Mary said, "Last night was the best night I have had in years. You were a perfect gentleman until the second bottle of wine, and thank God it only took two I was running low. I don't keep much wine in the house." She was smiling as she walked out of the bath room. "Breakfast is almost done; come into the kitchen when you are ready."

The table was a feast. Mary had made bacon and scrambled eggs with plenty of toast and fresh coffee. There was a bowl of sliced berries, some fresh cream in a small pitcher, and small boxes of assorted cereals. Arnold grabbed a cup of black coffee and sat down. Mary put a plate of bacon and eggs in front of him and sat down across from him with a plate of her own.

"Breakfast is the most important meal so make sure you finish it all." She chided in a mock stern voice. Mary smiled at Arnold, as she dug into her plate with fervor. Arnold followed and was surprised at how good the food was. They ate in silence. When they were done eating they got up. Mary asked if Arnold would be so kind as to drop her off at school on his way to work. Arnold smiled and nodded yes. Mary cleared the table as Arnold put on his sport jacket. The two walked out to Arnold's car and got in. At the school, Mary kissed Arnold on the cheek thanked him and got out of the car. Arnold watched her until she disappeared through the front door of the school. God I love that girl he thought as he put the car in gear, and headed for work.

Arnold could not think clearly all day. He was trying to figure out what he could about Sean's disappearance, but his mind kept returning to last night and Mary. She was some kind of girl. He could not remember why they broke up after high school, but he was beginning to realize it was one of his biggest mistakes. He filled out the necessary papers and put out a missing persons alarm on Sean, both state and local. He needed to wait a month before he could put it out nationally.

After work, he went home and called Mary. When she answered he was glad to hear her voice. He asked her if there was anything new with Sean and she told him no. They talked about their individual theories about the matter. Mary thought Sean had just decided to break out, she thought he might be out on some kind of binge, or left just to get some time alone to think things through. Arnold had more sinister thoughts about the matter, and he felt Sean had run into some kind of trouble. He believed Sean was dead or dying somewhere. Mary told him it was just the policeman in him that made him think such morbid thoughts. They made a date for Saturday night and both were happy as they hung up.

Saturday night came and still no sign of Sean. Mary and Arnold discussed the disappearance for a while, but their conversation soon turned to each other. They got to the movie theater, and opted to sit in the balcony. They felt like kids as they began necking in the back row. After the movie, the happy couple went out for a drink and late dinner. Arnold went home with Mary and went in for a nightcap.

"This is becoming habit forming, I could get used to this real easy, but it is getting late." He said as he kissed Mary on the lips. She smiled as she pulled away and said, "I kind of like having you around, too." She walked into the kitchen and returned with some coffee and cakes. "This should give you some energy; we need to talk about Sean. If what you say is true we are running out of time."

Arnold nodded and stuffed a piece of cake into his mouth. He washed it down with a sip of coffee, wiped his face with a tiny napkin that just about covered his lips and he said, "I think Sean is still around here somewhere. I seem to just feel him. Either we are just missing him, or maybe he is just hiding, I don't know but I feel he is close." "I feel it too" Mary agreed.

After an hour of bouncing theories off each other, Arnold got up. He said, "I think I need to go home and think out what we just said. Some of this could lead us to Sean." "Why don't you think it out here, then we could go to church tomorrow and let God help us put it together." Arnold smiled and followed Mary into the bedroom, this girl always had good ideas he thought as Mary pushed the bedroom door shut with her foot, and put her arms around her detective. She kissed him hard and long, and they fell into the bed.

Arnold got out of the pink bed and walked into the bathroom. Last night had been the best night of his life. Mary was some girl. He bounced into the shower, got the water just right, and broke into a happy tune as he lathered up. He heard the shower door slide open, and a fine voice join him in the singing of his song. He turned to see Mary and was startled. She put her finger to her lips in a sign of silence and then whispered, "We do have to conserve the water." It was a long enjoyable shower. Both had never been so clean as they were after this wash job. They had lovingly cleaned each other everywhere.

After breakfast, the pair went to twelve o'clock mass. As they were leaving they saw Mrs. O'Mally, and offered her a ride. She accepted, and they drove her home in silence. As she got out of the car in front of her house, she said, "Thank you very much for the ride. If you find Sean, you will tell me right away, won't you?" She left the car without hearing the answer, and walked slowly up the walk and into her house.

Arnold pulled up and into his driveway and said to Mary, "Come on in lunch is on me." Mary nodded her agreement and said, "Mrs. O'Mally is really having a hard time. She really misses her son." They got out and walked up to the side door.

Arnold stopped. He said to Mary. "Do you smell something funny?" Mary sniffed and said, "Yes it smells like something rotten." "It's not my garbage, I cleaned the cans Friday." Arnold said. Mary answered, "I think its coming from the O'Mally's house. Arnold walked over sniffed the air and said, "Yes from the cellar. We better check it out it may be a gas leak."

The pair walked to the front and climbed up the stairs to the front door. Mary knocked. Shortly Mrs. O'Mally answered the door. She smiled and ushered the couple in. "Did you find something?" the haggard woman asked with great hope. "No." Mary offered, "But we need to check your cellar, there may be a gas leak or something." The old woman motioned to a door in the hallway, "I hope it is alright," the old woman offered. "It may be locked. It's Sean's special place. He goes there when he needs to be alone. He does not want me going down there. He says the stairs are dangerous for me." Mrs. O'Mally continued, "That's okay though I have trouble with the stairs anyway, I haven't been down there in ages. Go ahead and have a look if you think there is a problem, I'm sure Sean won't mind."

Arnold stared at Mary and both seemed to think the same thing. Arnold put his hand on Mary's shoulder and said, "Why don't you and Mrs. O'Mally go in the kitchen and make some coffee, I'll go down and take a look, then I'll come back up and let you know what I find.

Nothing could have prepared Arnold for what he was to find. The naked, blackened, bloated corpse hung from a floor joist. A thick nylon cord was so tight around his neck; it seemed to be almost imbedded into the skin.

Arnold slowly backed up the stairs and closed the door. He walked into the kitchen pale as a ghost and poured a glass of water then drank it down. As the color returned to his face he said to Mary, "Why don't you and Mrs. O'Mally go over to my house for a while there are some things I need to do now, and it may be bad for you to stay here." Mary took the hint and ushered the surprised old woman out of the house and over to Arnold's.

Arnold called police headquarters and told Sergeant Griffiths what he had and asked him to hit a blotter card and have the medical examiner come to the O'Mally home. He found a bottle of whisky in the dining room and poured about three fingers of it into a glass tumbler. He drank it quickly then poured another, sat down to wait for the medical examiner.

Arnold was relived to see Dr. Maltese at the door only a few minutes after he had gotten off the phone with the desk sergeant. "What do you have Arnold?" the old doctor asked through blackened teeth clinched around a smoldering cigar butt.

"It's down the basement doc." the sick looking detective said, "It's pretty bad, it looks like a suicide, but I did not touch anything. It is all as I found it. I wanted to wait until you had a look to make sure there was no foul play." "Good work detective; I better go down and have a look." Dr. Maltese answered. The doctor opened his bag on the dining room table and took out some Vicks Vapo Rub. He smeared it under his nose, walked to the door of the cellar opened it, and went down the stairs closing the door behind him.

About an hour later, the doctor returned to the dining room and told Arnold what he had found. He said, "Arnold it is not a suicide, but an accidental death." Arnold was surprised. "How do you figure that?" he asked.

"There is no sign of foul play." The doctor said, "Plus there is a contraption, which appears to be home made that the dead man was using when he died. It is a machine used for auto erotic asphyxia, as the shrinks call it these days. It is a form of masturbation. It was made to cause a sexual release by creating a near death by strangulation situation. It is said to give the user the most potent sexual satisfaction possible when it works right. When it fails, well you see the results. It has two safety releases, but both failed. Come with me I will show you."

The pair walked down the stairs into the cellar and over to the hanging body. Arnold covered his nose and mouth with a handkerchief and looked to where the doctor pointed.

The doctor was pointing to a chain in the hand of the dead man and a cord dangling in front of the corpse. Doctor Maltese further explained, "The user sat on the contraption, and worked the pedals which slowly tightened the rope causing asphyxia by strangulation. Just before he passed out, the user would pull the chain and release the tension on the rope stopping the asphyxiation. The release failed. He could not reach the safety release, the rope in front of him, which was a second release in case the first failed, so he died of strangulation. I will have my livery people come, we will cut him down, take him to the morgue; I have already taken all the pictures I need. You can have copies for your reports if you need them, and I will perform and autopsy tomorrow, but I feel my initial findings will be correct. So you see detective this man did not try to kill himself, he died accidentally when he strangled himself because he could not operate that contraption the way he thought he could."

"Is this a common thing?" Arnold asked. "No." the doctor answered, "But this is the second one I have had this year so it may be becoming popular." The doctor shook his head as he walked to the phone.

After the body was removed, Arnold went to his house. This would be the worst part of this matter. The two people who probably cared the most for Sean O'Mally would have to be given the bad news. How could he tell Sean's poor mother. He would have to make up a story to spare the old woman grief and embarrassment he thought to himself as he entered his home.

Arnold made up a lie that Sean had fallen and broken his neck. He told the old woman that her boy felt no pain and died immediately. This seemed to give the stunned woman some comfort. Mary told Arnold that she would take Mrs. O'Mally home and spend the night with her. Arnold nodded his consent and flopped into a kitchen chair exhausted as the pair of sobbing women left his home.

In a few days, Sean was put to rest, it was a small funeral. Arnold had told Mary what really happened, and she cried; to her it was like Sean dying all over again, but after she was cried out she was able to move on.

The medical examiner had kept the particulars to a minimum in his press release, and the complete details were not released. The whole community was surprised and shocked at the young man's premature death. It is hard for a close knit community to lose a young man in his prime, especially one so involved with the community and its children. Sean would be missed.

Arnold and Mary would continue to see each other. They really enjoyed each others company. Poor Mrs. O'Mally, however, never recovered from her son's death and wasted away until she finally went to her reward about a year later.

Richard thought about the girl he had just killed. He was lying on top of her corpse. He realized he had done it wrong. He did much better with the first girl. The knife was much better. An ice pick was too fast.

The young girl had died instantly as soon as he drove the ice pick into her skull. He liked that she died, but he needed her to suffer like the first girl. He wanted to feel her pain, to drink her terror, and needed to dine on her hopelessness. The terror and hopelessness was not there in this kill. She just died. Anyone can kill; only a god does it with style he thought. If he were to become a god he would have to plan his actions during these meetings better. He needed more; he needed the death to satisfy his needs.

He dragged the corpse to the far extreme of the boardwalk and buried it in the sand. He took no trophies. All the way home he felt unsatisfied. His need was growing. But what this need was he did not know. He knew one thing; simple death did not satisfy his need. He required more, much more, and he would make sure next time he would get it.

Richard returned to the beachfront. He needed to begin his search for another lover tonight; the need he felt was compelling. Richard did not know that tonight he would meet someone that would change his outlook on how he picked his lovers. He walked to the boardwalk with his doctor's bag. He went to his killing grounds under the boardwalk, and made sure everything was in place, when he was finished he went up to his bench, sat down, and stared out to sea.

A small voice broke his concentration. He did not turn to look, he merely perked up his senses. Like a moth to the flame the young little girl approached Richard. She sat on the bench next to his and stared at him. He ignored her. Finally after some time, she asked him if he wanted to party.

Richard turned and looked at the girl. She was very young looking and scruffy. Her clothes were in poor shape and were dirty. Her coat was way too big for her, and was wrapped loosely around her skeleton like body. It had no buttons. She carried no purse. Richard thought surely that this young girl would be his lover tonight.

Susan Bakely had graduated high school in her home town in Nebraska last June. She was a pretty young girl, very smart with a bright future. She came to New Jersey to go to college. While in school she fell in with the wrong crowd and became a drug addict. She soon started missing classes and by this June she was lost. She dropped out of school and began the life of a junkie prostitute.

Over the Christmas break, the troubled young girl had gone home hoping to get help, fought with her parents, and ran away back to New Jersey. She became a Junkie prostitute because it was all she could do, and so here she was in the City Down the Shore with no money, no home, and no means to support herself but petty theft and prostitution. Things were going badly, and she was living in abandoned houses and on the beach. She was aging fast, her looks were going, she was dirty, she had been sick from the infections in her arm veins and was beginning to shoot up in her neck. Her clothes were in bad shape; her coat had no buttons, but it was long and warm. She held it closed with an old cloth belt she tied like a sash. She had not eaten regularly because she had no money for food or worse drugs. She was desperate, a typical junkie at the end of her rope.

She had seen Richard here before, and she figured on a cold lonely night like this she needed to make use of what was available. She was an expert pick pocket, and knew she could take advantage of this easy mark if she could get him right. Desperate drug addicts never make good choices.

Richard looked at the girl and said, "What did you say? I was thinking about something and did not hear you." The thin girl rolled her eyes, this is a thick one she thought as she answered, "I said would you like to party, you know like do the things you like best. I will do anything. I get one hundred dollars, and I will stay the whole night if you want." With the bad judgment of a junkie she thought that this would be an easy mark.

Richard answered, "Well I guess I am out of luck. I only have fifty dollars and I need to buy something to eat." The girl looked at him; she thought this would be a sure thing. She leaned against the railing, stared at him, and formulated this thin plan. I will offer him sex for twenty dollars, and steal the other thirty while he is coming. I will be gone before he knows what I did. She thought she had a perfect plan.

With her most seductive gaze the scruffy junkie looked at Richard and said, "I will give you a blow job for twenty dollars, but no clothes off, and then you can go get something to eat with what you have left." Richard nodded and quickly turned. As he turned he hit the girl full in the face knocking her over the railing and onto the sand.

Richard vaulted over the rail, and landed on his feet next to the stunned girl. He grabbed her by the hair and dragged her through the opening into his hell under the boardwalk.

The darkness on the beachfront was so great this night he was barely able to find the opening. Once inside, the excited psychopath pulled off her coat and was appalled by the open soars and putrid odor. Richard looked at the condition of the stunned girl's body and was angry. He flew into an uncontrollable rage and was wildly upset. .She was already dead he thought. Her arms were covered with rotting sores some oozing puss. He looked away. The abscesses sickened him. He lifted the girls head and punched her several times in the face and head knocking out all her front teeth. They spilled out of the bloody opening that had been her mouth onto the sand. Richard dragged the unconscious junkie out onto the sand, and down to the jetty. He looked out to sea, and he could barely see past the end of the jetty through the heavy fog. Richard hoisted the limp girl over his shoulder, walked to the end of the rocks, and threw the battered bloody addict into the ocean. She moaned as she bounced off the rocks and slipped into the cold, deep, choppy water. She quickly disappeared under the dark blue blanket that was the sea.

Richard stormed back toward the boardwalk, picked up the junkie's dirty coat and threw it far onto the sand. He stormed up onto the boardwalk, and made his way quickly home. He ran up the stairs and jumped into the shower clothes and all. When he was satisfied he was clean, he pulled off his clothes, threw them on the floor and took two more showers. First a hot steamy one then a cold one, like the ones he took in prison.

He went to bed and fell into a troubled sleep. A sore covered corpse was standing over him. She was smiling. Worms were crawling out of her eyes and ears. She was trying to grab him, but he was just out of reach. He awoke in a cold sweat. He was shaken from his encounter with the sickly young girl. He did not want this kind of person for one of his lovers. He had to be careful. It would not do to kill people that were already dead. He would stay away from junkies.

He tried to think of his first lover, but he could not see her face, only the worm eaten face of the junkie. He could not sleep. He got up and went to the freezer. He pulled out the head and unwrapped it. He took it upstairs and thawed it. The skin was rotting and the expression of fear was gone.

Richard removed the skin with the hair from the skull, and put them in a box of borax salt. He took out the cloudy eye balls and put them in a glass of vodka. Next he cleaned and washed the skull removing every trace of muscle and debris from it inside and out. When he was satisfied it was completely clean and totally empty he boiled it, dried it thoroughly, reattached the jaw with brass screws, and polished it with wood wax. He took this favorite trophy up to bed and caressed it in his arms. The mere touch of the polished skull put him at ease. The worm eaten face disappeared.

Richard shut his eyes and remembered the look of terror on the face of this lover, the look on her face when he had put the head in the freezer. Richard really loved that look and wished there was a way he could preserve it. He felt a calm flow over his body as he held this fine trophy He shut his eyes and stroked it gently and he relived the terror and pain he had given to this lover, and this put him at peace, and gave him renewed pleasure. He curled up around this wonderful trophy and held it tightly to his chest. Richard smiled as he fell into an easy dream filled slumber.

# CHAPTER FOUR

# The Murder

The city council had finished their weekly meeting. It was a hot summer and the chaos had started early. The powers that be in the city decided to add six new police officers. The Federal government had given them the money to add twelve after last year's riots, but the town fathers had already spent half on pork barrel favors to their political supporters. They opted to hire six. They called for a civil service test, and took the six highest scores after the list had been divided. The list was broken down into three categories: city residents, county residents, and state residents. All of the officers hired this time were local men. This was a good thing. One of the new officers was a lifeguard named John Height

Johnny had gotten the highest score. He was third in the written test but scored so high on the physical aptitude test that he moved up to number one. He was a lifeguard in town and had always dreamed of becoming a police officer. He was twenty –two years old.

When he was called and told to report for duty he was so proud he came in an hour early so he was sure to be on time for the swearing in ceremony. His mom and dad showed up just in time, and took a whole roll of pictures. He was known by everyone on the department, and went to school with some of the other officers.

After a week of working the day shift he was told to report for duty at 1600 hours; he would be assigned the 1600/2400 shift for the summer on a walking post. He would be sent to the State Police Academy in the Fall after the Summer rush.

At the same time as John was being sworn in the Milton brothers were beating up John Mayberry, who had caught them in his trailer. Mr. Mayberry was eighty –six. The two brothers beat him very badly and ransacked the trailer. All they got was six dollars in cash, a portable radio and an old Spanish American war pistol, that Mayberry had brought home with him after he left the marines. It was an old Smith and Wesson model 10 .38 cal revolver. The bluing was worn off, but the ancient pistol still functioned well, as Mr. Mayberry had kept it well oiled and in good working order. It was registered and legal. Mr. Mayberry was a law abiding man.

The Milton brothers were the reason this small neighboring township had a police department. They lived in a local trailer camp along the state highway and made their living rolling drunks and purse snatching old ladies. Once in a while they pulled a burglary like this one, when they thought the owners were unable to defend themselves. They were real punks. Tom was two years older than his brother. He was twenty and Billy was just shy of nineteen. They were biker wannabe's, but were not tough enough to join any of the gangs. They dressed like bikers. They even bragged that they were bikers, but everyone knew this was a lie. Most people just ignored them.

Tom said they should go to Newark and sell the gun. Billy disagreed. He wanted to use the gun to pull robberies. He said to his older brother," Why sell this for twenty or twenty-five dollars, when we could use it to make hundreds." Eventually Billy won the argument, and the two decided to keep the relic.

The two covered the revolver with an oil soaked rag, put it in a cigar box and sealed it with duct tape. They buried the box in back of their trailer. The two were busy for the next several weeks committing small thefts and other burglaries and soon amassed several hundred dollars.

During this time, two important things happened: Mr. Mayberry died in the hospital; he never came out of his coma. John proposed marriage to his childhood sweetheart Frances Dunn. Frankie was a tall beautiful girl; she and John had gone together since eighth grade. Frankie took a job in the local convenience store so she could save some extra money, and John continued his job as a lifeguard during the day for extra money. They planned to marry in the fall just before Johnny would leave for the Police Academy.

For most of the summer, it was hot and steamy. Things were much quieter this year then the past few years in the city. There were no major incidents, only few bar fights and one fatal accident, when a drunk hit a train, but that was it. There were no riots or social disturbances so far this summer

The first three months had gone smoothly for John. Both John and Frankie lived at home with their parents, so they were able to save most of their pay. He and Frankie had saved almost five thousand dollars, and they could not wait to wed. As Labor Day approached, both were getting nervous, but it was a good nervousness. They planned to be together for a long time. They would try to buy a house of their own as soon as they could. They were in love.

When the Milton brothers heard that Mr. Mayberry had died, the two brothers got scared. Tom wanted to dig up the gun and throw it into Shark River. Billy said no. He said he wanted to do one big job with it then they could throw it away. Billy won the argument. The two brothers went out and bought some drugs. They got high and planned the job. It would be a robbery of a convenience store.

The punks decided to steal a car, pull into a convenience store, and at midnight when the police were changing shifts they would rob the store. They would drive to the woods, ditch the car and make good their escape with the riches from the store. They figured they would get quite a haul it being Labor Day weekend. With the stolen car even if someone got the plate number it would not matter. They figured the plan fool proof. But fools rarely make fool proof plans.

On this Friday night, John was scheduled to work until midnight, but all shifts were being held over four hours. The Midnight shift would come in four hours early, and this would give them extra men for the crunch from 10:00p.m. until 3:00a.m., when the bars closed. The night was crazy. It was a full moon. There was fight after fight. Everyone was busy. There was a line at the hospital emergency room, and many people were sent to neighboring hospitals or given a number and told to wait in the waiting room.

At 11:45 p.m. that night, John asked the sergeant if he could run to the convenience store, and walk Frankie to her car. He had not had a break all night so the sergeant said, "Okay Johnny, but be quick its only going to get busier." John left police headquarters just as the Miltons were getting out of their car. He ran to the store so he could get done quickly; as he turned the corner he ran right into Tom Milton who was running out of the store. They both fell down. Billy, who had the gun panicked. He fired three shots. One of the shots hit John in the stomach knocking him flat onto his back. The two brothers ran back to the car and tried to run the fallen officer over, but he was between two parked cars and they couldn't get to him. Billy got out of the car, put the gun to John's chest and shot him twice more. Frankie hearing the shooting had run out into the parking lot only to see Billy killing John. Billy turned and shot at Frankie, but he missed. He had no more bullets so he threw the gun at the girl, and jumped into the car. The cowardly brothers sped away.

The owner of the store had called the police, and when they arrived everyone was in shock to see John lying on the ground bleeding with Frankie holding him. First aid picked up the fallen officer put a pressure bandage on his chest, attached oxygen and put him on a gurney. Frankie jumped in the ambulance with them. They sped away for the hospital radioing that they were coming in with a 99 gunshot.

John was already dead, but no one could tell Frankie. They treated him like he was still living. It was only after the emergency room doctor examined Johnny and sadly shook his head that Frankie realized the man she loved was no more.

Within seconds the whole state was looking for a white Corvair convertible with two white males inside who were armed and dangerous. Luck was with the police and against the two brothers. The police had blocked off all the main roads almost immediately. The weekend traffic was very heavy and the car was spotted stuck in traffic on a bridge. The police approached the car and the two brothers panicked, and they jumped out of the rolling car and ran in different directions. Both were caught after brief chases.

At police headquarters the two brothers were advised of their rights. Tom said," I don't know nothing about any shooting, we just stole this car." Billy did not say a word. He had defecated in his pants and asked if he could go to the men's room. When the store owner came to police headquarters he identified the two. He asked to be put in a room alone with the two of them he had some business to attend to. He was a large angry man. The officers told him no. The two were booked processed and taken to county jail in lieu of $1,000,000.00 cash bail each. They were put in segregation as cop killers and child molesters are often hurt or even killed while they are in jail.

The funeral for John was a very sad event. Most of the cops in the neighboring towns knew John, and many went to school with him. Departments sent representatives from all over the country. Even the FBI and the Secret Service came. Every State including Alaska and Hawaii were represented. A fund was started for kids of the City in John's name, but that does not ease the pain. Nothing could ever bring him back. The city would be a sad place for a very long time.

The forensics people had traced the gun beck to Mr. Mayberry. Billy's fingerprints were on the gun and in the old mans trailer. The two brothers were charged with Burglary and Felony Murder in the Mayberry case, as well as Murder of a Police Officer in the Line of Duty, Armed Robbery and Grand Theft Auto. With so many good witnesses, as well as overwhelming evidence, the two evil brothers were easily convicted.

When Frankie took the stand and identified the two men, and told how they tried to shoot her after they came back and shot Johnny, Billy jumped up and cursed her out calling her a fucking liar. The judge warned him to sit down and be quiet, and his lawyer pulled him back into his seat.

The Supreme Court had just repealed the death penalty and the Governor had commuted all sentences of criminals on death row to life in prison. The Supreme Court had upheld this so when the Milton brothers were convicted they were given three consecutive sentence's of life in prison. Even with this they would be eligible for parole in twenty years. The judge called this appalling, but his hands were tied by the Supreme Court. He felt this was not enough. The judge said at the sentencing, "This sentence is as big a crime as the murders."

Frankie burst into tears in the courtroom; Billy turned around and gave her the finger. As he started to curse at her, the Court officer knocked him out with one hard blow to the side of his head. The gallery cheered as two other officers dragged Billy's limp body out of the court room. The judge said he would not stand for cursing in his court, and thanked the court officer for acting so quickly and decisively in returning order to the court room, and left the bench. As everyone began to leave the courtroom, John's mother quietly said to Tom Milton, "You will both die screaming." Then she turned, and sadly walked away.

The Milton brothers were taken to Trenton State Prison and housed in the Vroom Building. They would complete their sentences doing hard time. Five years later Billy was raped and stabbed. He screamed and cried all the way to the medical ward, where he died of his wounds. Twenty years after his conviction Tom was granted parole. He said he did not kill the cop his brother did. The parole board believed him. Several years after his parole, while he was beating his girlfriend, she was able to castrate him with a pair if shears as he stood over her getting ready to hit her with a chair. He screamed and yelled all the way to the hospital with his severed organ in his hand. He died from loss of blood, just as the first aid got him into the emergency room.

It was just after Tom Milton had died that John's mother peacefully went to her reward. She had been sick for many years but had hung on long enough to see both men get justice for what they had done to her son.

It was a hot night, the moon was full, and it called to Richard. The lust was upon him and he knew he must heed the call. There was an unusually large amount of people around his favorite bench this night; it would be nothing more than a challenge for him. He knew he could do whatever he wanted. He was invisible, a god, and much smarter than anyone. He would be like a ghost in the night.

At about four thirty in the morning the area seemed to clear. Some people had left to go home, some for a quick snack that would begin a night of bliss, and others had to get their dates home. As Richard walked to his favorite bench he saw a young girl almost passed out on the next bench. She was leaning over almost falling off the bench. This would be too easy he laughed to himself as he sat down and watched the intoxicated girl. He had noticed her earlier at the Bootlegger Bar with two soldiers. She giggled with joy at their antics, and they plied her with drinks whenever she finished one. Now she was nearly passed out and her clothes were disheveled. It appeared they had left her. She was at Richard's mercy, and he had none.

Richard walked over to her and gently shook her. She opened one eye and groggily stared blankly at him. He said to her, "Would you like some breakfast little girl?" She smiled and answered, "I'll just eat you big man." It was the last mistake she would make in a mistake filled life. Richard sat down next to her and her head fell against his shoulder. He said, "Why don't we go down on the beach where you can lay down for a bit. We can get something to eat when you wake up." She half nodded and Richard helped the wobbly girl get up and leaned her on the railing.

Richard helped her down the stairs to the sand, then under the boardwalk. She passed out again. This is not what he wanted. He wanted her terror, her fear, and he wanted her to feel the sense of total hopelessness. Richard never gave one back so he would have to make do with this girl. He stared at the unconscious girl and decided to begin his work.

Now safely under the boardwalk, Richard ripped off the girl's clothes, she just giggled. This only infuriated him more. He tied her up with the ragged pieces of her ruined clothes and stuffed her mouth with her panties as she opened it to scream. He began to molest her roughly, but she was acting like she was enjoying it. He stood up, he wanted to scream. Instead he took out his pen knife and began cutting madly. When he calmed down, the girl was dead. It seemed like he had stabbed and cut her body in a thousand places. His shirt was covered with the girl's blood; he could not stand to have her fluids on him. He cursed her; he wished he had a bigger knife or a gun. He began to kick the corpse. Soon her body was a bruised oozing lump of flesh almost imbedded in the sand. He slit her throat to make sure she was dead, and he took no trophies. He rolled the naked, bloody corpse to the far back of the boardwalk supports and covered it with sand. The rats could have her. This was not what he needed, and now he needed it more, but the sun was rising, and he was covered with blood.

Richard came out from under the boardwalk and walked into the sea. He submerged himself in the cool surf repeatedly letting the cool ocean clean the gore and the debris of the girl from clothes and skin. After some time he returned to the beach, and he walked back to the boardwalk. He stared at the sea for about an hour, and then he headed for home.

Even with the soft morning sun he was dry by the time he reached his house. He could take no pleasure from this night. He tossed and turned all day in bed, He could not sleep; he could find no peace. The bloody corpse of his young lover taunted and cursed him in his dreams. He reached down and touched the skull under the bed. It calmed him. He shut his eyes and relaxed. He would remember the drunken girl for some time.

# CHAPTER FIVE

## The Cop Killers

The blazing sun rose in the sky like a crimson ball of fire. It signaled a hot time for all this day. Hectic turbulent times had been the norm this year and if it led to hot violence in the city, like in the last two years, the city police were in for a busy dangerous finish to the year.

The towns in the area had been warned by intelligence officers from the State Attorney General's office that there were militant groups operating in and around the state, and the word was out on the street that they planned to kill some police officers.

There was no further information at this time nor were there any details, but the information they had was considered unimpeachable. The main threats were believed to be directed at big cities and resort areas, and a major resort area was the City Down the Shore. The city had been the scene of three riots over the last five years. Add to this the fact that in the summer over one hundred thousand people visited the resort on the weekends; it was obvious that this was a perfect place for assassins to operate. They would be free to set up a base for future attacks on law enforcement personnel. The Governor decided to allow the State Police officers to patrol the beachfront areas during peak hours to help the local police departments for the remainder of the year.

The call came in a shrill yell over the car radio, Shots fired office's need assistance in the one hundred block of DeWitt Street, All units respond, Repeat, shots fired in the one hundred block of DeWitt Street all units respond officers need assistance. Tony and Lenny were on foot, but they were four blocks from DeWitt Street, they began a slow jog to the area. They could hear the shooting. They also heard police units responding from all through the city, their sirens a harsh scream in the hot Summer's evening.

The first car to arrive was Car Five with Barry Lamillo and Gary Aquirre inside. They immediately came under machine gun fire. Barry hit the brakes and both officers ducked as low as they could as the rear window, and side windows disappeared. They crawled out to the far side of the police car and tried to see the shooters. Lying in the street in front of them wedged under their patrol unit were two State Troopers. They signaled that the shots were coming from a house and garage on the west side of the street. Gary radioed the information to all the responding cars and to police headquarters.

Two of the responding cars, Car Two with J.W. and Davy, and Car Three with Bob Sara and Bobby Villa drove up Castalucci's Alley to try to flank the shooters, but the shooters had lined the narrow alley with piles of debris, and it was impassable with a police car. The Officers had to get out of the cars and try to proceed on foot. They went to the trunk and took out two shotguns and loaded them; they each took a bandoleer with twenty five additional cartridges of ammunition. The two officers proceeded up the alley on foot and they began to take fire even though they were a half a block away.

Earlier that day, six men had arrived in town. They were brought in by a girl Joanie Chesterman a cold blooded killer, who was already wanted for the death of two State Troopers earlier this year on the Turnpike. The men were escaped felons from the west coast and the Chicago area. Rahime Davis and TaJean Jones were part of the Weather Underground, Julio DiLugo and Cisco Bado were from the Mexican gang the Toro's, finally Sean McCarthy was an IRA member and his friend Sam Gronsky was an outcast from the Russian mafia, they were experts with explosives. All seven were armed and very dangerous.

They had taken up temporary residence in this vacant house, and had parked a van and a truck in the garage attached to the north side of the building. They had closed the doors tight to keep out prying eyes. They had an assortment of automatic weapons. Four Mac-10's, six m16's they had stolen from a National Guard Armory, and a dozen assorted pistols and revolvers. They also had thousands of rounds of ammunition for these weapons. They planned to ambush the first police units to patrol the area, shoot as many cops as they could and flee the area. They had safe cars in three spots in outlying towns.

The last car responding was Car four, Big Geno and Bonzoni. They had stopped to pick up Roy Mansky and John Koolman on the way. Both Koolman and Mansky grabbed shotguns from out of the trunk of Car four, and loaded them. They had them ready as they approached the ambush scene.

All of a sudden, the shooting stopped. There was an eerie quiet, which was suddenly broken by the revving of two car engines.

Two vehicles broke through the doors of the garage with a thunderous crash, first was a truck with a cab on the back, driven by Cisco, with Sean, Sam and Julio lying down in the back firing M-16's. The second was a van driven by Joanie with Rahime and TaJean shooting out the back with Mac-10's behind a steel barricade that replaced the rear doors. As they turned down the street Car four turned the corner and blocked the way. Joanie rammed the van into car four as the exiting officers dove for cover. She knocked the car out of the way, but the van stalled and steam jetted from the perforated radiator. She cursed as she tried to restart the van, but it was too badly damaged. Ray and John opened fire with the shotguns and peppered the van. They fired all six rounds from each of their guns through the windshield of the van, and reloaded as Joanie ducked for cover behind the passenger seat. The two rookies now reloaded, fired six more rounds through the opening made by the blown out windshield. They dove for cover as the truck barreled in with guns blasting from all the windows.

Cisco pulled the truck along the far side of the van and helped Joanie inside she was shot and bleeding. There was no hope for Rahime and Tajean. They were badly hit and could not make it to the door. There was no body armor on their legs and below their waist and they were badly wounded from the shotgun blasts. The five fled away in the truck leaving their wounded comrades to die in a hale of bullets.

About a mile away they pulled into a church parking lot and changed cars to a Cadillac they had stolen from a doctor's parking space at the hospital. They transferred all their weapons and ammunition to the Cadillac and slowly drove away. Sean examined Joanie and found most of her wounds were superficial. The one gunshot wound in her chest near her shoulder was hardly bleeding and it looked like the bullet passed clear through. Most of the blood came from a large cut over her eye, she received this when she crashed into the police car, and her head hit the windshield. Sean bandaged her with the first aid supplies the group had put in the safe car just in case they were hurt in the ambush, as Cisco drove them to a safe house in Camden.

At the scene of the shootout, the two troopers were shot but the wounds were not life threatening. They were lucky that the State had issued bullet proof vests to all their officers. The vests had stopped the hits in the vital areas. The troopers were taken immediately to the hospital for treatment of their injuries. Most of the city police officers were cut and bruised, but no one else was shot. That was lucky because the town did not have the money to purchase bullet proof vests for the officers, so most did not have them. There was no more fire coming from the van.

When the responding officers charged inside they found two men shot to pieces lying dead on the floor in the rear of the van. There were over one hundred bullet holes in the body of the van.

Sergeant Bolton responded to take charge of the scene. The trooper car and three of the police cars from the city were in ruins. They were shot up so badly that it was impossible to get an accurate count on how many shots hit the cars. There were twelve hundred and seventy six spent cartridges recovered by forensics in the rear bed of the van from the two Mac-10's and thirty one spent rounds from a 9mm Beretta auto pistol found on the front seat. The troopers and the responding officers were lucky, they could have been massacred. No one had any idea of the firepower these militant groups had at their disposal. The police were seriously outgunned.

41

The surrounding towns were alerted and the truck was found within an hour in a church parking lot a few miles away. It was sealed and watched until FBI forensics could get there to process it. An all points bulletin with all the necessary information was issued for the state and national wires.

This was the worst attack on police in the history of the city. When the officers approached the house, they were stopped by Sergeant Bolton. He ordered the men to secure the perimeter and called the military for a bomb squad. This was a good thing. The Marine bomb disposal unit found that the house was wired with explosive booby traps. They were disarmed by the military experts without incident. If the officers would have carelessly entered, they might have been blown to bits by the explosives, or burned up in one of the incendiary booby traps.

A new day has dawned in the City as well as the rest of the state. Police were now the target of these terrorists. The Police Departments of the state must adopt a strategy to combat this or face loosing many police officers unnecessarily.

Richard awoke to the sound of the gun battle. He wondered what it was. He was still thinking of his adventures in the city when the thought came to him that he had a tool at his mother's house that may be useful to him. He decided to make the trip up to see his mother. He would take the train.

The train pulled out of the station at about ten in the morning and by eleven he was crossing the Bay to Staten Island. The train station was over a mile from the house but Richard liked to walk, and a walk through his old hunting grounds brought back many fond memories.

What seemed like a moment was almost half an hour. Richard was so busy daydreaming that he almost walked past the old rickety house. It was clean and tidy but the cedar shingles had seen better days and the trim could use a coat of paint. Richard smiled as he walked up the driveway to the rear door. He opened it and walked inside.

The old woman at the sink slowly turned, smiled and said, "How is my good little boy doing? Sit down I was just making lunch." She motioned to a chair across from her at the small kitchen table. Richard silently walked over to the chair and sat down. The old woman reached into the pantry pulled a single piece of Silver Cup bread out of the package, smeared some peanut butter on it folded it and handed it to her son. Richard took it and put it in his coat pocket.

She turned back to the sink and continued what she was doing when Richard had walked in. Richard walked over to the oak key board and took an old rusted cast iron skeleton key off its peg and walked outside to the old four car garage behind the house in the rear of the backyard.

He put the rusted key in an old pad lock, turned it, and the ancient lock fell open. Richard walked inside. He looked around, walked over to the workbench, and stopped, as he searched the cabinets and shelves he thought to himself what a great time he could have if he had a place like this under the boardwalk. He walked to the corner and pulled down an old five pound Maxwell House Coffee can from the top shelf. He reached inside and pulled out an old oily rag. The rag was wrapped around an old Harrington and Richardson nine shot .22 cal revolver. He wiped off the oil, and the gun was like new.

This was one of his favorite trophies. He had stolen it from the prosecutor's house after he had killed him and his daughter. What great memories it brought back to Richard. How he made the badly wounded man watch as he sexually assaulted and killed his daughter, and how he had burned the house down around them. Could they have still been alive when the house burned down? The thought pleased him. The only thing that ruined it a little was the man's wife was out of town and had escaped his vengeance.

He pulled out an old box of q-tip swabs from out of the workbench draw took some out and began cleaning the gun He cleaned the cylinder and barrel and wiped the outside surface of the revolver; when he was done, it looked like a new gun. He stuck it inside his belt against the small of his back and left the garage. He relocked the door and walked into the old house, putting the key back on the board in the same spot, then he walked into the parlor.

The old woman was sitting in her rocking chair rocking slowly. Richard walked over, smiled at her, kissed her on the cheek, then he taped her hands and feet to the arms and legs of the chair with duct tape and kissed her on the cheek again and said "This should keep you busy for a while." She looked at him and said, "You are such a good boy Richard." Richard shook his head and walked out of the house back to the train station. He found he was whistling as he walked. It felt good to be home. While waiting for the train, he put his hands in his coat pockets and felt something. He pulled out the half of peanut butter sandwich. He grinned and ate it.

When Richard got home, he went upstairs and put his new tool in the dresser. He looked around and found what he needed. It was a driver's license for Mr. Robert Baker. He was a forty-five year old man but the description fit Richard perfectly. The license was good for one more year, and was just what Richard needed. He put it in his wallet and walked out of the house. He made his way to Kissling Sporting Goods and bought a brick of .22 long rifle ammunition.

He used the driver's license for identification without incident and walked back home. On the way, he stopped at the donut shop, bought a black coffee and a plain donut to go, and continued his walk home. All this walking had made him hungry.

He vaulted up the stairs to the porch, unlocked the door and flew into the house. Calm down he thought as he made his way to the kitchen. After eating the donut and drinking the coffee, he took the bag of ammunition up to the bedroom, took the brick of .22 long rifle ammunition out of the bag, and put the box on the dresser. He opened the top drawer and took out the revolver and placed it next to the box of bullets. He stared at them and smiled.

The brick contained ten small boxes each of which contained fifty rounds. Five hundred rounds, he thought to himself that should last me forever. He opened the brick, and then the first small box of fifty. Richard loaded the revolver carefully. He snapped the top lock action closed. He went to the bathroom filled the sink with water, wrapped a towel around the barrel and fired once. The bullet hit the water with a thud, and the towel started to burn. Richard dipped it into the sink and it hissed as the flames died out. The pistol worked. He dried off the gun, threw the towel into the bathtub, and went back to the dresser, and he carefully placed  the gun in the drawer next to the box of bullets. He closed the dresser drawer, walked over to the bed and lay down.

After a short nap, Richard went back to the dresser drawer, and took out the revolver. He examined it, took it back to the bed with him, and slid the revolver under the pillow. The revolver needed to be tested better he thought. If he was to use it as a tool for his work, he must know how it sounds outside, what it will do to a lover, and how it can best be used as a tool. He would think on this. He closed his eyes and slipped back into a restful sleep. He felt powerful with the gun under his pillow.

# CHAPTER SIX

## The Gypsy

Madam Moira was almost put in a trance watching the sea from the bench on the boardwalk as she planned her activities for the next few days. Sitting on the bench and watching the ocean soothed her and allowed her to put aside the troubles that plagued her and concentrate on business. Her business was surviving by her wits. She was an expert in the gypsy arts of conniving and deception.

Being a gypsy is sometimes a hard life. Being the Princess of the gypsy's is a full time job. Planning séances, doing readings, and completing astrological charts are among the legal jobs. Setting up scams, devising frauds, and setting up suckers for a big score are among the illegal jobs. Getting bail and run-a-way money for those wanted for more serious offenses are at best difficult. When you have been Princess for over twenty years, it begins to take its toll. Madam Moira was tired of life on the move and figured that she needed one last big score so she could retire and pass the leader role to her granddaughter Maria. She came out of her trance, stopped staring at the horizon, and left her perch on the wooden bench. She stood for a moment to get her wits, and walked back to her stall on the boardwalk. She was refreshed.

Gene Nunzio was getting ready to retire at the end of this tour. He would leave on vacation and retire when the vacation was finished

He was not retiring because he wished to retire, Gene would stay a cop until he died if he had a choice. He was retiring because he would be sixty five in three weeks and would be made to retire because of state law. He had been a police officer for forty-three years. He was finishing up his last tour today on the day shift. As he was patrolling his zone, a call came in to check out a suspicious vehicle in his area. He found the vehicle parked on Cook's Avenue, and when he got out to check it out four young subjects ran from the car and fled in four different directions.

In his frustration, he ran back to his police car. As he got in he saw three of the men ride by him in the opposite direction in another car. He immediately got the plate number and description of the car. He began to put the information out to all the other police cars and units on duty. In his excitement, Gene had trouble with the phonetic alphabet and the car description and plate number came out, "Blue 1965 Chevy four door with three male subjects, plate number 1 2 3 A-Atlantic X-X-ray Y- uh, Y – da, Y - um, Y - Wyoming." Well the car was eventually located behind the Grand Union abandoned, and with the radio missing. It, as well as the first car, had been stolen from a neighboring town. But as his forty-three year police career was coming to an end, and after all those years of good police work, Gene would always be fondly remembered by the officers that worked with him as Y-Wyoming Gene.

This last big score was at her door step. Mrs. Roisa from Allentown was the widow of a wealthy surgeon. He had left her millions in securities, and three large estates one in New Jersey, a second in California, and a huge ranch in Hawaii. The land alone was worth almost one hundred million dollars. The trust funds he left seemed a bottomless pit of money. She would make the perfect victim.

Her granddaughter Bonnie just dropped out of college, and she was living in sin with a man over twice her age. This was the favorite child of her favorite child and Mrs. Roisa was heartbroken. Mrs. Roisa had decided that if she could talk with her husband he would advise as to her what she must do.

After several sessions with Madam Moira, and a full astrological profile Mrs. Roisa was finally able to communicate with her long dead husband, who spoke through the medium Madam Moira. The

Madam advised Mrs. Roisa that her husband would get in touch with her personally. Several days later Mrs. Roisa received a letter from France addressed to her. It was signed Boinky Roisa. This was a secret name only she and her late husband shared. She was sure it was from him. He told her to give $1,000,000.00 to the Madam. She in turn would distribute it to a designated charity. Helping the poor was a sure way to begin the remedy for this problem with their granddaughter. After this was done she would receive another letter from her husband on what to do to further help Bonnie.

This was very comforting to Mrs. Roisa. She ran into trouble when she approached the family lawyer Mr. Carton with the proposition. Being a protective and suspicious man, he suspected that the wife of his best friend was being scammed. He promptly referred the matter to the police. He went to see Detective Captain Talon. The Captain took the basic information, and designated the matter to Detective Sergeant Berg to be handled by his best men. Detectives Arnold Fowler and Johnny Moose were given the case. They had been involved with Madam Moira and her confidence scams many times over the years, and they were familiar with her devious plots, but this scam was the biggest that had come to their attention. Because it would involve some multinational negotiable securities, the F.B.I was notified and asked to assist in the matter. Agent Campo and Agent Guida were assigned to assist the city detectives in their investigation.

It was decided that $1,000,000.00 in negotiable securities would be secretly marked, and given to Madam Moira. The marking would make them identifiable as evidence for the court case, and the registration numbers of all the bonds were recorded. This made them transferable but recognizable for any legal action later. It also made them traceable in case the con artists got away. The F.B.I could send out alarms to the international banking community to prevent them from being easily cashed.

These things would be unknown to the gypsies until they tried to liquidate the securities. Then the F.B.I. would be called in by the bank or institution, and take the possessors into custody, if the money was being used other than for the charity. The scam called for the securities to be given to Madam Moira to be cashed in for a certified check that would be turned over to the Salvation Army to be used in their general fund for the local poor.

At the bank, Madam Moira pulled the old pigeon drop and switched the brief cases. She gave the Bank worthless securities that had been printed to simulate the real ones, and made off with the genuine ones, as the bank and Mrs. Roisa counted the forged ones.

The Gypsy Queen was arrested in Newark Airport after attempting to cash one at the International Bank to give her some liquid walking around money. She had a one way ticket to London in her pocketbook. She originally planned to drive to Montreal first, meet her accomplices, and then fly to Paris with them where they would split the proceeds.

The plot failed when Madam Moira got greedy. The original plan may have worked because there was no way to guard the whole Canadian border, but her greed led her to make a bad choice, and in trying to cut out her partners, she had made a mistake in judgment that made it possible for the authorities to apprehend her.. The Canadian authorities had not been notified because no one knew that was their destination, and they may have been able to safely cash the securities in Canada if the gypsy's acted quickly as soon as the securities arrived.

Arnold and Johnny drove to the airport and picked up the Gypsy Queen at the federal holding facility outside the airport, and they brought her back to the city, booked, and processed her. The securities were taken as evidence, photographed and returned to the family lawyer Mr. Carton. A small portion of the securities were held in case the matter went to trial.

Madam Moira was held on Two Million Dollars Bail and after a long trial was convicted of Fraud and Grand Larceny. Because of her past record she was sentenced to thirty years to life.

Madam Moira was able to retire, knowing she would be well taken care of by the State of New Jersey for the rest of her life. Mrs. Roisa donated $1,000,000.00 to the Salvation Army through Mr. Carton and was happy she could complete her husband's wishes; but she never heard from him again.

Detective Fowler picked Mary up from school after he got off from work. He said "I am sorry I am late, but do I have a great story to tell you." Mary answered. "I hope it is a happy one. After the shoot out the other day I worry every time you go to work. I still think about poor Sean. It makes me cry to think of such a nice man dying such a horrible death. I need a real good nice story to ease my mind." The couple drove the rest of the way to Arnold's house in silence.

When they were comfortable with a couple of cool beers, and some chips and salsa Arnold told Mary the story. It amused her. They chatted about the greed and the brazen way the gypsies carried on their scams. Mary told Arnold that she believed that the Gypsies were so successful because most people were so greedy that they would do dumb things if they thought they were getting over on someone. "You can't con an honest man." Mary said. Arnold laughed at the cynical attitude his girl had. By the time Arnold finished his tale it was early evening and the pair decided to go out for dinner.

Richard gazed out at the ocean and began to fall under its spell. He entered a dream like state. He saw all of his lovers and relived their terrible deaths. He enjoyed again the pleasure they each had given him with their tormented struggles, and their painful deaths. When he returned to his senses he found he was grinning.

He had a painful experience with a drunken girl a few weeks ago and took no pleasure from her death. Within the week he had another innocent young girl, and she more than made up for the drunk. She cried and begged him for her life, and when he started cutting her, she urinated on herself. He found this amusing, and it aroused him. He raped her as she was dying, her painful death only magnifying his pleasure. The terror and the tears were getting better each time. He really loved his lovers. He had just finished visiting her again. She was beginning to smell and he knew he would have to do something with her soon.

Richard loved to visit his lovers for as long as possible after he had his way with them. He soon found that they rotted quickly unless he preserved them a little. He found that if he gutted his lovers, and buried them in the sand, they would last for a while. He would dispose of the entrails off the jetty or in the alleys and dumpsters on the way home. He would throw the organs into the sea for the creatures that dwelled in the depths to come and consume them, or leave them to the creatures that lived in the alleys, and stalked the night like him. Sometimes when he would take them home with him he would brazenly drop them off in people's garbage or an apartment complex's dumpster that he passed on the way home.

By preserving these corpses, he could visit them many times and also still use the killing grounds he was familiar with in the future. He could lay with them and do what ever he wished. Many times the remains were washed out to sea by the high rip tides that washed the shore of this city, or the frequent storms and hurricanes that visited the city especially in late summer and early fall. If the odor became too foul, he would move them to a deeper pit or the very extreme back of the boardwalk. Here they would disappear, probably eaten by the vermin that made this area their home.

He really enjoyed his lovers and yearned to keep them and their memory close, or at least something of them he could use to bring back to him the misery and horror he had caused these poor girls as he took from them all they had and all they would ever have.

Over the years he would collect and save eyes, teeth, scalps, and when possible complete heads. He would bring these trophies home and prepare them in his own special way, so they would be at his disposal when he needed them.

This was becoming a fine place for him to live. He could never run out of lovers. They were the lost souls, the dregs of society that were ignored by their families. They had been forced to strike out on their own to try to make a life for themselves. Once they met Richard, all they would make was their death, and it would be sure and painful. There was no one to miss them, no one to mourn them, only Richard to love them in his sick and perverted way.

Sometimes, especially in the winter, a lover could last for a whole month. This pleased Richard. He became attached to this area of the boardwalk. The bench above became his personal spot. The sandy dungeon that was the guts of the boardwalk became his love nest where he would do fatal unspeakable things to his innocent young lovers.

Richard returned from his journey and stood up. The glow of the morning sun was peaking over the horizon. He lasciviously stretched and began his trek home. He took no lover this night, but he had no need. He could choose his person, time and place because there was no end to the number of girls in the area trying to leave an unhappy past and find a better future. There were no time constraints; he could act as often or as little as he liked. There was only that forceful calling that came upon him every so often, usually during the full moon. This he could not resist.

He looked down the dark lonely boardwalk and saw at least four young girls wandering aimlessly back and fourth along the railing. They could all be lovers for him. It was like they were beckoning for his love. Tonight however he was not in the mood for love. He felt good and it made him feel powerful knowing he did not have to have a lover every time he went out.

When he arrived home, he made some coffee, took a slice of Silver Cup bread, and covered it with peanut butter; he folded it and ate it. He took a sip of the coffee then took the remainder with him to bed.

He thought to himself as he settled down for a restful sleep, its good to be a god. He put down his empty coffee cup, and turned on his side. Subconsciously he reached under the bed and touched the polished skull. It soothed his soul and comforted him. He curled up in a fetal position and fell into a deep sleep with his arm hanging off the bed and touching the skull. He dreamt.

# CHAPTER SEVEN

## The Axeman

The moon was hidden behind a curtain of dark clouds. The stars were also invisible behind this curtain; the night was as dark as the bottom of the deepest ocean. Tony was walking post one alone, but this was not unusual on a cold winter night. The workload was light, and the patrol units kept a watch for all the post men.

Tony had made his first check of post one, and all was secure. He was making his way to the callbox when he heard a distant thump. When he got to the call box, he checked in with Sergeant Harriman and told him all was secure, but he heard a suspicious thumping sound somewhere on Kimmouth Alley and he was going to look around to see what it was. Sergeant Harriman told him to be careful, and he would alert the patrols to head into the area in case Tony needed backup; and for them to listen for strange thumping sounds when they were in the area. Tony resumed patrol.

It seemed to him that he heard the pounding loudest when he was in the alleys so he decided to start at the east end of the business district and walk the alleys until he could zero in on the sound.

Just as he was finishing his last sweep, he heard the pounding as loud as he ever heard it. It was coming from above. Tony went to the fire escape in the rear of the Diamond King Jewelry store and climbed to the roof. It was the tallest building on the block, and he would be able to see the rooftops for two blocks from there.

When Tony reached the top the sound was much clearer. He looked towards it and saw a shape on the roof of the House Finance Building swinging a sledge hammer or something like a sledge hammer and hitting the side of the building next to it. He quietly climbed from rooftop to rooftop until he was next to the roof where the man was. He looked over the façade and saw Odie McDowell slamming a pick axe against the side wall. He had made very good progress and was about a foot into the cement side of the adjoining building. Tony ducked down and walked to the roof edge, He jumped to a nearby telephone pole and climbed down. The roof Odie was on was only four or five feet off the ground so Tony walked over to it, slid a garbage can against the wall and climbed up onto it. He stood up, pulled out his revolver and ordered Odie to stop and drop the axe.

Odie turned with surprise raised the axe and thought about charging Tony. The sight of the drawn gun changed his mind. He dropped the axe put his hands in the air and said to Tony, "Okay Officer you got me, but how you gonna come up and get me? When you put your gun away to climb up I'm gonna get away." "No your not." Tony answered, "I'll just shoot you a couple of times and say you tried to hit me with that axe. Who's going to believe a burglar on a roof with an axe over a cop anyway." Odie thought a minute and answered, "Okay you win just put down that gun and don't get too trigger happy. I will come along peacefully." Tony ordered, "Then lay down on the roof face down and put your hands behind your head." Odie reluctantly did as he was told. Tony quickly pulled himself up on the roof with the gun lying on the roof just between his hands in case Odie changed his mind.

Once on the roof, Tony put his knee in the center of Odie's back and began to cuff him. He could only get the cuffs on one wrist, he could not force the other wrist closer to the other arm with one hand. Tony barked, "Damn it Odie Put your hands closer." That's as far as I can go man." Odie replied.

Tony had no choice; he had to put his gun away so he could use both hands. He wrenched Odie's one arm hard in a hammer lock putting his full weight against the struggling felon, and holstered his gun. When Odie felt Tony's two hands on his back, he knew that the gun was in its holster, and he tried to get up so he could break free and get away. He began bucking like a bronco, but after a fierce but brief tussle Tony was able to get the two wrists cuffed, and Odie stopped his struggle. Tony then picked up the axe, and helped Odie up and walked him to the edge of the roof.

At the roof's edge Odie looked down and said, "You got to undo my hands so I don't get hurt, I could die from a fall this high." Tony laughed. He threw the axe onto the alleyway then turned to Odie put his arm inside his arm and said, "We jump on three: one, two, three." The two men vaulted off the low roof and onto the alley's pebble filled macadam. Tony was able to break the landing with his hand, but he was not strong enough to hold Odie up, and the burglar scrapped his face on the pavement. He got up and told Tony,"Look what you did to me you tried to kill me, I'm going to tell the judge first thing tomorrow what you did. You're in trouble now boy." Tony casually replied, "You do what ever you have to do it doesn't scare me. You're caught and you are going to jail, and that's a fact Jack."

Tony pulled the burglar to his feet and walked him the four blocks to police Headquarters. At police headquarters Odie complained to Sergeant Harriman about his treatment, The good sergeant looked at him with a glare that would melt the coldest ice and said, "You're lucky it was this rookie and not me that caught you on that rooftop with that axe. I would have busted a cap in your good for nothing ass and thrown you off the roof. If you lived I would have arrested you for burglary, if you died oh well."

When Judge Bianco called Odie's case in court the next day, Odie asked the judge if he could make a statement. Judge Bianco said, "It say's here that the officer arrested you on the roof of the House Finance Bank with an axe trying to break into the building next to it. Anything you say will be held against you and remember you will be under oath. What could you possibly want to say that will help your case? Bailiff, swear him in."

Odie stated after he was sworn in, "Well Your Honor that cop just climbed up on the roof, put me in handcuffs, and pushed me off the roof. Look what he did to my head." Odie pointed to the scrape on the side of his forehead. "He tried to kill me your honor. I was just trying to find a private place to go to the bathroom. The pick axe is my work tool. I go to work early in the morning and need to have my tool with me. That cop is just a mean man, and he should be put in jail for what he did."

Judge Bianco creased his eyes till they were barely slits. He stared at Odie for what seemed like an eternity. Then he calmly answered the burglar's query with these words. "You are to be taken to the county jail where you will serve six months for contempt of court for telling such an outright lie to this court under oath, and insulting my intelligence. You will be fined $250.00. You will also be held on $200,000.00 bail for the attempted burglary of the bank, resisting arrest, and possession of burglary tools. You will be confined in the county jail to await trial on those charges pending your indictment. You might consider using the six months to try and concoct a better story, or you just may get many years of hard time at the State Prison if you base your defense on a lie like the one you just told to this court. "

Odie's jaw dropped and the garrulous burglar was left speechless as Smokey the Bailiff walked him back to the holding area. A short burst of laughter came from the court gallery, but the judge banged his gavel and called for order and silenced the onlookers. Even the other prisoners giggled at Odie as he was cuffed and put in his seat. As Nancy Mauro called the next case she smiled to herself, she loved working for this judge she thought, but she would hate to have to appear before him.

Richard was still thinking about the girl a few months ago. She was a horror. She was dirty, filthy, a diseased junkie whore. He would have been in deep trouble if he caught some disease from her. She was a drunk and used drugs intravenously. He stared at the waves breaking on the shore, and he noticed a cloth rag that looked like the girls coat was still out in the sand half buried. He gazed at it and went into a trance.

When he was in prison, he had tried marijuana and it was alright but the other stuff, well it was just too hard to control. He saw many a prisoner die from an overdose of heroin, and flip out on too much cocaine or speed. He stayed away from that stuff. He never saw anyone rot away like the young girl did. And now, he was glad he had chosen to abstain. Maybe if he got some marijuana it would help calm him down and give him more control. He would have to check around for a connection.

Richard was directed to a biker named Bobby; he made arrangements to look over his stuff. After the meeting he left for home with two items. He had a nickel bag of marijuana and some new stuff. It was called LSD. It was a piece of blotter paper with decals of Mickey Mouse on it, one per inch it was wrapped in cellophane. Bobby told him to just bite off one or two squares of the paper and chew them. Soon, he would be flying; Bobby left with the admonition, "Be careful man this is strong shit." Richard could not wait to try this stuff.

At home, Richard rolled a small reefer and smoked it. When he felt he was relaxed, he lay down in bed and bit off two squares of Mickey Mouse and chewed them. He waited and nothing happened. He smiled to himself and fell asleep. What a dream he had. All the girls that were his lovers were running around taunting him to catch them. Just as he was about to grab one, she would turn into the rotting junkie girl, and spin around to chase him. He tried to wake up but found he was awake.

His lovers had found him; the girls were here in his house. He had to hide. He ran to the cellar and hid in one of the dark corners.

He was shaking. He stayed there for the rest of the day. He swore he could hear the girls running upstairs looking for him.

When he felt safe, he went upstairs. It was daytime. It was night when he had taken the LSD. He went out to the local convenience store and bought the newspaper; he found two days had passed since he had chewed the Mickey Mouse blotter pieces. Richard shook his several times to make sure he was reading the date right. Boy that was some strong shit he thought as he walked back home.

# CHAPTER EIGHT

## The Laborer

The sky was dark there was no light. Clouds had blocked the full moon and the stars, but its call was still on the lunatics. The city streets were lit only by the streetlights, and many of them were covered by fog. When the bars closed and their lights went out, the city became dark and still. On nights like this it is so dark it seems like the city dies, only to be resurrected when the sun arises again in the morning and scorches it back to life. True to the full moon, this night had been a busy night.

Matt Clakley was a mason's laborer. He once told the police sergeant while he was being booked, "I was born from labor, I labored all my life, and I will die laboring." It was a simple theory, and seemed to fit Matt's life. He worked hard all week carrying block, and he drank hard all weekend. He was a mild mannered man of tall thin stature, but he was as strong as the walls he helped build. He was not a bellicose man, but he never turned down a good scuffle as he came to call the many fights he engaged in, especially when he was drunk.

On this night, he was put out of the Orchid Bar, and he was angry. He wanted back in, and the bouncers would not let him back. The owner called the police, and they responded in force when they heard it was Matt. He could be a handful. Davy and J.W. were the first to arrive. Both had gone to school with Matt, at least for as long as Matt went to school. They knew him well. He knew and respected the two officers, but when he was in a stubborn mood he was unpredictable. Davy and J.W. talked him into getting in the police car, and they took him to his sister's house. They helped him inside, into a large easy chair, warned him to sleep it off, and they left.

Tony was just about to get some coffee, and he told Pete to pull in at the Coffee Break Diner, when a call blasted over the radio, "All cars respond to Joe Martino's Bar report Sanders Ervin is cleaning out the bar. When the officers arrived, they were greeted by the sight of Sanders outside the bar swinging a chair to hold off about fifteen angry patrons. He had a knife protruding from his leg and one sticking out of his back by his shoulder, but he was still game. He was swinging the chair like Babe Ruth hitting his 714 home runs.

J.W. threw his nightstick low into Sanders' feet, and Pete threw one at his head. Both clubs found their mark and then Frank, Vill, and all the other officers jumped on Sanders as he fell. Sanders screamed as the officers pounced on him, and bit Davy on the hand so deep Davy would need stitches to close the wound. But Sanders was loosing blood, and he was weakening quickly. Tony was able to get cuffs on his hands, and Sara grabbed his legs, and held them in the air.

Sanders yelled, "All right I give up!" then he passed out. The officers picked him up and put him on a gurney, that the First aid had wheeled to the fight as soon as they arrived. Sanders arms and legs were cuffed to the gurney rails and Tony and Davy went to the emergency room with the prisoner.

At the hospital Davy was treated, stitched up, and released for the bite, but Sanders would have to be admitted. He had lost a dangerous amount of blood. Tony called the desk, and the sergeant told him to stay at the hospital until relieved. J.W. came and picked up Davy.

It seems Sanders had beaten his girlfriend Joanie Morgan, and her six brothers found him at Martino's; as they argued with Sanders the fight broke out. Six against one would usually be a sure thing, but not when the one was Sanders Ervin. He was a true psychopath, and when he went off the deep end a whole gang would have trouble holding him. The loss of blood slowed him down or the officers might not have been able to hold him without breaking something on him, and that was usually the case when Sanders was arrested. He had many broken bones in his body from previous arrests.

The night was turning into one of those rare ones when you would be lucky to get through it in one piece. All the cars shot to their favorite diners to get some coffee to go, because they knew they would be hopping tonight.

This night Matt could not let it rest. He returned to the bar, and a huge brawl broke out. Right in the middle of it was Matt Clakley. The whole shift responded to the affray, and Matt was arrested along with several other participants. The police wagon was called, and about fifteen people were brought to police headquarters and booked. Most were released on summonses, the others posted bail. All that was left was Matt. The judge would not allow him to be released on a R.O.R. and set a ten thousand dollar bail. He would allow a ten percent posting in cash, but Matt could not come up with that kind of money. So he was sent to city yard for the rest of the weekend. He would be brought back before the judge on Monday.

This infuriated Matt. He wanted out; it was not to be. He was placed in a cell in the city yard by J.W. and Davy. J.W. admonished, "Be good for the rest of the weekend, and I will speak to the judge for you on Monday, okay?" Matt just nodded his head, lied down on the concrete bench, and tried to go to sleep.

In six hours, Matt decided he had enough of this concrete box of a jail. He called to Reggie the jailer, and he begged him to let him out. He yelled, "Hey preacher man save my soul and let me go home." Reggie Walker the jailer was a local minister of the "Bring your own chair on Sunday" Baptist Church. He supplemented his income as a preacher by guarding the jail in city yard at night. It was really the Second Baptist Church, but the parish was very poor and services were held in an empty abandoned store. There was a handwritten sign in the front window that read "Bring your own chair on Sunday.", so all the people in the area called it the "Bring your own chair on Sunday." church. Reggie came to the cell and decided that Matt could use a dose of the "Good Book" so be began to read him passages from the Bible. This calmed the unhappy Matt for a while, but it just did not last. When Matt realized Reggie was not going to let him out, he went back to sleep.

After a nap, Matt awoke and began thinking about being in jail for quite some time; Matt decided he had to leave. He began working on the commode. He pulled it and pushed it, kicked it and it loosened. He kept it up for several hours, until he pulled it from the floor. When Reggie made his last check of the morning, he saw the commode was loose, and all that was holding it down was a small water feed pipe. He called the desk sergeant to inform him. The shift was changing so Sergeant Harriman just passed on the information to the next shift and Sergeant Griffiths.

Reggie left and was replaced by Peabo Plummer. He advised Peabo about Matt and the condition of the commode. Peabo just laughed and said, "He will regret that when he has to take a shit!" Reggie just shook his head, and headed for his church.

Sergeant Griffiths sent Geno DeSanno and PuttPutt Petraglia two special officers over to city yard to check on Matt. He told them to call headquarters to let him know what was going on. Peabo and Matt were not the best of friends. They had once courted the same girl. Peabo had won out. Matt began to argue with him so Peabo ate Matt's breakfast instead of giving it to him, and then he began taunting him. That was it Matt had had enough. He pulled and pulled and finally broke the commode loose from its plumbing. Water squirted out of the feed pipe and flowed out under the cell door. Matt picked up the commode and began battering the door with it.

When Peabo saw the water flowing out of the cell block, and heard the noise of the commode battering the cell door, he got scared, locked the security door, and called the desk sergeant.

As Geno DeSanno and Putt Putt Petraglia walked into the call block, they were greeted by the sight of Matt out of the cell in the security corridor pounding the security door with the commode. They called for backup, and Sergeant Griffiths sent Big Geno and Bonzoni. The officers arrived, and they knew immediately that they were in for a tussle. Bonzoni called to Matt, "Okay Matt drop the commode, and stand up against the wall." Matt replied, "Kiss my ass, and if you open the door I'll kick all of yours." Big Geno walked to the door, and took out his mace. He sprayed Matt through the bars.

At first, it had no affect except to make him more enraged. But soon the strength of the gas took its toll on Matt, and he staggered over to the far corner, and he began to cry.

At this the officers opened the door, and charged Matt. There was a brief struggle, but soon Matt was handcuffed and shackled. The officers brought him out, and cuffed him to the back of a garbage truck parked in the city yard. Then, they sprayed him with water to wash the mace off him. Matt thanked them. He had regained his senses. Big Geno called Sergeant Griffiths. The angry sergeant told the officer to come to headquarters, pick up a commitment, and take Matt to county Jail.

The cellblock in city yard was a wreck. Matt's cell was totally useless. Water was dripping from the lead pipe to the commode, it had to be capped off, so two city workers were called from the beachfront to do the job. The steel door was bent beyond repair, and the commode was chipped and cracked. The other six cells were useable, but the whole place was flooded from the leaking pipe. The commode would never be used as a commode again all it would be good for was a boat anchor. The whole place stunk of mace for a week. Matt was taken to county jail until Monday. The judge fined him $200.00 and ordered he make restitution for the cell he damaged. It was just another busy weekend in the city down the shore.

Richard was pleased the night was gloriously dark. The bars had closed by the time he got to his bench, and the street light was still out over the bench. He loved the dark. He walked down onto the beach, and went under the boardwalk. His bag was undisturbed in its usual spot, the hammer was in just the right spot for a quick kill if he needed it, and the box cutters were still in the strategic spots he placed them. He was happy, everything was perfect.

When he arrived back to his bench, a little girl was sitting there. He said, "Hello." She did not answer. He sat down on the far end of the bench and gazed at the ocean. A blood red light shot across the sky. He turned toward the girl and found she was staring at him. She said, "I'm sorry, Hello, sir my name is Arletta, my friends call me Letti. I didn't mean to be rude when you said hello, I just have things on my mind." Richard said he understood and asked her if she would like some coffee. She said, "No.", and they both returned to looking out at the horizon.

Shortly, the young girl got up and walked down onto the sand. Richard followed; he then turned, and went under the boardwalk. For some reason the innocent girl turned, and followed him through the dark hole in the wall. It was like she was drawn to follow him. Richard would think of it later as his godly power that drew her in. She walked by Richard, and was dead before she took two more steps. The hammer blow was so brutal that the head of the hammer jammed in the back of her skull, and the force of her fall pulled the implement from Richard's hand as the dead girl tumbled to the sand.

Richard quickly cut away her clothes. He had his way with her corpse, then he laid on the still warm body and fell asleep. He awoke in a few hours refreshed. He gutted her corpse, put the entrails into a plastic bag; he pulled the hammer from the ruined skull , and then he pushed Letti's corpse to the far rear of the boardwalk, and into a shallow trench. He covered it with the dry fine sand. He put her clothing in a paper bag, and started to leave. No, he thought, he needed something more. He returned to the girl and pried open her mouth. He took as many teeth as he could knock out with the hammer; he put them in his pocket. Richard recovered her head with the cool loose sand, and walked out onto the beach satisfied. He began the walk home.

He threw the clothes in a dumpster on the way home, and left the entrails in an alley for the cats and stray dogs to dine on. As he left the alley to resume his trek home, he began whistling a song. This town was a really great place to live he thought, unless you were a young runaway girl. He joked to himself; then it was a great place to die. He walked home happily.

# CHAPTER NINE

## The Avenue

The steaming sun was hidden by the thick grey clouds that shielded it from view as it traveled across the sky this summer day. The late sixties and early seventies had been times of turmoil and great change throughout the country. Our culture was changing very quickly. There were riots and demonstrations in all the cities, and the city down the shore was no different.

Tony and Lenny were rookies. They had spent a month with the different training officers on the day shift and Midnight shift. They had made their first arrests; now they were ready to begin their first full post assignment.

Two more diverse people could not be found for a team. Both were rookies, but that is where the similarity ended. Tony was a local boy who grew up in the projects of this fine city. He was barely old enough to be a police officer. His uncles still had stores on the "Avenue" and everyone there knew him. Lenny was much older at thirty-four he only had one more year before he would be too old to be a police officer. He had always failed the physical because of his poor eyesight, but the State had revised its standards, and he finally passed the eye exam and became a police officer. Their first post was to walk the "Avenue" it was called post 5&6. A second round of riots had hit the city earlier that summer, the city still had not recovered from the first ones several years ago, but things on the street were getting back to normal. At least the businesses on the "Avenue" were beginning to recover a bit.

The Avenue was the heart of the city. The beachfront and the business district were the pretty parts, but the action was on the Avenue. It was what kept the city alive. As long as the Avenue kept pumping, the city would be okay. There was no place like it in the world. It was special.

There was no other street like this in the area, it was a piece of New York City on the shore. There was a bar every 100 feet and a different store every fifty feet. There were two or three tenements above every bar and store. To the south, north, and east were projects that bordered the street. One quarter of the people in the town lived around the Avenue. Hundreds lived in the street. The Avenue was a twenty-four hour deal; it never shut down.

Lenny and Tony began their walk up the street. Tony told Lenny not to walk to close to the street. Lenny said, "why not?" Tony answered something might fall on you. Lenny laughed. He said, "Kid I grew up in Washington D.C., which makes this place look really tame. I know how to walk down a street. Tony said okay and they continued their walk. In the 900 Block, they encountered Ms. Anderson, she was a local old maid, but that wasn't her fault. She would go after any man she saw. She had been doing this for thirty years, and although some of the shine had worn off the paint, the motor was still running strong.

She said, "Tony my boy who is this lovely man you are walking with, I have never seen him before." Tony laughed and said, "This is my partner Lenny we will be out here for a while." Ms. Anderson looked Lenny up and down like she was checking out a side of beef, and said, as she walked into her doorway, "Why don't you gentlemen stop up for coffee later, I have some fine blueberry cobbler I just made. Tony knows the way." As they walked away Lenny poked Tony and told him not to do him any more favors with any other of his acquaintances. Tony just smiled.

As they got into the next block, the two officers heard a "yo" coming from above, and as they looked up the contents of a chamber pot dropped out of the sky. Tony was out of the way he was in near the buildings and under the overhangs, but Lenny was by the curb, he took most of the debris as it splattered over his bright new uniform, and did it stink. Tony tried to keep from laughing, but he ended up braying like a donkey. The two rookies stopped at the next callbox, which was on the corner, and when Lenny told Sergeant Harriman what happened, the sergeant laughed and bellowed, "Okay rookie I'll send a car to pick you up. Go home and change, it will be your dinner brake." Lenny stuttered, "O o o okay sergeant." and hung up the phone.

He was really steaming. When car five came to pick him up, and Big Geno made Lenny ride in the back, he even put the prisoner shield up Lenny was really ripe.

Tony continued up the street, and went to visit his uncle at Eddie's Market. On the way, he stopped at Big Bo's Rib Shack and picked up two of Big Bo's famous sausage sandwiches. It was a thick southern type pork sausage fried with peppers and onions in an Italian role with Bo's secret hot sauce. It was a heart attack on a bun, but it tasted great.

Tony entered his Uncle Eddie's store, put the sandwiches on the counter, and called police headquarters on the phone behind it. Tony told Sergeant Harriman he was out for dinner at Eddie's Market.

Uncle Eddie looked at the counter and said to Tony, "You going to eat both those sandwiches kiddo?" Tony answered, "No I bought one for my favorite uncle." With that Eddie said "Go to the ice box and get me a Hires root beer, and get your self something." Eddie had opened this store in 1945 when he came home from the war. He had worked this store for over twenty-five years. Tony had often helped his uncle at the store in the past. His uncle took the root beer, placed it on the counter, he put the sandwich to his mouth. He looked seriously at Tony and said, "Don't you tell your Aunt Fannie I had one of these if she finds out she'll kill me. I'm supposed to be on a strict diet."

Outside Sadie Johnson was arguing with her boyfriend Tyrell Simmons. She wanted to go shopping, and he wanted money so he could go out with the guys. The noise was drawing a crowd so Tony went outside, and told the couple to take the argument off the street. Tyrell looked at Tony and said, "Hrumpf" and walked away.

Sadie said, "Thank you Officer Tony, you look real fine in your new uniform." This was the first time any person had called him officer, and Tony liked the way it sounded.

In about an hour and one half, Lenny was back, and the two continued on their post inspection. It was a routine night some other small disputes on the street, but nothing serious. Then around ten that night, the peace was shattered by a blast from the siren.

Lenny and Tony knew what that meant so they hit the call box on the corner of the 1200 block of the Avenue. Sgt Harriman told Lenny that there was a report of a woman screaming in one of the apartments of the Harris apartment building in the 1500 block of the Avenue. The building had been burned during the recent riots, and it was supposed to be vacant; so he advised them to be careful, and let him know right away what they had. The rookies closed the call box, and went off to see what they could find.

As they were arriving, they could hear the screams. Mrs. Harris the land lady of the front building said the screams were coming from the next building in the rear; the burned out Harris Apartments. It was a vacant building, and she was afraid to go back and see what was causing the noise. The two rookies walked to the side of the building crouched low and turned on their flashlights. They carefully walked through the alcove of the half gutted apartment house into the rear of the apartment building complex. In the rear they saw a half burned building apart from the main building. It was badly, burned but the frame was still standing; it was a left over from the riots. From the second floor, they could hear moaning, and an occasional scream. As they climbed the stairs both were very careful to watch where they stepped. The floor was not too sturdy. It creaked loudly in protest as they crept their way up the stairs. Burned out buildings could be a dangerous death trap for the unwary. The officers carefully made their way to the top of the stairs, and what they saw surprised and shocked them both.

Lying on the floor naked from the waist down was Lucky Mattee a local prostitute. Her legs were covered in blood and water. She was having a baby. Tony had never seen anything like this before, and neither had Lenny. Lenny quickly said, "I am going to hit a box, and get us some first aid you stay here and help Lucky." Lenny ran down the stairs leaving Tony who stood frozen staring at Lucky.

Between moans Lucky said to Tony, "Don't just stand there kid give me a hand the baby's coming." Tony slowly walked over and said, "Just wait ma'm the first aid will be right here." Lucky replied, "You tell him to wait he's half out already. Now grab his arms and pull." As Tony came closer, the screaming infant squirted out, and into Tony's arms. The rookie just looked at the baby all bloody and screaming, He froze like a statue. Lucky got up, and walked over to Tony and the baby just as the first aid arrived. She said to Tony,"Is this your first one kid?" Tony just nodded his head, and stared at the crying infant he was holding. "Well this is my seventh" Lucky stated, "and let me tell ya, it don't get no easier,"

The first aid men took the baby from Tony, wrapped it in a towel, then put Lucky on a gurney gave her the baby. They put the afterbirth on Lucky's belly, and took them both down to the ambulance, and off to the hospital. Tony was covered with blood, but he felt good. It was time to go off duty anyway.

By the time he got back to headquarters, everyone was waiting for Dr. Tony. They all razzed him for the rest of the night while he was completing his reports. As he was getting into his car to drive home, Sergeant Harriman came over to him. He looked the rookie in the eye and said, "Ya know Kid, now you're a real cop." Over the next twenty-five years, Tony was to help deliver eight more babies. It is something one never gets used to. It is an amazing thing to behold, and it always seems like it is the first.

Richard had just left the Bootlegger Bar, and decided to walk home along the boardwalk. He walked up to the rail, and looked out over the waves. A voice asked from behind him, "I can make you happy tonight mister." and he turned to see a young girl behind him. She said, "For ten dollars we can go under the boardwalk." Richard said, "Okay." He paid the girl with a twenty dollar bill and told her to keep the change. She smiled and hugged him vigorously. The couple walked down the stairs and onto the beach then through a small hole that led under the boardwalk.

The young girl knelt down and started to undo Richards pants. He kicked her hard; it knocked the breath out of her; she fell into the soft sand. In an instant Richard was on top of her. He grabbed her throat with his hands and she screamed, but no sound came out of her gaping mouth only a muffled gasp. The young girl struggled to free herself, and found she was fighting for her life. In a minute, it was over, but not before the girl had taken gouges out of Richards back with her finger nails. He had planned to choke her until she passed out, and torture her for as long as he could until she died. He had lost control and strangled her quickly because of the girl's fierce struggle and the way she had injured him. His back seemed on fire from the deep gouges made by the girl as she fought for her life; his shirt was even ripped. Now he was mad. No one had ever drawn his blood before.

He kicked and pounded the corpse until he was spent. Then he pulled a small knife out of his pocket and began cutting her. This made him feel better. He got up, took back his twenty dollars from the mangled girls remains. It was stained with the dead girls blood. He licked it and smiled. He dragged the corpse to the back of the boardwalk, covered it, and left. He made his way home.

He went up to the bath room, and when he looked at his back he was mad. He would have to find a better way to do his work. He did not like being injured but he loved when his lovers struggled.

Richard enjoyed his lovers much too much to ever stop. He would never let one of his lovers hurt him again. He promised himself this.

He would think up a plan to do it better next time. He went to the freezer and took out the scalp of his first lover. He put the cool trophy over his head and went to bed. It calmed him; he fell into a dreamy sleep. He saw this girl he had loved so well, and heard her muffled screams. He reached under the bed and touched her skull he became excited. The memories of her torment brought him pleasure .After he relieved himself, he fell into a dream filled sleep. He relived all the good times he had with his lovers, and enjoyed again the pleasure they had given to him. He felt he was a truly lucky man. He would wake up refreshed and renewed.

# CHAPTER TEN

## The Smurf's

This cool fall night the sliver glow of the moon was peaking through the clouds that once were a Hurricane in the tropics. This would become known as the night the Smurf's sunk the Coast Guard.

In the seventies, there was a cartoon called "The Smurf's". It was about a group of funny little men with white shirts and blue pants. When the 1600/2400 shift of the police department got off duty, they usually went out for a drink. They were not allowed to drink in uniform. They did not want to go home to change, and return to the beachfront again just to go out. It became popular for the officers to just take off their uniform shirts and their gun belts, lock them in their car trunks, then go out in their blue pants and their tee shirts. One observant bar maid had said they looked like Smurf's. Soon others picked up the nickname and it traveled from bar to bar. The name stuck. From that time on when the off duty cops were out on the town, the word would go around that, "The Smurf's were out".

On this particular occasion, it was Tony the Kid's twenty-fifth birthday. Tony was not a regular drinker, but on his birthdays, he made up for his abstinence. He could put them down with the best. His fellow officers decided to give him a party. This was the plan for this night. The whole shift would meet at the Quack Bar. They would start there and go where the whim of the night took them. If things went right, they might even convince Tony to mud wrestle the big blond in the topless bar down the street. There were ten bars in walking distance as the Quack was centrally located in the beachfront. This would be a great night all the officers thought as they began the party.

The guys decided to get Tony as drunk as possible as soon as possible. In this condition, he would be putty in their hands. They wanted to take advantage of this new fad called mud wrestling, and the goal of the Smurf's this night would see if they could get Tony drunk enough to try it out.

It was this night that sparked Mike's greatest invention. He invented a drink that came to be known as a Smurf. It was a shot of 151 proof rum, a shot of Blue Chartreuse, and some Bell's lime juice. It was blue and looked like the stripe on the Smurf's pants. It kicked like a mule. It did not take many to put one in the mood. This became the signature drink for this group.

When Tony arrived, a Smurf was waiting for him. The pool table was racked and ready for a game. The party had officially begun. Pool playing, joking and drinking was making the night speed by. Red the bartender wanted to close early as there was little business except for the Smurf's. So Mike and Tony moved the party to the Pony Bar. Tony was still sober enough to know he wanted no part of the mud wrestling the big blond, at least not yet

The Pony bar was on the opposite corner and was a real hot spot. Butch and Peety were at the door. When the Smurf's arrived and Mike told them it was Tony's twenty-fifth birthday, Butch told the bartender "Wolfman" that the first round was on him. Wolfie smiled and started to prepare the drinks. The guys went in, and sat in the corner. They continued the celebration. A bar maid Stacy, everybody's favorite, asked Tony to dance. Stacy was the dream girl of all the young men that patronized the bar. Stacy had the face of an angel, the body of a movie star, and the brain of a cucumber. She was the most beautiful girl in the club, about 5 feet 8 inches tall and built perfectly. She was as dumb as a hammer, but was a really nice person. She was just the perfect girl.

With the coaxing of the gang, Tony ambled out on the crowded dance floor with Stacy and began a jerking dance. They got into the rhythm; soon they were doing the bump, and other steps. After the dance, Tony went back to his stool and sat down to the cat calls of the Smurf's; Stacy went back to work. Slowly, the Smurf's left to go home. They realized Tony would never be convinced to try to mud wrestle the blond. Now only Mike and Tony were left. Tony had been able to outlast his comrades and escape the fate of mud wrestling.

Sixteen Coast Guard cadets had come to the Pony bar this weekend to celebrate their graduation from their last week in training. When they saw Tony dance with Stacy, they all asked her to dance. She said she was not allowed to dance while she was working. She told them that Tony was a friend, and her boss had made an exception He had okayed it because Tony was a very good customer, and it was his twenty-fifth birthday.

The Coast Guard would not take no for an answer. They badgered her for the rest of the night, and were finally asked to leave by the management. Reluctantly, they left at the threat of police action. Peety and Butch escorted them out, and Wolfman the bartender stayed at the door to make sure that they stayed out. The Coast Guard remained outside the bar on the sidewalk, shouting insults into the bar every time the door opened. They were disgruntled and acting like a small mob.

They told Peety and Butch they would be waiting for them when the bar closed. As was customary Tony and Mike stayed until closing. Then they began to leave. When they walked out they saw six of the Coast Guard guys threatening Peety and Butch. They went over to Peety and Butch's side with Wolfman, One of the Coast Guard cadets tried to hit Wolfman. He missed and Mike decked the Coast Guard guy; all hell broke loose.

Tony and Mike got back to back, just like they were trained to do on the job, and they hit anything that moved toward them. Peety and Butch did the same. Wolfman was big and mean enough to hold his own. In a matter of minutes there were Coast Guard cadets all over the side walk. Some were moaning some were bleeding, others were out cold. Some of the Smurf's pulled up in a big white van, and they pulled Tony, Mike, Wolfman, Peety and Butch inside and sped away, just before the sirens and police cars rounded the corner. The sidewalk was full of moaning and bleeding Coast Guard cadets. They were checked out by the officers responding, and all of them got up and moved away, none were hurt deeper than their pride. No one was arrested and all were allowed to leave. Some went to the hospital on their own for treatment of cuts and bruises.

The next day a Coast Guard Commander Payne came to police Headquarters to complain that a mob of police had beaten up his men. He said it was a gang of cops celebrating somebody's birthday. After listening to the complaint, Chief Tillman felt he knew who at least one of the cops was. He said he would look into the matter. The Commander said that the chief should be ashamed at the way his men acted, and that they all should be fired. The Commander left and said he would return at the end of the week to check on the progress of the investigation into this matter. He said he wanted the names of all the police involved, and he expected complaints to be signed. Chief Tillman did not like the Coast Guard. He had been a Marine in WWII and considered the Coast Guard a collection of rich boys, and draft dodgers. He liked Commander Payne even less, but he had his duty to perform no matter how distasteful it was.

Chief Tillman told Sgt Proud that when Tony the Kid got to work he was to report to his office at once.

When Tony entered Chief Tillman's office, he was told to sit down. The Chief said, "I know everything. Now I want to know the name of every cop involved, then I want to hear your side. Spit it out, and it better be good. We got sixteen injured Coast Guard men to account for". Just as Tony was starting to give his account, there was a knock at the chief's door. It was Mike. He said, "When I heard you were bringing in Tony I had to come; I was there too". The Chief said, "Alright sit down. I want the names of all the cops that were with you there." Tony said, "It was just me and Mike". Mike shook his head in agreement. It was true only the two of them. They knew that Peety, Butch and Wolfman were there, but since they were not cops why mention their names.

The chief said, "You mean to tell me you two kicked the shit out of sixteen Coast Guard Brats". The officers just nodded yes. Tony said, "We did not know how many there were; we were a little under the weather; we just hit everyone who tried to hit us." The two officers both insisted it was just the two of them. A check of the rumor mill by the chief confirmed what the two young officers had said before they entered his office, but he wanted to make sure of it before he acted further.

With this Chief Tillman stood up, slammed his hands down on his desk with a thunderous clap, and told the young officers, "I will deal with you two later. This kind of common brawling will not be tolerated on this department at any time. Get briefed, and hit the bricks." The chief decided he would discipline them later. When they left, the angry Chief looked out the window with a great grin on his face. The ex-marine hated the Coast Guard. During WWII he thought of them as rich pretty boys using their family's connections to stay out of the real fighting services. He often said they were without the guts to fight for their country. He was wrong of course they did their share in the fighting, as did all the military during the war. They certainly did their part and incurred their losses, but the chief was a Marine. He had Marine Corps pride, the Marines thought all other soldiers were second rate compared to them. It was part of their indoctrination. He could not help but feel some joy in what these two young officers had done; he thought he would have done the same twenty years ago.

The old chief calmed himself, sat down, and dialed Commander Payne. After a brief run around customary with the military, the Commander answered. The chief asked him if the cadets could describe the officers involved. Commander Payne answered, "They could only describe two, but I want the names of all the officers involved." The chief answered, "They can only describe two because there were only two officers involved". "That can't be", ranted Commander Payne, "no two police officers could rout sixteen of the Coast Guard's finest". Chief Tillman was smiling when he replied, "Maybe your finest aren't so fine. I really think this could be quite embarrassing for the Coast Guard, and their trainers. You might consider letting this matter drop. I mean when your superiors hear how your men acted, and how they were bested and all?" The chief let the question hang in the air.

Commander Payne sputtered on the other end of the line, and stammered, "May..may..maybe you're right , but you make sure you tell your men that that type of barbaric behavior will not be tolerated in the future." With this Chief Tillman said, "Commander , if you have any other problems I can ever help you with, feel free to call me". Then he hung up with a huge smile on his face.

Later that week, the Chief met with Tony and Mike and admonished them. He had waited several days because he felt it was good for them to stew a little. He told Tony that he was banned from celebrating his birthday in town again. He told both officers that they represented the department, and should conduct themselves honorably, and properly at all times. Then he walked away smiling. He was proud of these guys. They admitted what they had done, and they had done it well. They told the truth, and were willing to take the consequences.

So, this became the night the Smurf's sunk the Coast Guard in the city down the shore.

Richard was really having a good time in the city down the shore. There was an unlimited number of potential lovers arriving every day. They were just waiting to be selected by him for the honor of being one of his eternal loves. He must now perfect his craft. He hated to leave the wonderful tortured bodies. He must find a way to keep them near him, or at least parts of them.

He must find a place to keep them so he could visit them when he needed. They meant so much to him. They were his trophies.

He also needed to find a way to extend their suffering. They seemed to die so quickly. He loved the tears, and the look of sheer terror in their eyes. It made him want to kill them over and over again. He just could not get enough. He would have to plan more thoughtfully, be more thorough in his preparations, and be careful when executing his desires. He thought about eating parts of them, but he decided against that. Most of all, he must learn to control his temper. This would be the hardest, all his life he had been getting into trouble because he was unable to control himself.

Richard needed to think. He went down the cellar, and pulled a polished skull out of a gym bag. It was one of his favorite lovers. That is how he thought of his victims as his lovers because their suffering and deaths gave him such pleasure. He remembered them all even though he did not even know some of their names. As he stroked the skull, he heard the screams and saw the terror in the young girls eyes; the look of total despair. He became aroused. After he satisfied himself, he began to concoct a plan. He would think about it, perfect it, and use it in all dates with his lovers until it failed him.

He believed he made the perfect plan, and he used these rules:

    a. He would never begin until he was calm.
    b. He would be patient because he had all the time in the world.
    c. He would carefully confine his assaults to limited areas on the victims.

He could be patient and selective when choosing a lover, because there were so many lovers waiting for his touch. He would never run out; they renewed every day. Runaways always ended up in this city down the shore.

He went to the boardwalk that night to visit his special place. As he was going down to the beach, a young girl walked over to him, opened her blouse and propositioned him. She asked for twenty dollars. He told her he only had ten. She accepted, and he handed her the money. She told him they should go somewhere private. Richard suggested under the boardwalk. She agreed. He pointed to the hole that led to his special spot; the foolish young girl went in. The smell choked her, and as she turned to protest and ask to select a new spot Richard hit her with the hammer. She was fast and dodged the blow, but the blow glanced off her head and broke her collar bone. The second blow knocked her out. When she came to she was tied to a support beam naked. Her chest hurt and when she looked down she saw her collar bone protruding below her neck, and she fainted.

Richard revived her carefully, and began to make thin cuts in her chest with a box cutter. He licked the blood from her wounds, and the tears from her cheeks and eyes, as the suffering girl strained to scream through the duct tape over her lips.

One of her legs came free, and she kicked out hard. She caught Richard in the stomach knocking the wind from him causing him to drop his box cutter and fall to his knees. He looked up in a rage, took out a straight razor, and slit the girls stomach from her crotch to her breastbone. The girl died quickly.

Richard was mad, but he enjoyed the feisty ones. He left her taped to the post, and cleaned up the mess. Then he cut her down and buried her in a shallow furrow he made in the sand. He took the gore to the jetty, and threw it to the sea creatures. He left for home. This was getting too easy. These girls were practically begging to become his lover. He looked at the ten dollar bill he had taken back from the corpse; it had some blood on it. The blood was dried; it looked like a black smear across Hamilton's face. He kissed the stain, and when he got home he put the blood stained ten dollar bill in a small picture frame he had found in the living room closet. He put the frame on top of the television set and stared at it. He liked it; it added a nice touch to the room's furnishings he thought.

# CHAPTER ELEVEN

## The Stabbing

Joe Carbona was the son of Italian emigrants. He was born in Salerno Italy, and came here with his parents when he was two. He went to catholic school but did not do well. His parents died in a car accident when he was eleven. A friend of the family Frances Fafalardi took him in and raised him. He had no mind for learning. Joe was a problem in school, when he went to school.

Frances tried as hard as she could to raise him right, but Joe was a handful for two parents, he was just beyond her ability. He loved her dearly, and would try to do anything for her. Because of this, and because she loved him so, she would give him anything he wanted whenever she could afford to. She did as much as she could for the boy. She cared for him like he was her blood son.

Joe would walk the streets at night looking for easy money. At twelve he rolled his first drunk. By sixteen, he was the leader of a street gang, and they did small time burglaries and robberies. He came to the attention of the local crime boss, and so he picked up odd jobs for the local mob. Joe was a strong leader, and he was a brutal bully. Joe looked like a forties movie star called Taj Sabu so his friends gave him this as his street name. He was not a smart man, but he was ruthless, cunning, and powerfully built. He was a man who knew how to follow orders and keep his mouth shut. He had no conscience and would do anything his boss told him to do quickly and thoroughly. His boss considered him a good man to have around. His enemies as well as his boss's enemies considered him a man to be feared.

Joe would do anything if he could make money at it, sell drugs, rough people up, extort money, commit vandalisms, even murder was something he would consider doing, but all these acts he thought of as jobs, and they all had a price. He soon became the favorite of the local crime lord. It was only a natural progression that he became a personal enforcer for the local mob boss Carmine "Babe" Petraglia. Joe would report directly to one of Babe's consigliore, Corrado Russomano or Pasquale Lombardo.

He found he was very good at this job. He enjoyed his work. If you caused trouble or had trouble paying your bills to the bookies or loan sharks in the city, Corrado "Big Pussy" Russomano or Pasquale "The Plumber" Lombardo sent Taj Sabu to see you. The situation was either corrected immediately, or it disappeared. One way or the other a satisfactory solution was always the result of the visit.

This pleased the top boss very much. It made Taj Sabu a wealthy man, and a respected man amongst his peers. He became a man of honor. This honor meant more to him than his life. He could tolerate no challenges to his principles. They may not be holy codes, but they were the codes that he swore to, and they would be the codes he would die for.

If Taj Sabu had a flaw, it was his fondness for very young, very pretty girls. He consumed them two and three at a time. This was overlooked for a while, but Taj Sabu was now in his late forties and many nights he was making a fool of himself. None of his associates would say this to his face, but many said it behind his back. The bosses did not care as long as it did not affect his work; it didn't.

Vinny "Bag Of Donuts" Perrelli and Giuseppi "Joe Shoes" Montecalvo decided to check out the Giulio's Dance Palace, a new Go Go bar in the city's beachfront. They asked Taj Sabu to come along, and he readily accepted. There would be plenty of young girls dancing in the cages, and on the dance floor. It should be a good time for all.

For most of the night the three were at the side bar surrounded by young girls. Taj Sabu in particular was with two of the club dancers. He was shoving ten dollar bills down their bikini's and buying them overpriced drinks. As the bar began to close, the three men made offers to the girls to go home with them. One of the girls took offense. She told her boyfriend, one of the bouncers of the club.

This was a big mistake. When the young man, who was a college football  player and a bully himself, confronted Taj Sabu he was surprised when Taj Sabu just pushed him aside and told him to mind his own fucking business.

The boy made the big mistake even bigger. He grabbed Taj Sabu by the shoulders, and pushed him against the wall. Taj Sabu pushed out, and the young bouncer felt a soft pressure against his chest. When he looked down he saw a knife handle sticking out of his chest, and his shirt turning red from the blood. He passed out immediately.

Taj Sabu looked down at the bleeding youth, kicked him in the head, and grinned. Vinny "Bag of Donuts" and Joe "Shoes" grabbed Taj Sabu by the arms, and the two quickly walked the laughing man to their car. The two stuffed him inside and quickly left the area.

Tony and Mike were the first officers to arrive at the scene, they were across the street on the boardwalk when the call came in over the radio. They radioed police headquarters to send an ambulance to the bar, they had a possible code 99. Mike began to stop the bleeding with direct pressure as Tony controlled the curious crowd.

First aid arrived, hooked up a respirator, and sped away with the youth to the hospital. Davy and J.W. followed the ambulance in the police car. If the bouncer regained consciousness they needed to talk with him. If he died they needed to call in the State forensics unit. Sgt. Bolton stayed at the scene, and secured it with Tony and Mike until the detectives arrived.

Within two hours, detective Fowler, and the officers had it all sorted out. The bouncer was okay. He had a deep puncture wound, but it missed his lung, and it did not collapse, there were no major arteries or veins damaged. At the hospital the doctors easily stopped the bleeding, and several stitches closed the wound. The strength of the youth prevented any complications; the bouncer was treated and released from the emergency room, told to follow up with his doctor tomorrow, and he left with a card of symptoms to check for during the night. He was taken to police headquarters to give a statement to detective Fowler by Davy and J.W.

The actor was identified as Joe Carbona by the bartender and the victim's girlfriend. They were both able to pick his picture out of a mug book. This presented a problem. Sergeant Bolton wanted to arrest Carbona before the shift ended. Everyone knew where he would be, but no one wanted to pick him up. They knew whoever went would be in for the fight of their life. Joe Carbona never came easy. The sergeant had an idea. He called Tony over and asked him, "Joe Carbona lives with your aunt doesn't he?" Tony replied, "Yea, she raised him like a son." "Do you think you could go the Long Branch Diner and get him?" Tony frowned he knew this would be hard to do. He answered, "I could give it a try, but I can't guarantee anything. Joe Carbona is one tough customer, and he has a mind of his own. The last time he was arrested he put two of New Jersey's finest troopers in the hospital." The sergeant looked at Tony and said, "I realize that, but we have been catching hell this month. Our shift has been leaving too many open cases. We could sure use to close this one." Tony just shook his head and nodded. He said, Let me change my clothes, and take an unmarked car. I'll see what I can do."

All the way to the Long Branch Diner, Tony wished he had not taken on this detail, but he devised a plan. Here is what he did.

Tony pulled into the parking lot parked in front of the diner, and looked in to make sure Joe was there. Soon he spotted Taj Sabu, Tony sat quietly in the car,and waited for a while. Then he entered the Diner casually. Joe was in a booth in the back by himself eating. Tony walked to the back, and sat in the booth across from Joe. He said "Hey Mr. Carbona how are you doing? How's my aunt Frances?"

Joe looked at Tony and replied, "If you came here for me I ain't going nowhere, anyway, you got a lot of balls kid coming here to get me. I know why you are here. I won't chop you up right now because of Frances, but I will sure break you up some if you don't get the hell out of my face." Tony answered in soft voice, "Joe, I came here because of my aunt Frances. I could let ten six foot six State Trooper's come in and kick the shit out of you, then drag you off in a bloody heap, but it would hurt Aunt Frances worse than it would hurt you.

I know you are a tough piece of work. I am here to give you a chance to settle this the easy way, the manly way, a way with honor, and nobody has to get hurt."

Joe looked across at Tony, squinted, and stuffed a forkful of egg and a bite of toast into his mouth, "So what you got Kid?" Joe mumbled to Tony through the mouth full of food. Tony answered, "The kid you cut is out of the hospital and will be fine. All you need to do is come in get booked, processed, and then released on bail. I will go to the car outside and wait for you. You take your time, finish your meal, call Aunt Frances, and have her meet you at headquarters with money for bail. Then walk out of the diner and get into the car with me. I'll take you in, by the time you are booked and processed Aunt Frances will be there to bail you out. Nobody has to know anything, and then the lawyers can settle this in court. What do you say, we could get it over tonight, nobody here has to know what happened and you don't loose any face?" Joe put another load of food into his mouth, and sat back in the booth, shut his eyes, and folded his fingers behind his head.

In a few minutes, he opened his eyes and said "You know Frances told me you had a lot of brains kid, and I should listen to you. It took a lot of balls for you to come here by yourself just to give me a chance. I got to believe you are doing this for your aunt, so go wait in your car and maybe I will come with you, but no cuffs, no tricks, and no police lingo, okay." Tony nodded got up, hugged Joe, kissed him on the cheek as a sign of respect, and walked out to the car sat down in the drivers seat, and waited.

Half an hour later, Joe walked out of the diner waving to his friends, he walked over to Tony's car, and got in the front passenger seat. Joe looked at Tony and said, "Let's go kid. I ain't got all day, and I don't want to keep Frances waiting." The pair pulled out of the lot, and the made their way to the city police headquarters.

When Sergeant Bolton saw Tony pull into the lot with Joe Carbona, he was overjoyed. Tony walked in with Joe following and they went directly to the records room where Tony read Joe his rights, booked and processed the big enforcer. The sergeant called the judge and got a bail and filled out the forms for Frances. By the time Tony was finished Sergeant Bolton had the paperwork done.

The judge had set the bail high at ten thousand dollars cash or one hundred thousand dollars surety bond. Frances had come with twenty five thousand in cash just in case. She pulled out a packet of one hundred one hundred dollar bills, and handed it to the sergeant. He broke the bank seal and counted the money twice, then he gave her a receipt for her ten thousand dollars, and her copies of the bail forms. He told her to have Joe in court on Monday morning at nine o'clock. Frances got up and walked to the lobby and waited for Joe to be released.

When Joe walked into the lobby, Frances squinted at him, and she shook her finger in his face. She said, "I am getting too old to be doing this, when are you going to find a nice Italian girl and settle down, you ain't getting any younger you know? Now come on lets go home."

Frances led him out of police headquarters and Taj Sabu followed like a punished school boy leaving the principal's office with his mom after being suspended.

In court on Monday all charges were dropped when the bouncer told the judge that he had never seen Taj Sabu before, and anyway the man who stabbed him was almost seven feet tall and much younger. The victim said he gave the wrong information to the detective because he was in shock, and that the pain, and anesthesia from the stitches had made him hallucinate. The judge figured something was fishy in this story, but he had no choice but to dismiss the charges at Taj Sabu's lawyer's motion. The bouncer was admonished strongly by the judge, and the matter was settled.

Richard loved it when the police were tied up with the bars. This gave him free reign with no chance of being observed by an officer, not that this ever deterred him. He just felt more comfortable. He just hated police. He loved to see them work hard and loved it when they got jumped or hurt during these calls.

The boardwalk was filling with young people walking through to the beach for a fling in the sand with their date, some late night swimming, or just monkey shines on the beach with their friends. Times were always better for the kids, when the police were tied up at the bars.

Richard just sat and gazed into space. He did not see the shenanigans of the youths or the dramas of the young couples as they debated the course their passion would take this night. He just dreamed and stared out to sea. He thought about his lovers, the joy they brought to him, and the luck that had led him to the City. He wondered what would be left when the people were done with what they were doing. He knew there would always be something left. He loved to victimize the weak, or heartbroken girls that remained in the area, for whatever reason, after all the others left. They made the best lovers.

Richard got up and walked out to the jetty. The ocean was calm and the salty smell of the sea was strong. He was gazing at the horizon when he was surprised by a loud voice. "Hey Billy, where you been hiding?" the voice yelled. As he turned he saw a big young girl covered in tattoo's running toward him. She jumped on him, wrapped her legs around his body, hugged him, and kissed him on the lips hard and wet. Then, she stopped suddenly. Richard recoiled, he hated to be touched. He pushed her off him, and she fell onto the damp sand. The girl looked up at him and said, "Hey, you 're not Billy! Why did you push me in the sand? Are you too good for a beautiful young girl like me? Who do you think you are anyway?" Richard just ignored her, turned, and walked towards the boardwalk. He stopped for a second at the opening that led to his killing grounds, and decided to go in.

Within ten seconds, the loud girl was entering, his prey had arrived. She entered with a curse, "Don't you walk away from me shithead, I'm talking to you." As soon as she straightened up to face him, Richard punched her hard in the face, and then the stomach. She fell to her knees gasping for breath; she threw up in the sand. Richard kicked her brutally in the face as she lifted her head, and she flipped over on her back stunned. He grabbed a handful of her hair, and dragged her to the back punching her face and head as he dragged her. At the back he taped her mouth, and taped each of her wrists to her ankles. He started to cut off her clothes with his sheet rock knife. As she regained her senses the girl began to struggle. She soon tired as she realized her situation was totally hopeless. She began to sob as she lay naked in the sand taped in this awkward revealing position. Richard loved this. This would be one of his best he just knew it.

As he was walking home, he reached into his pocket and fondled the strip of flesh he had put there. Richard had cut the piece of skin off his latest lover. It was one of the girls tattoo's. He took it as a keep sake. It was a heart with the words "Fuck Mom" in it. Richard seemed to be able to relate to these sentiments himself.

Wow, she was great he thought as he walked into his house. She stayed alive for a long time even after her leg bones broke from the first rape. She was still alive and crying when he had sliced off her nipples and skinned her buttock to remove the tattoo; she was still breathing then, but sometime during the second sexual assault she had died. He was having such a good time he did not sense it. That was the only bad part. He liked to control when they would die, and feel their soul leave there body.

Richard bounced up the porch stairs and into the house. He could not wait to examine his trophy more closely.

After fondling the tattoo, and spreading it on the table, he decided to tack it out on a small piece of wood and stretch it like the Indians did with furs, then he put the tattooed flesh and the wood in a plastic baggie and filled it with borax salt. He put the baggie in the refrigerator and poured himself a glass of milk. He took a drink of milk and ate half an oatmeal cookie. Then he took the other half and went up to bed. He sat up in bed and finished the cookie and milk.

Then he laid down in the bed shut his eyes and relived the night in his mind all over again. It had been glorious. As he satisfied himself, he thought he must go back tomorrow and get her head. She was certainly a special one. Richard finished his thoughts he smiled with contentment, and then he fell into a deep dream filled sleep.

# CHAPTER TWELVE

## The Pussy Posse

The silver circle rose in the eastern sky. The first full moon of spring was a godsend. It marked the end of the cold dreary winter. The moon was surrounded by tiny dots of light that seemed to pulse in the hazy spring sky. It seemed to bring the city to life. After a slow cold four months this first weekend before Easter was a great time to get out and shake off the symptoms of cabin fever the winter can cause. It was also a perfect time to have a Pussy Posse.

Arnold called Mary to tell her that he would be late, and that maybe they should postpone going out for dinner. When he told her he would be tied up with a "Pussy Posse", she just laughed and said, "I'll cook something I can warm up later so you can have a good meal when you're done." Arnold said "Thank you, I will call when we are almost finished so you don't have to rush to get dinner ready. Now, I know why I love you Babe." Mary snickered back, "Well they say the way to a man's heart is through his stomach." Arnold laughed as he hung up.

Tony and Mike had been called to the squad room. Captain Talon decided they would be taken out of patrol for the remainder of the night, and used by the street crimes people in a Pussy Posse. This was the cities way of cutting down on the prostitution problem. These were called "Quality of life arrests." This was the fashionable political term for a "Pussy Posse" The city council ordered this from time to time to keep prostitution from getting out of hand. To be sure the police recognized that they needed these street walkers, because they knew everything that was going on in the town. Public pressure, mostly from religious groups and angry residents, made these crackdowns necessary.

A new batch of rookies had just graduated the State Police Academy, and so the City had some new meat to break in. There was no better way than in a Pussy Posse. They would not be recognized by any of the whores, and this should make for a productive night.

Herman Brown was the town drunk. He was known throughout the community as "Brownie," He had been a drunk for over thirty years. A once promising artist after World War II he took to drink and other than an occasional graffiti, he never painted professionally again.

What Brownie did do was direct traffic. When he went on a binge he would plant himself at a busy intersection and direct traffic. He was a sight to behold. He would flail his arms and spin around, it was like an informal ballet. People would stop and watch until the police arrived to take Brownie into custody. As he got older his balance and coordination diminished; age and alcohol had taken their toll. Soon Brownie realized he had become a danger to himself. Because of this he took to directing traffic in the wee hours of the morning at intersections with little or no traffic. He did not do it for the purpose of alleviating traffic congestion; he just really liked directing traffic. He thought of it as a natural skill. He would have loved to have been a traffic cop. He had done a little of that during the war when he was in the "Red Ball" express after Normandy.

The first detail of the Pussy Posse was to remove the hookers. The young cops were sent out in their own cars to pick up whores. They would be followed by a pick up unit that would take the hooker into custody after being signaled by the rookie that a proposition had been offered. This pick up unit would take the girl in to be processed. A proposition was any offer of sex for money.

On the way in to police headquarters, Tony and Mike came across Brownie lying in the gutter. He heard the officers coming, perked up his head, and gave them a salute. Tony and Mike picked him up and put him on a bench in the plaza park. Tony slipped a dollar into Brownies shirt pocket and told him to get some coffee when he could walk to the diner. Mike shook his head and said, "You're too good to the old wino's and lost kids. You will surely die poor." Tony just smiled, rejoined Mike, and the officers continued their walk to police headquarters.

As the officers continued their journey to police headquarters, they talked about the upcoming detail, and remembered their adventures on their first Pussy Posse, because just a few short years ago they were the rookies.

Tony and Mike had been told to report to the squad room. When they arrived they were told they would be taken out of patrol for the remainder of the night and used by the street crimes people in a Pussy Posse. They would be one of the catch teams. The officers had done this before so they did not need any briefing, they just left headquarters in an unmarked car and waited at the rendezvous point for the rookie baits.

At police headquarters, there was a team of ten people headed up by Detective Fowler set up to process the arrests, and a bus from the county jail to transport the hookers that could not make bail. This was a sight to behold. It was an assembly line to process arrests. During an average Pussy Posse there could be as many as fifty hookers crowding the security corridor. They would be cleaned out, their property put into paper bags with a copy of their arrest sheet stapled to it. Then they would be handcuffed to a security pole awaiting processing. After processing, they would be either released on bail after the posse was over or sent to county jail if they could not make bail.

The processing was a sight to behold and the conversation was as interesting as any soap opera. This night was no different. There were cat fights between the girls, screaming verbal assaults, and sexual propositions and unspoken innuendoes between the girls and the processors. There were numerous piles of narcotics, and the narcotics paraphernalia strewn all through the corridor as the girls tried to ditch the things before they were found in possession of it to avoid another charge. These items plus hidden weapons would also be found in the transporting cars when they were check in the sally port. Most of these items were extracted from the inner most hiding places of the girls arrested, by the girls themselves, in a surreptitious manner during their transport.

At one end of the corridor, "Little Bit" Parker slugged "Slo-eye" Bonnie Wright knocking the young hooker out with one punch. It turns out "Little Bit" did this because "Slo-eye" had called Smokey, one of the specials who was processing the girls, a bald old fat mutha fucka. Little Bit stared down at the dazed "Slo-eye" and stated, "He's a mature powerfully built gentleman to you girl!" Detective Fowler ran to the corridor just as two officers pulled "Little Bit" from over the groggy young girl; "Slo-eye" was helped to her feet and moved to the end of the line to get her wits, and to prevent a continuation of the hostilities.

The detective yelled, "Okay you girls cut that stuff out, the more trouble you make the longer it takes me to call the judge for your bails." This caused immediate silence, and the girls became much more co-operative from then on.

Smoky had once taken "Little Bit's" two children to her mother's house when she was arrested, and saved them from going into foster care. He did this on his own time because he loved kids and knew the hooker's mother. The working girl never forgot that curtsey, and respected Smokey for that even though she had long ago given up the two children for adoption. She knew that as a junkie prostitute she was not fit to properly raise her children, and she wanted the best for her kids, so she gave them up hoping they would get a better break than she got. Because of this, she felt a need to defend the kind old cop's honor.

It was a good night, over seventy girls, and three drag queens had been arrested. Only fifteen made bail so the bus was filled with the remainder; as it sped off to the county jail, the rookies were called in for phase two.

Arnold and his people were relived by Detective Moose and his crew. When he got to Mary's house, he could smell Italian food as he walked up the walk. He loved Italian food, and he was hungry enough to eat an Italian bear. When he walked inside Mary bid him hello from the kitchen and told him to sit down. She quickly brought out some pasta with meatballs, and on the side  an Italian salad of roasted peppers, sharp provolone cheese, olives, and artichoke hearts.

Arnold said, "This is great Babe, I am very tired, but not too tired to enjoy this great meal." Mary smiled and answered, "I hope the pasta restores some of your energy, I have plans for dessert." As she walked away Arnold noticed she only had a sexy black lace negligee under her apron.

The second phase was to arrest the "Johns" Eight undercover police women and two of the youngest male rookies were sent out as street walkers waiting for hits from the Johns that frequented the area. One of the rookies, Robbie Roberts was beautiful. He was just twenty-one about six feet tall thin, but well built. He had the face of a movie star. He would make great bait. The group went out, and when the detail was over they had over sixty Johns in custody. Robbie Roberts had ten Johns himself.

A funny thing happened the next morning at the arraignments. A Doctor Bailey from the next town had been arrested twice for propositioning Officer Roberts in the same night. The court clerk Nancy Mauro confirmed to Judge Bianco that this was in fact the case. The judge was puzzled at first and asked the doctor why he propositioned the same undercover officer twice. The judge figured the doctor must have known the young man was a police officer the second time. The good doctor nodded and said, "Yes, I did but he was such a beautiful young man I couldn't help myself. However, I did offer him much, much more money the second time." The judge just shook his head, as the gallery in the courtroom broke into a short laugh. He banged his gavel and called for order, then he fined the doctor $1,000.00 and warned him not to be arrested again. As he walked outside to pay his fine the lonely doctor winked at Officer Roberts.

Richard loved his trophies. He had teeth eye balls, the skulls and even the few heads in the freezer that he kept so he could be near his lovers. He had several prize possessions like the skull under his bed, and the two scalps he had in his collection in the refrigerator. He had cured the scalps in borax salt and they had preserved very well. He used a chemical that furriers use to soften the skin and keep it from shedding the hair. He did a fine job, and the scalps looked good. The memories they brought never failed to arouse him.

Tonight, he would go out, but he had no need. He would of course take whatever came to him, but tonight he needed to think. There was a young hooker working the beachfront; she interested him. She was black, and he had never had a black lover. The problem was the two beat cops on the boardwalk patrol were always moving him from his bench. They also seemed to be friends with the young girl.

Richard knew that his harassment by these officers would end in five or six months, because after Labor Day the nightly beach walking patrol would end. Most of the hookers would also disappear, but this young girl seemed to live in the area. He might never get a clean shot at this fine young girl, but he would try, if not then there was always another girl.

He would have to play this one carefully. He had the whole summer to get a chance at her. He was plotting his attack when a young hooker approached a drunk on a bench about half a block from him. As the pair began to walk down to the beach, two officers sprang from an arcade doorway, and approached the couple. The couple was frisked, separated, advised, and sent on their way. The officers did not have enough for an arrest, but both parties were strongly advised. The hooker was actually an undercover officer, and her backup was hidden on the roof of the candy factory. They could see most of the boardwalk from this location, even Richard and his bench.

Richard had been lucky. The police officers were staking out this area. They were all cops even this hooker was a cop. They must be running a Pussy Posse this weekend Richard thought. If he had tried to make her his lover, he would have been caught. This made him think. He would have to be careful in the future. It seemed wise to eliminate street walkers as a source for potential lovers. He would just stick to the young girls that propositioned him. They could not be police if they asked for money for sex; Richard knew that would be entrapment.

A careless move could cause him much inconvenience. Of course no dumb cop could outsmart him; nevertheless he did not need any trouble or added complications. The pickings were too good in this city. He decided that he must be more careful.

Richard stayed for the night watching as the pussy posse performed it's sweeps, and by sunrise the area was as clear as it could be. He got up and began his walk home thinking to himself how good it was to live in a town where the streets were so safe for a citizen to walk late at night. Then, he smiled at his sarcastic thought as he climbed up to his porch and entered his doorway. He would surely do all he could to make it a little less safe. He went in, made some coffee, and smeared some peanut butter on a slice of bread. He took his snack up to his bed and sat down.

Richard put down the refreshments, and he pulled a favorite skull from under the bed, and stroked it. It brought back fond memories, that he enjoyed while he sipped his beverage and finished his snack. He loved to think about his lovers. He put the unfinished coffee on the floor, sat up in the bed, put the skull in his lap, folded his hands behind his head, leaned back, and gazed at the ceiling. The touch of the skull against the skin of his stomach put him at ease. It brought back wonderful memories and satisfying moments. He became aroused.

After he was satisfied, he put the skull back under the bed and laid on his side in a fetal position. He shut his eyes. Soon, he was in a deep dreamy sleep.

# CHAPTER THIRTEEN

## The Candy Kids

Tony and Mike were walking the beachfront patrol. It was called Post 4. They just passed the convention center when they spotted Denise Chambers sitting on a bench near the boardwalk railing looking at the ocean. Denise was twelve years old, and it was two in the morning. Tony and Mike knew this little girl very well. Her mother was a heroin addict and a prostitute. The young girl and her mother were on welfare; they lived a few blocks away in the motel on Sixth Avenue and Kingsly Street. Denise's brothers and sisters were taken away from her mother; she was the only child her mother was raising. That is because her mother made an agreement with the child welfare people that she would give up all her younger children, and agree to have her tubes tied if she was allowed to keep her oldest Denise.

"Good morning Mr. Tony and Mr. Mike." Denise said as the officers came over to the bench. "How are you this morning?" replied Tony to the little girl. She was one of his favorites, and he always gave her something. Denise got up looked at the officers. She said, "You gentlemen look very handsome tonight." Mike said, Flattery will get you everywhere little girl, but you should be home in bed." Both officers knew that Denise could not go home, but it was a clear warm night, and it would do her no harm to stay on the boardwalk.

98

They would keep an eye on the area, make sure she was safe, and keep it clear of any dangerous people. Girls had been disappearing from this area all summer, but they were mostly runaways. Those kind of girls usually leave on their own when the pickings get slim so it was hard to tell just who was missing and who just left to move on. That makes it hard to find out whether or not something has happened to them.  This summer it seemed to the officers that there were much too many girls vanishing this year.

As the officers were leaving, Tony said "What is that dollar doing in your hair?" then he rubbed Denise's hair and pulled away a dollar bill. Denise quickly grabbed it from him, and said, "It must be mine it was in my hair." The two officers smiled and walked on.

As they walked to the Municipal Pool, they saw Tiger Morales. He was standing by the doorway, and he started to walk away as the officers approached. Mike yelled to him to stop, but he would not. Instead he said walking backwards carefully watching the two officers, "My mom's old man just kicked me out, and I ain't goin' to no jail." The two officers knew Tiger being out might get him into trouble tonight, but with the lead he had on them they could never catch him so they let him run away. He slowed down as soon as he saw the officers were not going to chase him. Then he, "cool walked", down the boardwalk and out of sight. Tiger was eleven years old. His mother was twenty-six. She was a dancer in a topless club, and her boyfriend managed her. He hated Tiger, and Tiger despised him. They were mutual enemies. Tiger would get into any kind of mischief he could so both officers walked to a pay phone and called the desk.

When Sgt. Harriman answered Mike told him, "Sarge, you better alert all the cars and patrols; we just saw Tiger Morales out and about, and he can be a one kid crime wave if he has a mind to." The sergeant grunted, and said. "Okay, but you guys don't start no stuff tonight I need some rest." When Mike hung up he said to Tony, "The Sarge sounds hung over tonight so we better go easy or we could be counting seagulls for the rest of the summer.

The rest of the night was routine, and at five in the morning the officers were completing their final check of post four. When they saw the door of the candy store on the south side of the municipal pool was open, they went inside. The place was ransacked. There was debris all over the counter; the storage closet had been forced open, and the boxes of candy broken open. They used the phone in the store to call the desk, and Sgt. Harriman was not pleased. He said, "I didn't mean for you guys to go to sleep just keep it quiet, well you better stay there until I get the owner to the scene.

Nick Pappas was a third generation candy maker. He made candy and sold candy bars from the major companies. His candies were far better than the manufactured bars, but some kids will only eat certain things. He was never unprepared. He hated to lose even one customer. When he entered the ravaged store, he looked around, pulled his hair and moaned, "yei yei yei." He shook his head and continued pulling his hair. When he was done checking everything he said, "Those kids they really got me good this time. They got about 4,000 candy bars." Mike and Tony said in perfect unison, "They got what?" Nick repeated they got thirty boxes of candy with a gross of candy bars in each box. Well needless to say Tony and Mike caught hell when they turned in their report that morning. As they left to go off duty, but both officers knew they would be receiving a call from the chief sometime that day.

Detective Fowler relieved the officers and took over the scene. He said to them as they were leaving, "Did you guys see anyone suspicious last night?" Mike and Tony answered in unison, "Tiger Morales."

After he was done at the scene, Arnold stopped by the middle school to see if Tiger was there. He was not. He stopped by the high school to see Mary. The pair had been together for several years since the O'Mally incident. They were in love.

Mary knew Concetta Morales very well so he would talk to Mary about Tiger. Concetta had been one of Mary's favorite students until the young girl got pregnant and left school. When the detective walked into the office Mary looked up from her desk and said in a mock stern voice, "What can I do for you today sir?" Arnold winked and said' "Meet me after school I need some help with my sex education class." She answered, "Mr. Conover handles sex education for the boys I will see if he is free for tutoring this afternoon." Arnold laughed, and walked over and kissed her on the cheek. He told her what happened, and they sat down and discussed the matter.

Captain Talon called Tony and Mike at home during the morning and told their wives to have the officers report to the chief at two in the afternoon. Both officers were outside the chief's office at one thirty that afternoon. All the other officers that saw them walked away smiling, and thanking God they weren't on post four last night.

In the chief's office were two men, Nick Pappas senior the owner and founder of the candy factory, and Father Cutross the priest from the Greek Church. They asked if there were any leads, and if the security at the boardwalk needed to be beefed up. The two men were mainly there to emphasize that these types of things would not be tolerated, and they were very dissatisfied with the police performance so far in this matter.

After the two citizens left, the chief really gave it to Mike and Tony. He said that they had better get to work and find out what happened last night. They better hope that the candy is found. He said, "How could you let somebody walk away with thirty boxes of candy? Are you guys blind or what?" The angry chief turned to them and said, "I could catch a guy carrying that much stuff. Get out there tonight, and you better get something. I have Detective Fowler working on this case. If you get anything, see he gets what you get."

Mike and Tony walked out of the office, and they were as low as you could get. Mike said, "Come on let's hit the street now and see if we can find out anything. Then, we will go and talk to Arnold. He's a good guy and together we should be able to clear this up pretty quick."

The two young officers road around for several hours in Mike's car but found nothing. They checked the street, and talked to people, but nothing turned up. Mike said, "Lets go over to Jim's Diner in Bradley and get something to eat then we can come back and continue our work." As they pulled into the restaurant parking lot, they saw Denise Chambers on the corner. She had on a very new and expensive skirt with a classy blouse, and new high heel shoes, which she was carrying in her hand, along with a large heavy shopping bag.

The young officers walked over to Denise, and Tony said, "My you look pretty today Denise." The young girl smiled and said, "Thank you Mr. Tony." They asked her if she needed a ride, and she answered, "No thank you kind sirs."

Mike said, "What do you have in the bag little girl?" and with that Denise dropped the bag and shoes. She started to run but Tony caught her by her arm. She said, "I was going to tell you guys tonight please let me go. I didn't do nothing." Tony put Denise in the back of Mike's car, and got in next to her. When the officers looked in the bag, they discovered several boxes of candy bars. Mike looked at Tony, and the pair drove to police headquarters with Denise Chambers and the candy.

After a cheeseburger, some fries, and a Pepsi, Denise told Tony and Mike, that after they left the pool area Tiger came back to see her. She told them that Tiger was her boyfriend. She said they were leaning on the door to the candy factory, and it just opened. They went inside and saw all the boxes of candy piled right near the door. They just couldn't resist it. The two kids took the boxes of candy, and dropped them over the railing down onto the sand. Then, they climbed down and ate some. But they could not eat that many boxes of candy, so they decided to hide them. They put the boxes of candy in a trench under the boardwalk and lightly covered them with sand. Then, Tiger got this great idea. They would sell the candy.

Tiger had taken fifty dollars out of the register, and he and Denise went to Steinbach's department store and bought new clothes. Not their usual cool clothes, but real square clothes. Then, they each filled the shopping bags with candy, and went to the neighboring towns. They sold the candy bars for a dollar. Denise said she told the people she was selling the candy for the local catholic school. Tiger said he would tell his customers he was selling the candy for the Little League. Denise had almost six hundred dollars in her purse. She told the officers that she was going to meet Tiger at the North Bridge.

Tony and Mike went to the north bridge, to wait for Tiger to come back to town. As Tiger crossed the bridge, Tony, who was hiding behind a tree, jumped out and grabbed him, and Mike ran from behind a car, cuffed him, and the officers put him into the back seat of Mike's car. Tony picked up the shopping bag Tiger dropped, put it on the front seat, and got in the back seat next to Tiger, and the trio was off to police headquarters.

At police headquarters, Tiger was cleaned out he had almost one thousand dollars on him as well as some of the candy still in the shopping bag. The officers teamed up with Detective Fowler, and interrogated Tiger. The brazen boy agreed to tell where the rest of the candy was only if the officers agree not to charge Denise. The detective agreed, but only if they got the remainder of the candy back today. Tiger answered okay, and said he took the candy alone anyway, and Denise had appeared after he had broken into the store and that she just stood watch while he removed the candy. The young cops agreed with the detective's not charging Denise if the candy was recovered and Detective Fowler added, "But Denise does not leave police headquarters until we get all the candy back." Tiger shook his head in agreement, and he took them to a spot on the boardwalk near the candy factory, then down into the sand to a hole in the boardwalk base. Under the boardwalk there were almost twenty cases of candy covered over with sand in a shallow trench. The two young burglars had sold most of ten cases this day. They had worked hard.

Since these kids had sold almost fifteen hundred bars of candy in the neighboring towns this day, and had been up all night moving the candy, they were both very tired. They had done more work than they ever had this day. But it seemed it was all for nothing.

The remainder of the candy was returned to the Pappas's, along with all the money the kids still had on them. Mr. Pappas was amazed at the amount of candy the pair had sold, and was very satisfied with the recovery of the remainder of his property; in gratitude, he gave the cash recovered from the kids to the local boys club. Then when he went to court for the case against Tiger, he asked the judge to let Tiger work for him, to work off the cost of the damage to the door and the cost of the candy he had stolen instead of sending him to the reformatory. He was impressed at how hard the youth worked to make money after he took the candy. The judge agreed to release Tiger into his custody under the supervision of a youth counselor. Tiger worked for the Pappas's until he graduated high school.

The police never had to arrest Tiger again. He went to school regularly. He participated in sports; baseball was his favorite. He never used drugs. He worked, hard and stayed out of trouble. He was a favorite of the Pappas family. They treated him like he was their son. After high school, Tiger could not afford to go to college so he joined the Marines. His hard work allowed him to do very well in the Marines. He soon rose through the ranks. He was chosen as a presidential guard. He was promoted to lieutenant and put in charge of an elite anti terror unit, then then he was promoted to the rank of Captain, and he was put in charge of an Embassy Guard. He was one of the marines killed at the American Embassy in Iran during the revolution against the Pshaw. .

Tony and Mike had many encounters with Denise in the years that followed. She helped the officers many times as an informant. Unfortunately she followed in her mothers foot steps, and first became a prostitute, and finally a junkie. She was always a friend to Tony and Mike, and they helped her as much as they could. She died just before the turn of the century. Her body was found badly decomposed near the bench she often sat on at night as a young girl. It was on the boardwalk across fron the Pappas's candy factory, looking out at the sea. Her body had been covered by a pile of snow. Some joggers came upon what was left of it in the early spring.

Arnold picked Mary up from school, and told her about the outcome of the great candy burglary. She laughed. "Concetta was a very smart girl, it's good to see her son has her brains. I just hope he doesn't screw up his life like she did hers." Arnold smiled and replied, "Well he won't end up pregnant if that's what you mean." Mary frowned at the poor joke, and punched him playfully on the arm. The pair then drove to Arnold's house for some fun in the afternoon.

Richard was sitting in his usual place when the two policemen walked up to him. He hated these two officers. They asked him for identification frisked him roughly, pushed him around a little, they warned him not to loiter in the area, and sent him on his way. As he walked off the boardwalk, he wondered how he could kill these two annoying men. If he brought his gun, could he shoot them both before they shot him? He thought about this all the way home.

Richard could not sleep. These two police officers really were getting to him; he needed to do something about them that was for sure. He would give it some serious thought.

After about three hours, Richard left his house, returned to the bench on the boardwalk, and stared out to sea. Something had interrupted his thoughts. He was surprised to hear a sweet voice behind him. It was a young girl, and she was crying. He turned and said, "You are too young and pretty to be crying like that." She looked at him and smiled. "I'm drunk, and can't find my mom's car. When I get home, she is going to kill me. I can't call the cops because I'm only 17 years old." Richard said, "I'll call them for you." She answered. "Thanks, but I can't drive it anyway, I'm too drunk." Richard said, "Lets go under the boardwalk, you can get some sleep; when you wake up, I'll call the cops for you, okay?" The ingénues young girl said okay, and they walked on to the sand. Richard pointed to a small opening at the base of the boardwalk, and the pair walked through it. As the two sat down in the sand, the inebriated girl fell down in the sand and passed out. Richard could not believe his luck. She was a beautiful young girl, not like the runaways he usually caught. She was clean well dressed and polite. This would be a prize lover for sure.

He dug up some duct tape he had hidden in the sand sometime before. He pulled some off and sat on the girls chest pinning her in the sand. He plastered the tape across her mouth as she awakened. Her eyes opened wide with terror. She struggled, and bucked like a bronco trying to get Richard off, she almost succeeded. When Richard hit her on the side of the head, she went limp. He got off turned her on her stomach, and taped her wrists to her ankles. This was just like the boys did to him the first week in reform school. Then he turned her over and penetrated her. He had sex with her for a long time, but something was wrong. He looked down, and her head was turned to the side in an odd angle. He looked at her chest. She was not breathing. When he felt for a pulse, he realized that her neck had broken from the force he used while molesting her. He knew she was alive when he started, but he could not tell exactly when she died. No matter he thought; he had enjoyed her for three hours.

He would have taken her head if he had his things, but instead he dug a shallow trough in the sand, rolled her in, and covered her. He would save that for another time. It was getting light out. He worked best in the dark. He left with mixed feelings. He was glad he had met a lover on a night he thought was lost, but he was sad she did not last longer. He could have loved her much more.

He was worried that someone would have seen him with her. This was his first local girl known to the people in the area.

The next night, Richard returned to the girl with a large knife. He must destroy her corpse so if it was found she could not be recognized. He took apart her body. He separated her arms, legs, and head from the torso; he gutted her. He put the guts in a plastic bag and the plastic bag into a paper bag, and put the head in his doctor's bag. After he buried the arms, legs, and torso in separate spots along the back of the boardwalk in the soft sand, as deep as he could; he picked up the bag with the head and guts of the girl, and walked to the opening. He looked back and was satisfied with his work.

He carefully left the killing grounds, walked to the end of the jetty dropped the entrails into the ocean, balled up the bags and put them in the doctor's bag with the head, and returned to the boardwalk. He climbed up the stairs and onto the boardwalk and headed home. In a few minutes he walked past a couple sitting on a bench looking out at the ocean. That's strange he thought a middle aged couple on the boardwalk this late. The couple looked at Richard, and the man watched him suspiciously as he walked off the boardwalk.

"That's a strange looking fellow to be on the boardwalk this late at night." Arnold said to Mary, I would give a hundred dollars to see what that weirdo has in his doctor's bag. He sure isn't a doctor." Mary just laughed and said, "you are always so suspicious of everyone, remember we are here to find out what happened to Janet Morrow not to harass citizens. Arnold just smiled at the jibe, "I guess you are right." He said, "It's just the cop in me. I am suspicious of anything that's not normal."

Richard casually walked home taking his usual rout through the residential areas, and he threw some left over pieces of the innards and some loose debris in the alleys along the way home for the stray animals to enjoy.

When he got home all that was left in the doctor's bag was the head. He cleaned it off, and thought as he admired his new trophy, what a beautiful lover this was. He carefully wrapped this prized trophy in butchers paper, then plastic wrap. He carefully put it in his freezer. He showered and went to bed. What am I going to do about those two cops, he thought, as he fell into turbulent, but dream filled sleep?

# CHAPTER FOURTEEN

## The Missing Girl

Mary called Arnold at work. She asked him to meet her for lunch it was very important, and she believed it could become a police matter, He was always glad to meet his favorite girl for lunch so he agreed to meet her at the deli on Main Street at about one o'clock.

Mary and Arnold had been seeing each other for many years now. There were no plans to get married or to start a family. They really enjoyed each other but both were reluctant to make a total commitment. The pair had been single for many years, and they also enjoyed their time alone.

When Arnold walked into the deli he saw Mary already seated in the back at the corner table. He could read deep concern on her face. Arnold kissed Mary on the cheek, and he sat down. Mary looked him in the eyes and said, "Do you know Horace Gamboll?" Arnold answered, "The guy who owns Microchip and half the world, no not personally." "Come on Arnold I am serious" Mary countered, "this is important." "Yea, I know of him. His niece is always getting in trouble here; she is a drunk, and an easy piece according to the other kids, He always sends his lawyer to get her out of trouble, and to straighten things out after she messes up." "Well she has disappeared!" Mary offered. "She was one of my problem children, but she was a nice problem. She was very close to working out most of her personal issues, and now she is gone. She would have graduated this June with honors, and was going to go to college. She has already been accepted. She was excited and could not wait to go away to school."

"Arnold I am worried something bad has happened. I don't know what exactly but I just feel it. Her name is Janet Morrow, and her mother is Gamboll's youngest sister. They live on Third Avenue. You know that big house on the corner. The girl's father was killed in Viet Nam. Since her husband was killed, her mother has become a basket case. Gamboll loves his kid sister, and Janet is his favorite niece. He has no children of his own. His security men went to look for her when she did not come home last night. They found the car she was driving on the beachfront this morning. The girl had been using the car as a reward for making the honor roll. No one has seen her since she left the Bootlegger bar last night around midnight."

"Her mother says that she has been gone all night before, but always came home the next morning, or called from where she was. Arnold, Gamboll does not want the police involved, he has his own people looking into this, but I don't think they will get very far. He has offered a one thousand dollar reward for any help that leads to finding her. I know she did not run away. I was with her two days ago and we made plans for her to live in the dormitory, and to even go to school early to become familiar with the area. Something bad has happened I can feel it. I don't know what to do. I really cared about that little girl. I saw her through some really tough times and now she is gone."

"Take it easy Babe" Arnold said, "I'll look into it discretely, and fill you in on what I find. If it gets bad we will get involved whether Gamboll likes it or not. I'm sure the girl is alright, probably just sleeping late with a friend." Mary nodded she looked a little relived. "I always feel better after I talk to you." Mary said to Arnold.

Arnold offered to buy the lunch. Mary grinned a brave smile and said, "I'll just take some coffee." Arnold ordered a hot corned beef sandwich, and the pair ate in silence. When Arnold finished, the couple got up, they kissed and Arnold reassured Mary once more, and each returned to their work.

When Arnold finished his shift, he went down to the beachfront to look around. He went into the Bootlegger bar and talked to the owner who told Arnold he knew the girl, and she was a regular although she was never served because they did not believe the age on her proof. He advised Arnold to come back in the evening and speak to Matt the late night bartender. He might be able to help him.

Arnold went back to the school after work and picked up Mary. He said to her, "Babe how would you like to spend a night on the town with a worn out old cop." Mary just smiled and replied, "Just as long as he's not too worn out I think I can find the time. How did you make out looking for Janet?" "That is why we need to go out tonight, so I can mix business with pleasure." Well let's just hope you are not too worn out for the second part." Mary chided in a sarcastic voice. They both laughed, and Arnold left to go home and put on something more comfortable. Mary walked home after she was finished at work and waited for Arnold to pick her up.

The couple went to the Marine Grill and had a great seafood dinner. Then, they walked the boardwalk all the way to the south end of town. They walked down to the street, and into the Bootlegger Bar.

Matt was tending bar. The place was jammed. The couple sat down and had a few drinks while they waited for the crowd to thin out. After a few hours, most of the young people were gone. Mary and Arnold walked up to the bar for a last drink.

Arnold asked Matt if he knew Janet Morrow, he smiled and said, "Everyone knows Janet Morrow. When she gets old enough, she will be the town drunk. I kicked her out of here last night. She tried to come in here, and she was already so drunk she could barely stand, plus she is only seventeen." "Where did she go?" Mary asked in a concerned voice. "What are you her mother?" Matt asked.

Mary answered, "No, I am her teacher; I just want to find her, Janet is a very good friend of mine." "Who's the big old guy with you, your father?" Matt joked as he nodded toward Arnold. Mary laughed as Arnold stood up and said to Matt, "No, I am Detective Fowler, and you will be snickering out of the other side of your face if I start checking I.D's on some of these kids you got in here tonight!"

Mary grabbed Arnold's sleeve, and guided him out of the bar, still giggling at the jibe the bartended threw at Arnold. Although they were the same age Arnold looked much older than Mary. She looked about ten yours younger than him.

"You are supposed to be helping me find the girl, not harassing bartenders." "Well, we were getting nowhere fast with that guy anyway." The irate detective said, "Let's go back on the boardwalk and walk back, maybe we can see something." They sat down on a bench about halfway back and looked out to sea. "It sure is peaceful on the boardwalk this time of night." Mary said. "Yea" Arnold replied, "but it can be explosive at times." Soon, an odd looking man passed with a doctor's bag in his hand. He seemed to slide out of the darkness. The pair stared at him, especially Arnold. Arnold looked at Mary and quipped, "He sure isn't going on a house call with that doctor's bag." and after some conversation about him the couple got up and continued their walk up the boardwalk north to the top of the town, and their car.

On the north end they ran into Tony and Mike. They said hello and Arnold asked them about Janet. They knew her but said they hadn't seen her for many days. Mike said some of the kids said she had met a nice boy and cleaned up her act.

Back in the car Mary said, "See, just like I told you even Mike said she had gotten straightened out. That's why I am so worried." Arnold just nodded and squinted his eyes, a sure sign he was thinking. In a few minutes, he turned to Mary and said, "You are right. Every sense I have tells me something bad has happened to that girl. I don't know what yet, but I feel it just as sure as I feel we should go to my place for a nightcap, and discuss this further." That's a great idea!" Mary said, as their car pulled out of the parking lot and into the sparse traffic.

Richard was in bed with his favorite skull. He did not feel like going out again. He had gotten home with his trophy, and after treating it properly he was tired. He thought about the pretty girl's agony and her fear. This caused him to become aroused. After he satisfied himself, he just wanted to think in peace. He remembered many of his lovers, the taste of their tears, the smell of their blood, and the look of terror in their eyes. He was aroused again.

He would spend the rest of the night in bliss reminiscing about his lovers. He found sometimes this was as rewarding as having the girl here with him.

That brought up a new thought. He needed to get a girl alive into his house. He needed to hold her prisoner. He needed to be able to keep her alive and torture her for extended periods. She had to be a strong girl so she would last. His own personal slave to torture and mutilate at his whim.

This would surely be the perfect reward for a god, to have his own personal slave. To be able to totally possess another body and soul, to hold their future in his hands, to have the power of life and death, and pleasure or pain, that is truly godly power. The taking of the last girl had shown him that he could get anyone if the conditions were right. It boosted his already inflated ego and added to his already excessive confidence. This is why he was such a powerful and dangerous person. He really believed that he was so smart that he would never be caught. He was careful, and never tried to plan too far in advance, rather he simply reacted to the situations as they presented themselves.

He would rest now, and dream those wonderful dreams. It was good to be a god he thought as he settled down with a cup of black coffee, and a slice of bread smeared with peanut butter. He knew it was his destiny to find the perfect lover, and to bring her home to control and love for as long as he wished.

He knew he would dream about this; and he knew his dream would surely come true. He wished the girl from last night could have been his slave; she had been his best lover so far, but he had made her an angel far too soon, and now she was gone. He would strive to make his dream come true, and he would surely find another perfect girl. He felt it deep in his black perverted soul.

# CHAPTER FIFTEEN

## The Duchess

The sun rose through the steaming mist, and burned a path from the eastern horizon to the sandy shore. It beckoned the city's residents to arise. The city was the home to many diverse people and Charles Furman was one of them. He was six feet three and two hundred twenty five pounds of athletic skill. He was the fastest boy in High School, and he was one of the strongest. He had to be; he was Gay in the late nineteen fifties. This was a bad time to be a gay young man. He was mild mannered, but his sexual preference forced him to be aggressive. Kids are cruel to those that don't fit in or are different. He left school at sixteen even though he was smart enough to have finished it easily.

He was drafted on his eighteenth birthday. He did two years in the army. It was there he got his equivalency diploma, and then did one year in Viet Nam. Two years later he was honorably discharged. At twenty, he was filled out and beautiful, but he had little formal education or work skills. He wandered from job to job unable to find one that would provide him a proper living or career, and soon, he found himself walking the streets at night, at first looking for love, then to make a living. He became a prostitute, began to dress like a woman, and took the street name Duchess.

On a weekend night in seven inch heels, and a beehive hairdo no one could anchor a corner like the Duchess. He was a perfect queen.

His friend Morris Bates, known as Chantille on the street, had nothing but envy when Duchess approached his corner. If Duchess had a flaw, it was in his choice of lovers. He loved a thug named Oscar Poindexter, a brutish man who made a good living by pimping Drag Queens. Duchess adored the man, and would do anything for him. Love is strange and compelling wherever you find it.

Poindexter was a greedy aggressive man, short squat and filthy. He would have broken Duchess' legs for some of the indiscretions he had committed. But in his own way, Poindexter loved the Duchess too, and The Duchess was also Poindexter's biggest money maker. The two fought regularly.

Poindexter had supplemented his income with a small crack distribution racket, and was doing very well with it. The problems began when Poindexter became hooked on the crack himself. The mood swings of this already violent man were unbelievable. He had brutally raped and beaten two of the older drag queen's whose production had fallen off. There is nothing sadder than an old drag queen trying to stay young and make a living on the street. Poindexter knew it, but he was loosing touch with reality.

The relationship between Duchess and Poindexter steadily deteriorated. Finally Duchess was arrested in a Pussy Posse sweep, and because of his past police record, the bail was set extremely high. Poindexter did not have the money for bail, because he was blowing it up his nose. So, the Duchess was sent to the county jail. County Jail was no place for a drag queen. After a week, The Duchess tried to hang himself, and for his own protection was released from jail, after a short stay at the County Jail's mental ward.

When the Duchess returned to the city, he was reluctant to return to the street. This infuriated Poindexter, and the two had a falling out. Duchess went his way and Poindexter went his. It was not an amicable parting.

Over the coming weeks, the Duchess kept more to himself than ever. He rarely went out, and when he did, it was never in full dress. His looks deteriorated; he became sloppy. He was becoming a recluse. Poindexter was missing his best moneymaker, and he also missed his lover. He decided to find Duchess, and try to patch things up. He asked around, and no one could tell him for sure where the Duchess was. Soon, both men were missing.

Davy and J.W. had been given a call to see a lady on Elizabeth Avenue near the Youth Center. When they arrived, they found Ms. Jenkins with two young boys. One was Rabbit Johnson, the other was Twig Anderson. She said to Davy, "I should be a cop. I just solved the great school hooky, and pie stealing gang of this city. If these good for nothing's were in school where they belong, they wouldn't be stealing' honest, hard working folk's pies."

Both boys had pie on their hands and faces; they were caught in the act by Ms Jenkins. She told the officers, "When you see Beverly Johnson and Cecelia Anderson you tell them I expect two new pies, one apple and one blueberry. They can give them to me at church Sunday." The two cops laughed and took the boys to school to face the wrath of Principal Parker at the Middle School. "This could be worse than the wrath of Ms. Jenkins!" J.W. said as they entered the school with the boys. "Between Principal Parker and their mothers, the boys would be sore for a long time to come." Davy added.

Just as the shift was ending, all cars were called to the attic of the old Griffiths Cleaner's store. There was a seldom used one room apartment there, and a strange smell was coming from the stairway door. Vill and Sara were assigned as the primary officers, and Davy and J.W. arrived as backup. Upon entering the attic room, the officers found a gruesome scene. The Duchess was tied face down to an old four poster bed. He was naked. He had been tortured and castrated. There were over one hundred deep slashes across his body. In a rocking chair across the room, was Poindexter's body. The head was tilted back and a revolver protruded from his mouth. The top of Poindexter's head and a good portion of his brains were splattered on the wall and ceiling behind him.

The officers notified police headquarters, and Detective Fowler was sent to investigate the scene. Arnold had known both men all his life, and he knew their relationship would come to a bad end. A tragic end to a pair of tragic lives, Arnold thought as he watched the coroner's livery men cart away the body's of Charles "Duchess" Furman and his lover Oscar Poindexter. They were both less than thirty years old.

Richard found himself stroking the skull from the last girl he had made his lover. He had returned home with the whole head, but he could not save it. He did the next best thing. He skinned it and put the skin in a box of borax to preserve it. Then, he removed the pretty blue eyes and put them in a jar of vodka. He meticulously cleaned and emptied the skull. He reattached the lower jaw with brass screws, and there it was a perfect trophy. He was happy with his work.

This would become one of his favorite trophies. He would keep it near all the time, either under his bed or sometimes on the television. He cleaned and polished it often. It became something he needed to have around.

Richard had been taking many trophies. He had jars of vodka filled with teeth and eye balls; he usually displayed them on the television in the den. The heads he kept in the freezer for as long as he could keep them fresh, and skulls he kept in various places that he could easily access.

Richard arrived at his bench just as the beach was clearing. He gazed out at the ocean. He pretended to be sleeping until the area was clear. Then, he took up his usual vigil to see if there was something left that would interest him. He dreamed for a while about his lovers, and how lucky he was to have an unlimited supply. He could actually choose there were so many easy marks. He felt he was very fortunate to be in a place like this. He relived the screams and the tears, oh those tears tasted so good he thought. He had such power; he was so smart. This could go on forever; Richard was beginning to believe that he was truly immortal. Nothing caught his eye this night, and as the sun began to peek over the horizon; he decided to go home.

At home, he fell into bed. He instinctively reached underneath and brought out the polished skull. He rubbed it, and he soon dropped off into a restful sleep. Richard could tell just from the touch of the bone which victim the skull belonged to.

Richard would dream dark, sordid dreams when under the spell of one of his lover's skulls. The dreams would calm him, and add to his happiness. They pleased and inspired him. Runaway children beware;

Richard's dreams spell danger for the lost young girls coming to the city down the shore, for Richard makes his dreams come true!

He curled up on his side and hugged the skull close to his chest, and he fell into a dazed stupor. He could see the pretty young girl's tears slide down her cheeks. He could feel the bones of her legs break as the weight of his body pressed upon her. He could feel her squirms of pain as she convulsed to try to make the pain lessen. He awoke from his trance fully aroused. He felt invigorated. He satisfied himself and walked to the window. It was light out. A glance at the clock showed him it was almost mid day.

Richard went down to the kitchen, and he made some coffee. He looked out the back window, and watched the neighbor's cat toying with something it had caught. He enjoyed the sight. The cat crippled the little furry animal, and teased it for some time before artfully killing it, and haphazardly eating the poor creature almost as an afterthought. Richard understood the cat. Food was not the important thing in a kill; it was the death that was important. Killing was an art; there was nothing more artistic than a beautiful kill.

Richard poured some coffee into a cup, picked up a slice of bread, smeared it with peanut butter, and he went back to the bedroom. He thought about what he would like to do this coming night. He smiled, and then he finished his lunch and took a nap.

# CHAPTER SIXTEEN

## The Sergeant

The winter sky was clear. The morning star was on its way to its perch in the steel blue sky. Soon, it would be spring, and the city's churches would come alive with the joyous voices prepared to celebrate Easter. Father Michelli was at the side door to the alter sacristy. He always walked into the sacristy this way, when he entered the church, for whatever reason he needed to go there. This night he had returned to the sacristy to finish his chores.

Father Michelli heard a loud crack from the back of the church. He had come to the church to get the vestments that were soiled, and needed to be cleaned from the sacristy drawers. He looked out the doorway, and he saw that the poor box lie broken on the floor in the back of the church. As he examined the scene, he saw a dark shape run out the rear church door. He calmly walked the side entrance of the sacristy down the stairs and outside to the parking lot, he leaned flat against the wall of the church and waited. When he heard the rush of footsteps approach, he stuck out his leg, and tripped the mystery man as he ran by.

A symphony of change flew from the thief's hat which he had folded in his hands, and jingled a tune across the church parking lot. Father Michelli looked down to see Angelo Rocco sprawled on the pavement. The thin, old priest said, "Angelo, go pick up the change, and put it back where it belongs; then come to the confessional you need to speak with the angels." When the scruffy youth walked over to the confessional, Father Michelli's eyes commanded him to sit down. The priest blessed the young man and said, "You need to come to church everyday after school and say the rosary in front of Saint Anthony. Go and say one now then go get ready for school. I will see you this afternoon."

Angelo Rocco was the twelfth and last child in his family. His mother died shortly after he was born. His oldest sister Loretta raised him. His father Guido was a big brute of a man. He was a heavy drinker and a nasty drunk. He beat all of his children so most had left his house as soon as they were able. Just Loretta, the oldest child, the youngest girl Mary, and Angelo were left living in the house with the miserable old man. Loretta was a secretary. She worked for the town judge in the Municipal Court, so the old man left her alone. She stayed mainly to keep an eye on the last two kids. The old man was dying of a lung disorder, and most of his time was spent sick in bed or drunk, and he was drinking even more than usual now. Mary was going to graduate in June. She was accepted to the Dominican Convent in Coldwell to begin to train to be a nun, this coming summer. She would be leaving the house and Loretta would only have Angelo to look after. Looking after Angelo in itself, was more than a full time job; it came with much overtime.

Angelo went to the rectory after school, and Father Michelli put him to work around the church; then, he sat down with Angelo, helped him do whatever homework he had from school, fed him, and sent him home. He did this for the rest of the year.

During that time, Angelo's father died, and his oldest sister took custody of him. This year had changed his life. He began doing well in school. In two more years, he finished grammar school. Angelo graduated High School four years later with honors and joined the Marines. After four years in the Marines, two in Viet Nam, he returned home, and joined the local police department. A few years later, he married his high school sweetheart Jeanie Fafalardi. As soon as they could, they saved up and bought a small home. Now they had three children, and things could not be better. Angelo had been promoted to sergeant, and he was in charge of the 2400/0800 shift. His first ten years on the job had been hard, but he had shown he could do the job. He was a natural leader of men. He came out on the top of the list for sergeant, and because he was a veteran he locked the list. He would have been made anyway, but this had assured the promotion.

On the quiet cool spring nights like this, Angelo often thought of that night over twenty years ago that changed his life. Father Michelli was over eighty now and he was a Monsignor. Angelo still dropped by to see him from time to time. The old priest was one of his best friends.

This had been one of those quiet slow nights. Spring was in the air but it was still very cold. It was just after 0400hrs that the sergeant was brought back from his dream world as the police radio squawked 837 to car ten, 10-27 Headquarters. The sergeant figured the deskman needed relief so he answered, Ten-four and turned the police car towards headquarters.

When he got to headquarters the first aid wagon was there. Captain Munny got out and walked up to the sergeant's police car as Angelo was pulling into the police lot. He said to the sergeant, "We have a problem on First Avenue.". Angelo new this would be bad, Sick Dick, the town psycho, lived on First Avenue, and it was a full moon. Angelo asked, "Sick Dick?" the captain nodded. The two men went upstairs and planned their action.

The problem was Joseph Richard Benny. He was known in the community as "Sick Dick". He was a mental patient that had been freed when the State deinstitutionalized the patients housed in the mental institutions through out the state. He was a lunatic, and the full moon was calling, so he was out of control. He was four hundred pounds of lunacy kept under control by a concoction of thorozine and valium. The strongest doses available were prescribed. But even these failed when the call of the moon came upon him. He lived with his mother, who was over eighty, in a small house on First Avenue.

His mother had called first aid to take him to the hospital emergency room. When the ambulance pulled up, Sick Dick ran out of the house naked, and jumped on the hood of the ambulance. He rolled off into the street, and before he could get up the first aid men pulled away. He chased the ambulance down the street, but he was not built for speed, and after a brief sprint soon stopped. He was in a very aggressive mood.

Angelo called his men to the Squad Room and briefed them. They made a plan to try to take Richard into custody with as little trouble as possible. Angelo set out for First Avenue with the whole squad. The ambulance followed.

There were five cars rolling that night. Car 2 was Tony and Pete, Car 3 was Davy and Frank, Car 4 was Bob and Bonzoni, Car 5 was J.W. and Big Geno, Angelo was in car 10. They would all be needed on First Avenue this night.

When the caravan arrived at the First Avenue address, the house all was dark. It was as quiet as a graveyard. Mrs. Benny was on the porch sitting in a rocking chair. She had her head in her hands, and she was crying.

When Angelo walked up to the old crying woman, she sighed, and sobbed, "I don't know what to do with my boy Angelo, he just won't listen to me any more." Angelo asked where her son was, and the old tired woman just shrugged her shoulders and pointed at the front door, "In there", she said.

Angelo said to his men, "I don't want anyone hurt if possible. Tony, Pete, Bob and Bonzoni go around to the back door. We will let you in if it is locked. Dave, Frank, J.W. and Big Geno you will go in the front door with me. Okay let's go, and be careful."

As they entered, they saw Sick Dick on the landing between the first and the second floor. He was sitting on the floor naked cutting thin lines in his chest with a kitchen knife. Angelo and J.W. had grown up with Joseph Richard. They had gone to school with him until Joseph Richard was sent to the mental institution for strangling cats.

Angelo walked over to the stairs; he said, "Hello Joseph". The disturbed man stood up quickly. He pointed the knife at the sergeant and said, "Don't you come no closer Angelo or I'll cut ya." With that Angelo stopped. He said, "Joseph Richard just put down the knife, and let's talk". The agitated psycho just laughed and said, "You sound just like my mother, you must think I was born yesterday. I know you want to take me away, and I ain't goin'." He waved the knife like a fencer, and unexpectedly lunged at Angelo. The sergeant stepped back. As the edgy psycho lowered the knife to his side, he fell back against the wall, and started to cry. Angelo slowly climbed back up the stairs, and reached Joseph Richard's side. The sobbing man had his face buried in his chest. Angelo said to the sobbing man, "Just give me the knife, buddy and we can talk this out." Suddenly Joseph Richard stopped crying, he looked up with his eyes wide with anger, and backed tight to the wall. He held the knife with both hands out in front of him and pointed it at the sergeant. He yelled, "No" and pushed the knife at the sergeant.

Angelo backed away to the edge of the stairs. Both men looked each other square in the eye. J.W. pulled out his baton. Joseph Richard glanced away, and pointed the knife at J.W. and he said, "Put that away J.W. or I'll cut Angelo". J.W. put the baton behind his back.

Angelo turned to the men, and signaled them to be ready. Joseph Richard became edgy when he saw the sergeant make the furtive motion. He began a loud sob, almost a cat's screech that turned into a banshee yell, then, unexpectedly Sick Dick lunged at Angelo plunging the knife into his shoulder. Angelo pulled out his revolver, and shot six times into the lunatic's chest. Joseph Richard backed away, yelled, and jumped again toward the sergeant, he stabbed the sergeant again. The Psycho plunged the knife into the top of Angelo's chest just above the collar bone. J.W. pulled out his gun and fired once. The .357 magnum roared. The shot hit Sick Dick in the center of the chest, and the force of the bullet knocked the crazed man to the wall where he died, as he slid down to the floor, leaving a bloody mark on the wall.

The men ran to Angelo who had rolled down the stairs. There was very little blood. Angelo said he was fine. Captain Munny told the men to put him on a gurney, and they fastened him down with the safety straps, and loaded the grogy sergeant into the ambulance. With the wail of the siren, they were off to the hospital. J.W and Dave went in the ambulance with Angelo. Captain Munny had called ahead to the hospital to alert them they were coming in with a "99".

During the ride, Angelo said he felt sleepy. He said to Dave, "I'm flying with the angels." Dave said, "Don't go to sleep Ange, we are almost there". Angelo laughed. At the emergency room, Angelo looked at his friends smiled, and shut his eyes. The nurses rushed to him, and started an I.V. in his right arm. Angelo had stopped breathing. The doctor began C.P.R., put the wounded man on a respirator, and tried for half an hour to revive him with no success. Monsignor Michelli had arrived just after the ambulance, and had given Angelo Last Rites. The whole hospital seemed to go quiet.

J.W. had called Sergeant Harriman on the desk and told him what had happened as soon as they arrived at the hospital. The Chief had been notified, and went immediately to the hospital. He was shocked when he was told by the doctors that Angelo had expired. The Chief and Angelo had been friends since childhood. They played worked, and raised their families in the same neighborhood. It seemed so unbelievable.

The Chief left the hospital to go to Angelo's house with the tragic news. Angelo's wife passed out when she was told. The children came down the stairs with sleep in their eyes, and began crying at the sight of their supine mother. Their aunt, who the Chief had brought with him, hugged the children to her as Angelo's wife lay prostrate on the floor. The Chief tried to revive her and Captain Munny came to his aid.

An autopsy revealed the first wound to be nothing more than a deep, painful cut. The second wound had nicked the jugular vein deep in Angelo's chest. He was bleeding all the way to the hospital, but the blood had spilled inside his chest so no one could see haw badly he was bleeding. He was dead from loss of blood when he reached the hospital. There was nothing that could have been done to save him. His journey with the angels had been quick and painless.

This had been a busy night because of the murder of the sergeant, and the police were tied up the rest of the night. A young girl named Valerie had arrived in town this week. She had been sleeping under the boardwalk with two other runaways; she was fifteen, and from upstate New York. She only had two dollars left from her escape stake. Her father had died when she was two and her mother soon after. She was passed from relative to relative until she got to her mother's oldest brother. No one in the family liked him. He was a recluse. He took custody of her, and he had made her his prisoner and slave. He locked her in the shed next to the barn, and rarely let her out. When he did let her out to clean the house or do chores he did not wish to do she was chained to his belt with a heavy boat anchor chain padlocked around her neck. She was not missed at school because she had moved so many times. He would sexually abuse her whenever he wished. She would not resist any more because he stopped feeding her until she consented. When she was good, the uncle would chain her to the barn door, and let her out to get some sun.

She got out of the shed one night. She slipped into the house while her uncle was out drinking. She took what money she could find and fled the farm. After a week of wandering, she ended up in the city down the shore. As she walked along the boardwalk, she was thinking of becoming a prostitute to earn money to live on. The others kids she had met were doing this. It did not seem that bad to a person who had been sexually abused most of her short life.

This night the city's other sick Richard was sitting on a bench looking out to sea. As Valerie approached, he turned and asked her if she would like a beer. She said yes. After two beers and some small talk, Valerie asked Richard if he would like some sex. She had never done this before, and her proposition was awkward. She asked for twenty dollars. Richard offered five and she agreed. As the couple went down onto the sand Richard said that they should go under the boardwalk. The young girl foolishly agreed.

Under the boardwalk, Valerie began to remove her cloths. As she slipped her sweatshirt over her head, Richard knocked her down, grabbed the bundle, and taped the girl's arms to the sweatshirt so she could not get them out. Her face was covered and she could not see.

He taped her ankles to a broom handle he had cut for just such an occasion. He had hidden it with his other paraphernalia in the sand. It barely fit between her ankles. It hurt her. She felt like she was being split in two. It spread her legs apart as far as they would go.

Richard cut off the crying girl's pants and underclothes. Her screams were muffled by the sweatshirt. Richard found he enjoyed the muffled sounds. He molested her and sodomized her for several hours torturing her with small cuts and battering her when the mood pleased him. He really enjoyed himself with this girl; she had great stamina; but he found he was getting bored because she seemed not to be struggling enough. He heard the girl beg him to stop in her plaintive muffled voice; he became aroused again. His attacks were more brutal. In a few minutes, the young girl changed her plea. She begged him to kill her. This pleased him even more. This is the greatest one ye, he thought, as the girl grew quiet and stopped moving.

When he thought she might be dead or near death, he gutted her. He loved the way her body convulsed as the remainder of life drained from her body. Finally, he pulled the .22 caliber pistol from the waist band of his pants, pushed it into the sweatshirt against what appeared to be her head, and shot her once. It made soft muffled sound. This pleased him. He had placed the pistol hard against her sweatshirt to soften the sound. It had worked; the noise the gun made what sounded like a loud pop.

He dug a shallow trench in the sand rolled her into it and covered her body. He took her clothes, jewelry and all her meager possessions, and put them in a bag. He lay down on top of the mound of sand and went to sleep. He had a dream filled sleep. He relived the incident in his dreams. He awoke several hours later refreshed. He left the area, and whistled as he walked home. It had been a good night, he thought, as he made his way through town; he would return another time for trophies.

No one would ever miss Valerie Hobbs; it was as if she never existed. Her name may have never been remembered, except that her welfare identification card from New York State was found several years later along with other souvenirs in Richard's house.

This was one of the saddest springs in the city down the shore. There was no joy during Easter, and in the Memorial Day Parade this year there was a terrible new reason to remember. The town would be in mourning for a long time. A warrior had fallen in the battle to keep the city safe and secure. His death was a great loss to his family and to the community. He would never be forgotten, and Valerie Hobbs, the poor girl Richard had brutally made his lover certainly would.

# CHAPTER SEVENTEEN

## The Shootout

The yellow sun blazed over the city. It had done so for seven days in a row. Summer would be early this year. This was great for business, and a real hardship for others. On this hot steamy May day, there was little comfort for those that had to be out in the weather. The police cars had no air conditioning. Thank god for the beachfront Vill thought as his patrol unit made its way to the ocean front. There was always a breeze on the north end of the boardwalk. He could park off the jetty and get some relief, while he and his partner started their daily reports. Sara and Vill would never make it to the north end this day.

Roberto Sara, and Robert Vill were partners. They had been police officers together for fifteen years. They grew up together, and they went to school together. Sara went into the Marines, and Vill into the Army, when they got out they both became cops. The both married, and they bought houses next to each other. On the job, they became partners and worked together regularly.

Their last call had been in the projects. May Graham had had it with her good for nothing son. She told him to get out and not to come back until he got a job. She told him it was almost summer, and there were jobs to be had all over the town.

Leroy "Bean Pole" Graham was six feet ten inches tall but weighed only 150 lbs. He had long arms and long legs; he had hopes of being a professional basketball player. His problem was he was lazy. He had the size; all the skills needed, and was always the first one picked at the playground for games. Scouts from local semi-pro leagues would stop by to watch him play. They were always put off by his lack of hustle. He could not read well because he dropped out of school at 16. Leroy would never be anything but a common laborer. He was twenty now and had few prospects. He had lived with his mother all his life.

His father died when he was ten. His mother May got a job at night so she could be there for him during the day. She stocked shelves at the local supermarket. She worked hard, and made enough for them to get by, but now she was beginning to feel her age; she realized that she could use some help. She was always ready to take a part time job if they were available to make a little extra. Bean pole never worked. It was probably her fault because she had babied him all his life, but he was all she had left. She loved him dearly. She knew it was time for him to make his own way. She hated to see him leave, but she knew he must. It was the hardest decision of her life.

Bean pole was not ready to go. He was very comfortable at home, and did not want to look for a job. He did not think he needed one. May disagreed, and a fight erupted. During the fight, Bean Pole did the unthinkable; he called his mother a "Bitch" and pushed her down. That was the last straw. May reflexively picked up a frying pan from off the stove, and smashed Bean Pole on the side of the head. He collapsed like a house of cards. All those years of stacking shelves had given May the strength of a wrestler. Bean pole did not stir, and May thought she killed him. She franticly called the first aid, and the police responded with them. Bean Pole was just coming to when they all arrived. May had hurt her wrist when she had fallen, it looked like it was broken. First aid convinced her to go with them to the hospital.

Sara and Vill arrested Bean pole, and the first aid took May to the hospital. Later they found out her wrist was in fact broken so Bean Pole was charged with assault, and sent to the county jail. May wanted to get him out but her sister would not lend her the bail money. Her sister said to May. "Let him stay in jail for the day and tomorrow we will see about bail." May reluctantly said okay, what else could she do, and so she let him go to the county jail. She returned home and cried all night with worry about her boy.

Sara and Vill were on their way to the North End, and as they approached the light at Fifth Avenue, a van shot across four lanes of traffic and cut them off. It appeared to be loaded with kids. Sara put on the overhead lights. He called in the license plate number, and the traffic stop to headquarters. Vill got out on the right side and stood by the front of the police car just behind the opened door, while Sara prepared to exit the patrol unit to walk to the drivers door to ask for the driver's credentials.

As Sara got out of the police car, he heard a noise like a firecracker and the police car door window shattered just below his hand. He ducked by reflex, and the next blast went over his head into the headrest of the front seat. Vill pulled his gun, and fired into the van. The van full of shooters sped away.

The shocked officers got back into the police car and began to chase the van. Vill called headquarters and advised that they were in pursuit and under fire. All cars were directed to respond as backups. Suddenly, the back door of the van flew open, and two youths lying on the floor began firing at the police car. Both officers ducked low behind the dashboard of the police car as the windshield shattered in the hail of bullets. Sara began to drive in an "s" pattern so the youths could not get any more straight shots at the police car. They were heading for the Border Lake, and four units had set up road blocks there. They were ready for the van. Cars four and five had the north road blocked, and cars three and ten had the west road blocked. The only place for the van to go was in the lake or onto the beach.

Tony and Pete got out of car five with shotguns, and fired into the front of the van as it sped toward them, trying to knock out the engine. A plume of black smoke shot from the front of the van, and it came to a screeching stop with a gush of steam like a Yosemite geyser escaping from the grill just as the van struck the police car. Sara and Vill almost crashed into the rear of the van, but swerved at the last minute to avoid the collision. Six young boys jumped out of the side of the van, they all had guns, and they were shooting as fast as they could pull the trigger. They ran in all directions.

Two boys jumped into the lake, they surfaced to the sight of four police officers with shotguns; they put up their hands and surrendered. Two more boys ran out of ammo, Cried "Don't shoot we give up!" and they put up their hands and knelt down in the street. Two others had ran into a housing development and disappeared.

Neighboring police departments had heard the transmossions and responded to the area to see if they could assist. Sergeant Bolton asked them to surround the development. Then Detective Fowler, and four officers began a search from house to house for the armed youths.

The first of the missing boys was found hiding in a dog house in the yard of old Mrs. Mitchell. She had heard her dog crying at the back door, and knew that someone was in her backyard. She signaled to the police to go around back, and the boy's shoes were spotted through the dog house opening.

The second boy was found hiding in a tree house behind a vacant house. He fired two shots at the police, but missed. He then yelled, "Don't shoot. I surrender; I ain't got no more bullets." He threw out the gun, and stood up with his hands in the air.

The youths fired over 150 bullets during this incident, and luckily no one was hit. There was damage to two police cars, and several buildings bore the scars from the impact of the stray bullets.

Vill and Sara were lucky to escape unhurt. They returned to police headquarters to begin the preliminary report. The crime scene had been turned over to the detectives for processing, under the supervision of Sgt. Bolton.

The teenagers were taken into custody. The boys were from a wealthy community bordering the city. Their parents were middle class professionals, doctors, lawyers and teachers. In most cases, both parents worked. The oldest was fifteen, two were fourteen, two were thirteen, and the youngest was twelve. They had been drinking and dropping acid. They had gotten into one of their parents personal stocks of drugs and consumed a large quantity. They burglarized the house of a neighbor who was an F.B.I agent, and they jimmied the gun cabinet. The boys had stolen the guns and ammunition from him; they had set out on an adventure. They decided to commit a robbery.

The twelve year old went shooting with his parents and knew how to use the guns. He loaded them for the others, making sure the right ammunition was in the correct gun. After their capture, the boys were cocky. They were heavily under the influence of the drugs they had ingested. They smiled and joked during their processing. The first parent to arrive was Doctor Shamsky, the father of the twelve year old. He defended his son saying, "I taught him how to shoot; you are lucky if he wanted to hit you, you would be dead." With parent's with this kind of attitude no wonder the boy did what he did.

The next was the stepfather of the fifteen year old boy. He was Municipal Judge in the next town. He was very upset. It was his neighbors van the boys were using. They had stolen it from her driveway that morning. He told the officers, "Send the little bastard away. I have had nothing but trouble with him since I married his mother." He refused to take him at first, but relented at the urging of his wife, and took the boy home.

The other parents came to claim their wayward sons, and take them home. Finally only one boy was left, Gene Bono. His father Dr. Bono was the man who's drug stash the boys raided. About six hours later, a lawyer arrived. He said he represented Dr. Bono and would like to take custody of the boy.

Sgt. Bolton stepped forward. "Where is the boy's father?" he commanded. The lawyer said, "I do not know." Sgt. Bolton said that Judge Bender from county court said the boys were only to be released to their parents. The lawyer reminded the sergeant that Dr. Bono was the congressman from this district, and that he was a very powerful man. The sergeant ignored the implied threat, and he told the lawyer, "I have a commitment from Judge Bender right here, and if the boy's father does not show up to get him, I will send the boy to juvenile detention until he appears before Judge Bender next week.

The lawyer left, and walked to the phone in the lobby. He returned about a half an hour later, and told Sgt. Bolton to send the boy away, Dr. Bono chooses not to come in.

The shootout in the city down the shore was over. The boys had robbed a 7-11 in the next town, and they left the owner and his helper tied up in the store room. They had beaten him and threatened to kill him after they tied him up. They panicked when they saw the police car pull behind them. Being high on drugs they thought the police were looking for them for the robbery. This probably precipitated the shoot out because of fear of being arrested. They thought the officers knew they had robbed the 7-11 store. The officers were lucky to get away without being shot. The six young men had ruined their lives, but their lives may have been ruined already.

The district got a new congressman the very next election. On the evidence given by the teens, a search warrant was issued for Dr. Bono's home and office. A large amount of illegal drugs along with two unregistered guns were the proceeds of the raid. The case against the boys proceeded to trial, and a new case against Dr. Bono began. Soon, everything went beck to normal for a while. Nothing lasts forever not the good or the bad. The poor store owner was so scared after the robbery he retired, sold the store, and moved to Florida.

Richard had been anticipating his next conquest for several weeks. He had his eye on a pretty young girl he had noticed sleeping on the beach. To him this was a good sign she was a runaway. He would look into this discretely; he did not want to be connected to her in any way if something should come up in the future.

Two nights later, he spotted her alone on the beach crying. When Richard approached her, he could smell she had been drinking. He said to her, "It can't be that bad." She looked at him, and gave him a weak smile. "No, its just I miss my home so much." These were the words Richard wanted to hear most. He told her, "Listen, Here is five dollars, go to the donut shop, and get some coffee and donuts. I will wait for you here." She said, "You trust me? You just met me?" He said, "Yes." As she got up to go she thought what a nice man this was, he trusts me even though he doesn't even know me, I think this is the kind of friend I need in this strange town.

This act put the ingenuous girl at ease, it made her feel better. I think I will have a good friend after tonight, the young innocent girl thought as she walked to the donut shop. Young girls can be so naïve.

She returned with the coffee and four donuts. As she handed Richard the change he told her to keep it. The girl smiled. It would be the last smile of her short hard life.

Richard suggested they get out of the night chill, and go under the boardwalk to drink the coffee. As she ducked to enter, Richard kicked her hard in the behind sending her sprawling into the sand. He jumped on her back, and pushed her face into the cool loose sand. The young girl found herself suffocating, and she could not breathe; she struggled fiercely until she finally passed out.

When she came to she was tied with her wrists to her ankles. Her clothes had been removed. There was a rope around her neck, and her mouth was duct taped closed. She whimpered. Richard was sitting across from her smiling. He had a razor knife in his hand. He slowly walked over to her and lightly cut her on the breast. She screamed but the duct tape gag muffled it. Her eyes were wide with fear, Richard liked this. A tear rolled down her cheek, and Richard licked it off. He thought this is a beautiful taste, the taste of fear. He slowly slit her other breast cutting deeper as he slowly moved down to the tip. He brutally cut off the nipple. The terrified girl passed out from the terrific pain. This upset Richard, and he flew into an uncontrollable rage punching and kicking her limp hanging body. Finally in his fit of anger, he gutted her from her crotch to her breastbone. He cut the rope that was holding her up, and as she fell he slit her throat.

He penetrated her as she was dying. He heard her legs break from his weight, but she was already gone. Too soon, he thought. She died too soon. I have to control myself better; the terror should last much longer because when they suffer it feels so good. He buried her in the back of the boardwalk, and put her entrails in a plastic bag, then into the bag that had contained the coffee and donuts. He sat down on the covered body and finished his coffee, and ate a donut. When he was ready, he got up and left with the bag of entrails that he would disperse on the way home.

As he walked home he thought about ways he could make his lovemaking last. He needed a way to keep them alive. Even if they passed out, he needed to know that they were still suffering. He loved to give pain and see terror. It was his food, it nurtured him. It would take some thought to work out a plan, but he knew he would find a way. He threw the plastic bag into a dumpster in the rear of an apartment building he passed on the way home.

At home, he thought about the girl, her tear, and how special it tasted. He found that the thought of the taste of the tear had aroused him. He began to think about his other lovers and how they never fully satisfied his needs. No matter how much he got from them, he always needed more. His search for the perfect lover must still continue. He had become so aroused with these thoughts he thought he would burst. He reached under the bed, and pulled out his favorite skull. He kissed it and put it next to him. He became aroused thinking of his new lover. After he satisfied himself Richard caressed the skull. It put him at peace, it always did. He smiled; then, he turned on his side and curled up around the skull. He fell into a deep dreamy sleep.

# CHAPTER EIGHTEEN

## The Car and the Kid

It was a steamy scalding day, and it would be muggy all night in the City down the shore. The temperature had been in the nineties all week, and on some days touched over the century mark. The night had to be cooler, and there was, as always that beautiful zephyr of a breeze off the ocean that made it bearable. This night had been a busy one with many bar fights and disputes, but all the bars were closed now. Tony and Pete were finished checking their post. They parked the patrol car in the north point municipal lot to take advantage of the cool ocean breeze and were starting their daily report. Ronnie and Frankie pulled along side. The young officers began telling war stories about the night, and they compared notes on the calls they had handled.

It had been busy from the start this sweltering summer night. Silky Martin had been slashed by his girlfriend when he tried to take the week's food money for a night on the town. His girl Lenore loved him dearly, but she drew the line at sacrificing the weekly food money for their kids. It was a love cut across the shoulder and chest. It needed almost thirty stitches to close the yawning wound; Silky said he cut himself shaving, and did not want the police. He was taken to Fitkin Hospital emergency room where he was stitched up. When the doctors were done working on him, he left the hospital. Before

136

he left the hospital the officers advised him not to go back home until after court tomorrow. It was more than a warning. Silky agreed.

Lenore was brought in to police headquarters and booked, but she was processed and sent back home to her children. There was no purpose in keeping her in jail overnight. She was needed at home to tend to her children. Lenore would come in to see the judge in the morning. Eventually, charges would be dropped. A small fine would be paid to cover the court costs, and an admonition to cease further hostile acts would be given to both parties by the judge.

After that start, the night seemed to level off. There were the usual bar fights, and several fender bender accidents with no major injuries, but nothing too severe, just steady work. The patrol units were kept hopping, but there were no more serious calls. After the bar closings at 0300 hours, things settled down, and now the officers were catching up their reports during the lull.

"Meet you guys at my uncle Harry's for breakfast later?" Ronnie said. Pete answered, "You buying?" Ronnie just laughed. He new his uncle, who owned a local diner, would not charge them as long as Ronnie did the cooking, and the cops were in and out early before the breakfast rush. Ronnie said, "Sure." As the guys were talking, a soggy, dripping wet young man slowly approached the police cars. He nervously said, "Excuse me". All the officers turned to look at him. They all knew this was going to be a problem.

Frankie said to the young man, "Go over to those guys kid it's their post." He pointed to Pete and Tony's police car. The sopping young man trudged over to Tony's window and asked, "Excuse me sir but could you please help me? I seemed to have driven my car into the lake." Tony looked at him and said, "Where?" The youth pointed a waterlogged finger, and dripping arm over the roof of the police car toward Border Lake. He said, "Over there." Frankie and Ron began to laugh. Ron said, "See you guys at my uncle's if you're dry enough." And he and Frankie sped away laughing. There would be no break time for Pete and Tony this night.

They told the young man to get in the back of the police car, and the two officers pulled out of the lot and headed to the lake. Tony called Headquarters; Sergeant Simon answered in an annoyed voice, "Don't you guys ever stop?", like they called just to disturb his rest.

They told him what they had and asked for first aid to be sent, but the crotchety sergeant said, "Just let me know what you have when you get there. I can't tie up the ambulance if it's not needed."

As the patrol unit pulled to the lake front, the youth pointed out the window, He said, "Right there." All the officers could see was the mirror surface of the lake reflecting the stars and the summer sky. It was as still as if it were frozen. Pete said to the youth, "If you are making this up you are going for a swim." The young man pointed to the right and said, "Right there see my antennae?" Tony got out and looked. The surprised young officer called to his partner Pete, "He ai'nt kiddin' buddy its there alright." Pete just laughed and said, "I guess you are the one going for a swim tonight buddy."

Pete called back police headquarters. He advised the desk sergeant there was a car in the lake, and as he was doing so the kid said to Tony, "I think my three friends are still in the car."

With that, both officers jumped out of the patrol unit and ran to the lake edge. There was a two foot high concrete embankment at the shoreline. Pete said, "I can't go in there I can't swim that good. You're the lifeguard you go." Tony wasted no time, he took off his gun belt, and took his wallet and keys out of his pockets. He locked his things in the shotgun box in the police car's trunk and jumped into the lake. The smooth water split, and Tony was in up to his shoulders. He made his way out to the car wading and swimming as fast as he could.

When he got to the car, he stood on part of it. He called to Pete, "I am going down to take a look." Tony disappeared under the cool blanket of water. Pete had called back the desk sergeant and advised him what they were doing. Sergeant Simone said he had called for divers, but they would not be there for about an hour. Tony surfaced and said, "There is nobody in the car." Pete yelled, "Are you sure?" Tony responded, "Yea, the driver door was opened so I swam in and looked it over. I looked all around. The car is empty." Tony held up the ignition keys. With that, the kid jumped into the lake, and he started to swim for the other side. Tony quickly caught him and grabbed him by the hair, and shook him. A handful of hair came away in Tony's hand but the kid stopped his swim, and perched himself on the roof of the car. Tony said very firmly, "Think carefully kid what happened?" The kid said he did not know. He told the officers someone gave him some cardboard to chew on, and now he is in the water. That was all he remembered. He did not even recall walking over to the police car.

Tony was standing on the roof of the car holding the young man by the arm. There was a yell, "Smile" and a flash. The press had arrived. Denis the press photographer was ecstatic. He had a great front page picture, and plenty of time to get it in before the deadline. When Pete saw him arrive, he jumped into the lake so he could get into the picture. So did Ronnie and Frankie who had pulled up with the photographer. Denis snapped and snapped until he was out of film he thanked the officers and said, "I'll send you guys copies. These pictures are great." True to his word, Denis provided several pictures to the officers the next day as promised.

These did turn out to be great pictures, and one was even on the front page of the Newark News, and the City Press. Inside they had a two page spread in the Newark News. It had been a slow news night.

It turned out when the divers arrived that there were no other people in the car. The lake bottom was dragged, and the divers searched the area, but there was no sign that there were any passengers in the car. A tow truck with a boom was called, and the car was fished out of the lake. All the other doors were still closed. Only the driver's door was opened.

The young man was a student from a local college, and he was tripping on LSD. His estimated speed, to go that far out in the lake after hitting the concrete embankment, was calculated at over one hundred miles per hour. The car may even have flipped in the air as it flew into the lake. How he wasn't killed God only knows. He was sent to the hospital. The doctors committed him for thirty days to the psychiatric ward for observation, and then released him to his parents. The officers never met for breakfast. They got instead a memory that will last a lifetime. So ends another night in the city down the shore.

Richard would be busy this night. He had met two young girls in a bar and had convinced them to meet him at around four in the morning to drop some acid. Bonnie and Betty Kreel were from West Virginia. They had run away over a year ago. They had been established in the city for a year. They had false driver's licenses. They were known as Darla and Dina Christianson. They worked at a local burger joint and went out drinking when they could afford it. They never took a date home, they were very careful girls. They always dated together because they thought they could look out for each other. They thought this would protect them.

They had always wanted to try acid so they could not resist when Richard made his offer. They had seen him in the bars many times, but never paid any attention to him. He seemed harmless enough he was too old to be out for sex. He looked like an old biker. They knew that they had each other, and so they felt secure. Richard left the bar after making the date.

The girls were late; they hoped he would be there when they arrived. Richard had gotten the acid from a motor cycle gang member named Bobby Ward. He had let Ward crash in his house once and they struck up a kind of friendship. Occasionally, Ward supplied him with drugs, and Richard let him crash at his place from time to time; it was a relationship that benefited both. Ward assured Richard that this was the top notch stuff.

Richard was waiting at his bench when the girls arrived. He questioned the two to see if they told anyone what they were up to. Both girls said no. He told them that the acid was strong stuff, but the girls were not deterred, it only made them anticipate it more. Richard could not believe his luck.

Under the boardwalk, Richard told the girls he would give them the acid one at a time, so the other girl could help him if the one taking the acid had a bad trip, and were to get out of control. The girls giggled. He had Darla tie up Dina, for her own protection of course. This was so she would not hurt herself if she had a bad trip, and he and Darla would be able to help her.

The girls laughed and giggled as Darla tightened the knots on Dina's wrists and ankles. Richard slopped a piece of blotter paper into Dina's mouth and covered her head with a paper bag. He then pulled a hammer out of the sand and smashed Darla across the face, as she was watching her sister. She collapsed to the sand like a sack of potatoes. When he removed the bag from Dina's head, she spat out the paper, and started to scream. Richard plugged her mouth with a wad of paper from an old bag and tied a bandana around it to keep it in place.

Dina's eyes were wide with fear as Richard lifted her sister's bloody face from the sand. He licked the blood from around the oozing wounds around her face. Darla's eyes fluttered quickly, and the young girl let out a low moan as her body went limp. Richard felt for a pulse, but there was none. She couldn't be dead he had hardly hit her. Richard yelled, "No." but it was too late the girl was gone. Her nose had broken and the bone had penetrated her brain. He cut through the girls clothes, and stabbed and slashed the corpse with fury. Then, he punched the corpse in the face continually knocking out her front teeth. He picked up some of her teeth that he had knocked out and put them in his shirt pocket.

Richard then turned to Dina and said, "Watch and see what I am going to do to you." He turned and ripped some of the clothes from Darla's bloody corpse and sexually assaulted her. Then he cut off her bloody head. He lifted the grotesque trophy, turned around to face Dina and he smiled a wicked smile. He lifted it high to show it clearly to the petrified girl, but her eyes were closed and her face was wet with tears. Richard yelled at her to open her eyes, but she did not answer. He yelled, "Open you're eyes Bitch or I'll cut off your eye lids!" He approached her with his sheet rock knife preparing to cut off her eye lids, but something was wrong. He stuck the blade deep into her leg but she did not move. The young girl had partially swallowed the paper gag during the rape and torture of her dead sister, and had choked. She was dead too.

Richard went crazy. He slashed and ripped the two corpses; then he cut off all the clothes from the girls limp bodies. He took all their clothes, and identification, put it in his carryall and closed it. He scalped both girls and put their hair in the carryall too wrapped in some of the ruined clothes. Then he dismembered the corpses, and brought the pieces to the far back area under the boardwalk. He dug a deep trench and pushed the parts into it. He wrapped them with the cut up clothes and covered the remains with sand. He put their entrails in a plastic bag and took them out to the end of the jetty for his friends in the depths. The creatures of the ocean rose for this free meal. Richard returned to the sister's mound and rested on top of it. When he was refreshed, he took his trophies and left.

On the way home he tried to figure out what went wrong, but he could not think clearly. It seemed it was easier to kill his lovers than to keep them alive. When he got home he washed the scalps and dried them. He went to bed with the dried scalps on his head. It would be a dreamless, and uneventful sleep. This night had exhausted him, and he needed to rest.

He would return another night and collect the girl's skulls. He felt he needed them. He did not understand why, but there was a need. The pair had actually satisfied him. This was the first time he took two lovers in one night. He would relive this night many times in his dreams. Their end was so enjoyable to him that he would look back at this as one of the finest nights of his life.

Exhausted, satisfied and physically spent, Richard fell asleep.

# CHAPTER NINETEEN

## The Catamount

Mary had noticed that two of her favorite girls had stopped coming to the G.E.D. Classes in the evening. She decided to ask Arnold about the missing girls at lunch. She told Arnold about these two sisters Darla and Dina.

"Two more scatterbrained girls you could never hope to meet." Mary said. "They had come to summer school to get their G.E.D.'s. I believe they were runaways, but that does not matter; they have identification saying they are over twenty-one, and they both have jobs and driver's licenses. They were doing very well. It was a real battle for them to keep focused on their lessons, but they worked hard at it, and they were passing. Just after they took the test for their diploma, they disappeared, and no one has seen them since. They both passed, and I know that after working so hard they would never just leave without finding out how they did. I know they would want their diplomas. I am worried that something bad has happened to them. I am sure Darla and Dina would be proud to know that they got their G.E.D.'s. I can think of no legitimate reason for them to leave before they found out, and I am worried."

"Girls like that move around quickly, and for no good reason. Just a new boyfriend could be why they disappeared. Although, I will admit it is highly unlikely in this case that both girls fell in love

143

at the same time. I will keep an eye out for them." This seemed to relieve Mary. Arnold kissed her on the cheek and turned to leave to return to work. Mary grabbed his face in her hands, pulled it towards her face, and kissed him on the lips. Then, she sat back down, and finished her lunch in silence. She was very concerned that something bad had happened to the young girls. She sensed it right down to her core. She shrugged, cleaned the kitchen table, then, returned to the high school to finish her day.

A mountain lion is one of the most efficient killers among the large cats. It is not a stalker nor a runner, but a patient hunter. It stakes out a territory, and learns all the well used game trails. It then picks a spot near one of these trails, and waits patiently for its prey to wander by. A stone outcrop or a large boulder along one of these trails will serve very well. It will seldom wander from it's territory, and will usually use it's favorite killing sites over and over again. It rarely chases it's prey because the prey always seem to come to him.

Richard looked at the jar on his dresser and smiled. There were six or seven teeth and an eyeball in the jar suspended in vodka. These were the trophies of some of his best lovers. Then he looked out the window of the bedroom and thought how lucky he was. He had settled well into the house in the City Down the Shore. The trust his mother had set up for him while he was away was more than he needed to live on; he put the left over cash into a box in his dresser. He had had great luck these first few years. He had killed many girls, and all the kills were very satisfying. He could not help but feel that there was something missing. He felt he was just scratching the surface on what horror he could inflict on his lovers before they succumbed to his mutilations. He also needed something to help him to remember the good ones, and help him plan the deaths better. He would need to take more of these fine reminders home with him.

He needed to find a way to keep his lovers with him. He shut his eyes and laid down; he thought about the two girls last week It was the first time he did two at once. Another one of his favorites was the girl last month, and how she screamed until he put the tape across her mouth. He loved how the blood trickled from the slits across her breast that he had made with the sheet rock knife. He had bought this tool to try it out. Yes, this tool was a keeper. He smiled as he remembered how metallic the blood tasted when he licked the wounds. He remembered the taste of the tear of some of his favorite girls. Then, he thought of his last girl's tears. It seemed she continued to cry even after she was dead.

He must remember to be careful not to gut the girls so viciously they never lasted long after they spilled their insides into the sand, but the warm blood felt so good on his hands, and his desires were so hard to control. The salty tears let him taste the pain and horror of his lovers as they suffered for him, their blood warmed his soul and brought him much pleasure, and their pain and suffering helped him reach his sexual climax. These girls were truly his lovers because people always suffer for the ones they love the most. With this thought, Richard fell into a dream filled sleep; he was smiling

When Richard awoke, he was totally refreshed. He went down to the kitchen, took a slice of bread, and smeared some peanut butter across it. He poured a cup of tepid coffee from the pot he had left on the stove. Just like in the Joint, he thought as he sipped the tepid beverage, and nibbled on the bread. Several weeks had passed since his last lover, and even though it had only been several weeks he felt he needed something. This need pulled at his soul.

It was dark already and he wanted to get to his bench early. He put on his jacket, grabbed his doctor's bag, and set out for his spot on the boardwalk. The bench he had grown to trust to produce his lovers. He felt it would be a rewarding night. It was getting toward the end of the month, and most of the young runaway girls would need a little extra money to help them to the next month. He was right.

He was pulled to this last bench on the south side of the boardwalk by the yellow orb rising over the ocean. The moon was large and full, the need was upon him, however he did not feel anxious because he knew someone would ask to be his lover tonight; someone always did. If not, he would be back tomorrow. He would sit and watch the golden moon dance in the cool fall night and think of all the things he would do to his next lover. He fell into a relaxed, trance like state and began to dream.

Richard really began to believe he was a God. Only a small God he thought as he gazed into the glowing moonlit night. He certainly

145

had the power of life and death. He surely was much smarter than anyone else he had known. He knew he could be invisible. The authorities did not even know that he was taking a girl a month, sometimes more, from the crop of runaways that came to the city to find their fortune. The supply was inexhaustible. These girls always came to him. They had no past, no real name, and certainly no future after Richard was done with them. He never had to search or set traps for them. They always approached him, they trusted him, and he always rewarded their trust with his love. He began to think that as a God, he knew what was best for these misguided and confused little girls, and he enjoyed helping them find their salvation. He enjoyed it very much. They were certainly better off with the angels than in this cold cruel world, and he would provide their hell here and now to make sure they got to heaven. There would be no need for purgatory for his lovers.

His peace was broken by a series of shouts and giggles. Richard suddenly became alert. Like a catamount on a boulder waiting for prey to wander by, tensing as it heard the snap of a twig.

Richard waited for his new prey to appear, he knew she would. Then he silently would prepare himself and pounce when the time was right. There was never any hurry or necessity because there were so many girls available. The careful way was the best way. Prison had taught him patience and calmness, and he had mastered these traits perfectly.

A chubby young little girl fell against the bench, she looked at Richard and blushed, then put her finger against her lips as if to signal Richard to be silent. Then she broke into an uncontrollable giggle. Richard just stared and smiled.

The girl fell against him and sat down. "Hi, I'm Debbie" she slurred, "I'm sorry that I bumped you sir, I may have had a little too much to drink." Then she broke out into another series of uncontrollable giggles.

Two young boys that looked like soldiers came to the bench, and one said, "Come on Deb or the diner will close, we're hungry!" She looked at Richard smiled, and pointed to the young men. Debbie said, "They love me; so I have to go. It was nice meeting you sir." She got up and left. Her guardian angel was with her tonight. Richard just smiled as the girl got up to walk away with the two boys.

Debbie felt a chill all the way down her spine right to her deepest nerve as she turned back to see Richard's gaze upon her as she walked away. She walked off the boardwalk with her two friends, she did not know why she had this feeling; it was as if death was with them. It made her frown. She became sober.

She would not look back. It made her feel like she just left the devil. She shook her head, smiled again, and followed the two boys to their car. She would have to watch her drinking she thought as she got into the car with the boys.

Richard continued his contemplation, it seemed like only a few minutes, but several hours had passed. The chubby girl seemed like a dream. Why did he become alert? The answer was on the bench next to him. A thin young girl was sitting with her head in her hands sobbing. She looked like a skeleton in baggy blue jeans and a sweat shirt. Richard softly suggested, "Would you like some coffee? It may make you feel better." The girl looked at Richard and she stared at him for a few moments, then she nodded.

The thin girl walked over to his bench and sat down at the far end. Richard handed her twenty dollars, and he asked, "Would you go to the diner and get a couple of coffees? I would love to go with you, but I am hampered by an old war wound. Get yourself something for breakfast, too" he added, "I'll be fine with just a large black coffee." She slowly took the money, got up, and left without a word. Richard could see by her desperate look that she would be back. He would enjoy saving this girl tonight.

As Rachel walked off the boardwalk, she thought about just leaving with the money and not coming back. She knew she could not do that. Her strict Jewish upbringing had prevented her from such larcenous actions, even though she was desperate, and at her wit's ends. Instead she went to the diner, ordered a full breakfast and ate it quickly. When she was about to leave, she ordered two large black coffees to go. While walking out, she passed two police officers coming in, she brushed against one of them, nodded, and softly said good morning as she left the diner.

The thin young girl slowly walked back to the boardwalk, and she began to think of her home and family. She missed them very much. She never would have left if her father would have let her choose her own husband. She knew she could never marry the old man her father had chosen for her, she left home after her father threatened to disown her if she failed to comply or worse yet send her to a relative in Israel. Now, she was on the street alone with no job, no money, and no home. She hoped this nice man would let her stay with him for a couple of days until she could get on her feet. She would offer him sex. It was all she had left.

Richard smiled as he saw the thin girl walk back up onto the boardwalk. He knew she would come back to him. "I hope you feel better now." Richard said as the girl returned to the bench, "You can keep the change." She nodded, said "You are very kind sir." smiled, and kissed him on the cheek. He did all he could to keep from recoiling from her kiss. He hated it when the girls touched him, even with the kiss. He smiled a tight lipped smile, looked away, and started to drink his coffee.

After he composed himself, he asked the girl why she was crying. The young girl told him of her plight, and how much she missed her home. The two talked for a while, and the ingenuous girl suggested they go down on the beach to get out of the wind. Richard nodded and they walked down to the sand.

On the sand, Rachel saw the opening under the boardwalk, and she suggested they go in and see if it was warmer there. Richard just grinned and followed the girl inside. She never knew what hit her. When she came to she was taped to the supports of the boardwalk. She was naked and cold there was a strip of tape across her mouth. She saw Richard to her left with his back to her. Rachel began to sob. She struggled fiercely to free herself, but she was taped fast to the supports.

On his way home, Richard was whistling and swinging his doctor's bag vigorously, after dumping the bag of innards from the young girl in a dumpster. He was pleased with his night's work. He had sent the girl to heaven for sure, because he made sure he made her hell her last hour on earth. He remembered the sound of her fingers breaking as he bent them back to her wrist, and the loud cracking of her arm and leg bones shattering after he struck them with the hammer. He could not recall when exactly she died. She had stopped whimpering soon after the first leg broke. She had bitten through the cloth gag. He was too busy enjoying his lovemaking; he must learn to pay more attention to his lovers needs. As satisfying as this was, he knew it could be much better.

He had the girl's head in a plastic bag inside his doctor's bag. He had left his tools at the killing grounds to make room for his trophy. He buried her headless corpse in a deep trench at the back of his killing grounds. He would put the head in the freezer until he decided how to preserve it. He had her jewelry in his pocket. It was a very fine gold necklace, and a large gold six pointed star. This was his first Jewish girl, and she was a fine one at that. She did not try to scream, but whimpered deeply through the gag. She fought fiercely, and continually tried very hard to break free. She almost succeeded in getting her right hand free, she was so skinny. But when the hammer blow broke her arm she stopped wiggling it and Richard was free to do what ever he wanted without fear of her getting loose. She just whimpered and moaned occasionally.

Richard had raped her brutally, and gutted the corpse when he had finished, then removed the head with an army surplus survival knife. She may have still been alive when he began to remove it he thought. This brought a huge grin to his face.

He buried the body in a sandy grave after he cut it apart, and wrapped the pieces of her body with her slashed clothes. He buried his tools in a spot near the entrance to the boardwalk supports. He took the entrails, and put them in the coffee bag then into a plastic bag. He then put the head in a plastic bag and stuffed it into his doctor's bag. He walked out to the ocean, and washed his hands in the quiet surf. Then he returned, picked up the two bags and left for home.

When he arrived home, he washed the head in the bath tub. He made small holes in the nose sinuses and stuck a hanger into the brain case. He liquefied the brain matter like he read the Egyptians did with a bent metal coat hanger on a power drill. Then he flushed out the head until only clear water came out of it.

He cleaned the flesh of any blood residue, dried it, and wrapped it in butcher's paper tying it tightly. He then placed the wrapped parcel into an extra large freezer bag, and put it into the freezer in the basement. He felt pleased. He hoped that this one would stay preserved for a long time. He liked the look of terror in the cold lifeless grey eyes. He went upstairs and fell asleep as soon as his head hit the pillows. Making love to the thin Jewish girl had exhausted him. He relived the wonderful night in his dreams.

Mike and Tony had just finished their tour. As they finished their reports they remarked how busy they were when the moon was full. The night had gotten off to a slow start, but it soon picked up as the bars filled, and the patrons liquored up.

The first fight was at Jay's Bar between two members of rival motorcycle gangs. Both fled prior to the arrival of the police, but not until the bar was trashed and the bartender and one of the bouncers were cut by the combatants.

Joe Martino's was soon to follow with a fight between several Irish steel workers, a pimp, and two of his girls over payment for services. One of the girls, who was stiffed had slapped one of the workers. The problem was that she had three razorblades between her fingers to increase the effectiveness of the slap.

What resulted was a bloody fight with two of the iron workers and Sweet King Barnes going to the hospital. None of the girls were at the scene when the police arrived, but the bartender gave Big Geno and Bonzoni the street names of the two girls. Kelly O'Rourke had six deep cuts across his face and neck; Kelly was not a good looking man, but the scars and stitches would make him a horror for the rest of his life. Patsy Kelly had a broken nose and a long cut over his left eye. This was just another scar on an already marked and broken face. Sweet King suffered a broken arm and shattered jaw, physically he was hurt the most, and it would be some time before he would resume his status as a force on the street.

None of the participants wanted to talk to the police or pursue the matter, but that was usual in these cases. They had to be treated at the hospital, arrested, and charged just in case the event was worse than what the officers now saw. The judge and their lawyers could sort out the particulars in court.

The last call involved two students from a local college. The loving couple had come to the Pony Bar to hear a well known rock band, and decided to go onto the beach after the bar closed and have some fun. After an interlude on the sand under a blanket, the two decided to take a swim au natural to cool off. It was a bad choice.

When they returned from the sea, their blanket and all their possessions including their clothes were gone. After a brief search and despite the embarrassment, both of the naked young kids approached Mike and Tony to ask for assistance. They both blushed as they told the grinning officers their tale of woe.

Tony told the two kids to sit down, and Mike notified police headquarters. The first aid arrived soon with blankets, and took both youths to the hospital to be checked for exposure. Tony went with the first aid, and got all the pertinent information he needed for the report. When he was done, he returned to the city with Big Geno and Bonzoni who were at the hospital with the fighters from the earlier call. Two of them had been held at the hospital because the staff needed more time to treat their injuries, so Bonzoni would return later, and serve them with summonses for the fight.

"That girl sure was built!" Tony commented to Mike as the two finished their reports, and prepared to go home. Mike nodded his agreement, "Just another night at the North Jersey Shore's premiere resort." Mike quipped as the two young officers left police headquarters to get some food; they found that busy nights usually made them extra hungry.

Tony and Mike went to the diner, and both ate a good breakfast then went home. Mike had bumped into a thin young girl as they entered. He said, "Good morning young lady." And the girl nodded and said "Excuse me, good morning sir.", and walked out into the dark still night. Both officers remarked to each other later on how thin and gaunt this young girl was. She was soon forgotten by the officers and was never seen again.

# CHAPTER TWENTY

## The Raid

It was a cool night; the breeze was whipping off the ocean, and the sky was clear. The sand on the beach glowed; it was lit by the light of the full moon and all the stars in the ebony sky.

The siren sounded so Tony and Pete knew they must hit a call box, or use the nearest pay phone. They walked up Kinmouth alley, and Pete used the pay phone at the City Service gas station. He dialed "O" and told the operator to connect him to police headquarters; he gave the operator his badge number. Sgt Harriman answered. He barked, "Both of you get your butts upstairs, and make it yesterday."

Pete knew this would be a good night they were only called in when something like a raid or special detail was happening. While Tony and he walked to police headquarters, they wondered what was up. The young officers were hoping they were being called in for a raid. That would keep them busy the whole night, and maybe even mean overtime. When the two young officers arrived at police headquarters, there were police cars parked down the street, and into the municipal parking lot. They knew this would be a raid. When they got upstairs to the squad room, Sergeant Bolton was waiting. He told them to sit down and listen. They were the last officers to arrive, and when they were seated, Captain Talon began the briefing.

They were told that they would be raiding "Sugar Bear", the local drug kingpin. Sugar Bear was a Jamaican Rastafarian whose given name, as far as anyone knew, was Classford Greene. He was born in Jamaica, but he lived in the city most of his life. He was about thirty years old. Sugar Bear was about five feet two inches tall, and was well over three hundred pounds. He wore his hair in long dreadlocks, and looked like a bear. He was strong and ruthless. As with most successful drug dealers, he ruled with an iron claw.

Where there are hookers, there are drugs. In this city where there are drugs, there is a Sugar Bear. A price war developed on the supplies of drugs for the hookers, so a pimp called Lensy decided to save some money. He went out of town for his drugs. He sold the leftover drugs to his girls and their johns. He was doing very well. He knew that when Sugar Bear found out about his little enterprise, he would not let it go unpunished. Lensy knew could never stand up to Sugar Bear by himself so Lensy met with the detectives, and Sugar Bear was set up.

Lensy Hilton was really named Dewey Hilton; he was tall, skinny, and nearly blind. He had to wear glasses with thick coke bottle lenses. Because of this, on the street, he was known as "Lensy". When you looked at him his eyes were like slits, because he was always squinting. He was six feet tall and about one hundred fifty pounds. He was a pimp by trade, but never passed up a chance for some easy money; selling these drugs had been easy money. Whether the enterprise was legal or questionable did not matter to him, as long as the profits were there. He only had to get the drugs, and his girls did the rest. If Sugar Bear found out that he was selling drugs, Lensy knew he was dead or at least badly broken, so for now Sugar Bear had to go.

Lensy told the detectives where the Rastafarian hid his drugs, and even went in and made a controlled buy for them. With this information, the detectives filed an affidavit in county court and were granted a search warrant.

Sugar Bear lived in the "penthouse" on the fifth and top floor of the old Slade Hotel. The old hotel was once the biggest whorehouse in the county; now, it had been converted to an apartment building. The first floor had a large lobby. There were no apartments other than the owner's residence. The owner lived on the first floor with his family. At the east side of the lobby were the stairs to the apartments, on the upper floors. The stairway ran up the east side of the building. There was a hallway on each floor. At the end of each hallway, was a door that led to a fire escape with one exception. The fifth floor had no hallway. The top of the stairs ended at that apartment door. The stairs were the only way to this penthouse apartment other than the top landing of the fire escape, which only ended to a large window.

The fire escape clung to the west side of the building. The top landing of the fire escape was like a steel balcony for the fifth floor apartment, accessible only from the door on the floor below or a window in the penthouse apartment. The landing had plants on it against the window, with a close line strung across its length. The landing was about five feet by ten feet. The only way into the apartment from the fire escape landing was through the three foot by six foot window which opened into the living room of the penthouse apartment. The building was five stories, and had a large front porch that rapped around the west side of the building. The fire escape bottom sat on the porch roof.

The raid would begin with an assault on the apartment door using a battering ram. The detectives were told that the drugs were stored in the pockets of coats hanging in the large closet next to the entry door. The main body would hit the door with a battering ram, enter and secure the drugs. Everyone in the apartment would be arrested. Tony and Pete would be out on the fire escape to prevent any evidence from being thrown out the window. Sugar Bear could never fit through the window, so only two men would be needed there. The captain told Tony and Pete, "You don't have to go in, unless he tries to flush the dope before we get the door down. If you see him getting the dope out of the coat pockets, go inside as fast as you can, and yell to us so we know that you are in there." Pete and Tony looked at each other and smiled, this would be as great a night as they had hoped.

At four thirty in the morning the unmarked police cars quietly rolled up to the Slade Hotel. The tour cars had closed off the block so no unwanted traffic could enter the scene of the raid. One officer stayed in each car. The ambulance, which responded with the police to every raid, was parked on the corner. The team went into the building, and up the stairs. On the fourth floor they split. The main body went up to the fifth floor. Pete and Tony hit the fire escape. Pete told his partner to go up to the landing, so he could see into the window. Pete did not like being out on the fire escape; he was afraid of heights. When Tony was in position Pete poked his head inside the door, and whispered to the team that Tony was in position. The team charged the door with a concrete filled pipe they used for a ram. Then all hell broke loose.

Tony could see Sugar Bear lying on the floor watching a boxing match on the television. When the ram hit the door, the crash brought Sugar Bear to his feet. He was fast and agile for a fat man. The door was knocked off its hinges, but the team could not get in because there were three thick chains that spanned the doorway. The chains were padlocked to steel eye studs in the beams on the sides of the door. Sugar Bear ran to the closet, and started to grab the packets of drugs from the pockets of the coats. Tony yelled down to Pete that he was going in, and Pete reluctantly began his climb up the fire escape. As Tony jumped in through the window, he yelled to the team at the door, that he was in the apartment, and that Sugar Bear was trying to flush the drugs. Sugar bear stormed out of the closet with as much drugs as he could carry. The fat Rasta froze when he saw Tony in the apartment. He shoved the packets of drugs into his mouth, and grabbed a decorative sword from the wall.

The panicked drug dealer charged Tony. Sugar Bear was an awful sight with the drug packets in his mouth, powder all over his face, and the sword in his hand, like a Rasta Teddy Roosevelt charging up San Juan Hill. He ran toward Tony with the sword pointed toward him trying to make the young officer move, so he could get to the bathroom.

Tony put out his left hand to deflect the sword, and brought down his night stick on Sugar Bear's head. Tony hit him so hard that the blow lifted the young cop off the ground. The nightstick struck with a resounding click. But during his charge Sugar Bear had managed to put the sword through the palm of Tony's hand.

As Sugar Bear collapsed to the floor, Tony looked at his ruined hand and screamed. Tony fell to his knees just as the team entered the apartment. There was blood, white powder, and drug packets all over the floor.

The captain told the sergeant to call the first aid men who were in the lobby, and told Tony "Leave the sword in until first aid gets here you might damage something; they are coming up the stairs now." When the First aid men arrived they told Tony to leave the sword the way it was so he would not do more harm. They took him down to the ambulance, and told him to sit on the gurney. The ambulance sped away to the hospital, so Tony could be treated for his injury. All the way to the hospital, Tony sat on the gurney holding the sword, and cursing every time the speeding ambulance hit a bump. Looking at it alone hurt; it felt like he was holding lightening in his hand.

When they arrived at the emergency room entrance, Tony was wheeled into the hospital, and put in a booth with a curtain drawn around it. A nurse rushed in; she walked over to Tony smiling as she pulled the sword out of the wound, then she wrapped a large thick gauze bandage around the bleeding, aching hand and said." Hold this tight, the doctor will be right in." Tony said, "You just pulled it right out?" The nurse replied "Sure why didn't you do it before you came here? It would have hurt much less." Tony felt like a fool, but was relieved to have the offending blade out of his rapidly swelling hand.

Tony received two stitches in his palm, one in the back of the hand, and a tetanus shot for good measure. Pete came to the hospital to pick him up, and they returned to police headquarters, so they could complete their reports. Sugar Bear was treated at the hospital for the wound to his head and taken back to police headquarters by Sergeant Bolton. Sugar Bear was printed and new mug shots were taken, then he was sent to county jail in default of bail, after the detectives were finished with his processing and his interrogation. He now sported a bald spot where Tony's baton opened his head. The doctor had placed seven stitches there to close the wound.

Sugar Bear was charged with Possession CDS, Possession with intent to distribute CDS, Assault on a Police Officer, Destruction of evidence, and Attempted Murder. His bail was very high, and he would be in jail for a very long time until his trial.

Sugar Bear had his charges eventually merged in a plea bargain to Possession with intent to distribute CDS, and Assault on Police Officer. He pled guilty, and was given twenty years by the judge. He was paroled seven years later.

Lensy Hilton got his reprieve, and did well with his new business, but it was short lived. He was stabbed by one of his new girls several months later in a dispute over money, and he bled to death in the back seat of a taxi cab before the taxi driver could get him to the hospital.

Tony went back to work the next day, and was a celebrity for about three days. Then, another officer was injured in a scuffle, and the new war story, that went with the injury became the center of attention. It just continues day after day. Crime never stops, even though the police do their best to control it. Everybody gets their chance for attention, but that attention does not last. Someone else is always next. It always changes, and it goes on forever. Every day is different, but it is always the same

Things were picking up in the city, and there seemed to be an endless number of runaway kids in town, but only for a short time. They seemed to disappear quickly much more quickly than usual.

Richard was mobile. He had met up with Johnny Fitzpatrick a cell mate from prison. Fizz, as he was called, was an ex-biker. He was so bad even his biker friends were glad to see him go away. When he got out they avoided him, and he needed wheels. He bought an old used car from a widow that lived next to his sister's house. It was an old Chevy Bel Air four door with a huge trunk; it was twenty years old but only had 25,000 miles on it. The old lady had kept it in the garage since her husband died fifteen years ago. It was in bad shape outside with rust in all the usual places but it ran like a dream. Fizz borrowed some money from Richard, and bought the car cash. He paid the widow $500.00 for it. This car would come in handy when the pair was working.

After getting plates and insurance, he drove the car to Richard's house. Fizz and Richard cleaned up the old car, then Fizz returned to the old woman's house wearing a stocking over his face. He broke in beat the old woman, and took back his money, and about $3,500.00 in cash she had around the house along with her TV set. He got away free and clear. Fizz considered this a good omen. Things were finally going his way.

Fizz was a perfect sleazebag. He was sexual degenerate with no honor or honesty. He would do anything. He had no guts, and he needed a leader; but he was as good a follower as anyone could want. Richard took him in right away, and they lived together in Richard's large house. Fizz had his own room. He loved the work Richard was doing. They were a pair made in hell. They would work well together. Life for the runaways that came to the city just got worse.

Within a week, Richard had worked out a plan. He wanted to be able to keep his lovers with him for the longest time possible. He also wanted to expand his loving, at least he thought of it as loving. He now had a good use for the luggage he had stolen from his mother. He loved the car. It was an old 4 door Chevy Bel Air, and four people could hide in the trunk comfortably. There was no limit to the number of lovers Richard could store there if it were done right. His excitement was almost too much to contain. He smeared a slice of bread with peanut butter poured some coffee into a cup and went up to his room. This would be a great year, he thought, as he finished his snack. Then he reached under the bed to bring out his favorite skull; he curled up around it, and dropped off into a troubled sleep. The moon was almost full.

Two days later, he was sitting on his usual bench on the boardwalk, when he was surprised by someone calling him. She said, "Richard, you are Richard, how are you tonight?" He turned and was surprised to see Johanna one of his earliest lovers. He was stunned, but soon came to his senses. There was no one there. He was sweating. He looked around, and he saw faint shapes that resembled his lovers gliding around the bench. He got up and slowly backed off the boardwalk.

Richard began a slow walk home in a daze from the encounter at the bench, when he heard the sound of a horn. He looked and there was Fizz motioning him to get into the car.

Richard got in the car and noticed a naked girl passed out on the back seat. Fizz said, "She's dead drunk, you wanna fuck her?" Richard replied, "No I just want to make her one of my lovers. I need something good tonight" The two degenerates laughed at the pun. Fizz parked in a dark lot behind a vacant building, and raped the unconscious girl again, then he turned her over to Richard, and he left the area for a long walk.

Richard was prepared. He had what he wanted in the spacious trunk. He went to the trunk, and took out his doctor's bag. In it he had all he would need. First he spread a plastic painter's drop cloth over the back seat, and then he put the girl on it, and put a piece of duct tape over her mouth. He put her arms over her head, taped them together, and then to the arm rest. He then cut off what remained of her clothes.

He brought her back to consciousness, breaking an ammonia capsule under her nose. He tortured her until she passed out, then he revived her and tortured her more slicing and cutting until the poor young girl painfully expired. She lasted for a long time. Richard was pleased. He was so aroused that he sexually assaulted her dead corpse in all three orifices; he was pleased with his work.

When Fizz returned, he found Richard asleep in the front seat of the car. The girl was gone. He woke Richard up and said, "Where's the broad? I wanted to fuck her again." Richard said, "You can still fuck her I'll show you when we get home."

# CHAPTER TWENTY—ONE

## The Train

The midnight shift had left police headquarters, and the day shift had just finished their briefing. They were preparing to begin their patrols. Sara and Vill had just made a stop to get some coffee when they heard over the car radio, 837 to all cars call me by phone. Vill went to the nearest phone booth, and dialed the operator he gave her his badge number. She connected him to police headquarters. Sgt. Griffith answered, and said, "Go to the high school and meet Sergeant Bene there he'll tell you where to go, someone called in a bomb threat, and the janitor has found something suspicious."

When the officers got to the high school, the kids were outside joking and jostling in lines down to the end of the block. The officers met Sergeant. Bene at the front door. He looked pale. He said, "Guy's we got a live one. The janitor says he found what looks like a piece of pipe with batteries and a clock attached to it in a shoe box." "We have got to close the school", the Principal said, as he was walking toward the officers. "We can not risk the safety of the children." The Sergeant agreed. Sergeant Bene took a loud speaker out of his car, and he said over it, "Everybody walk in an orderly manner to the football stadium and meet your homeroom teacher." At the stadium, the principal directed the teachers what to do while the officers secured the area around the high school, secured the suspicious item, and closed the school.

The bomb squad from the nearby military base responded about two hours later, and went to the suspected bomb. The Captain, who was the leader of the bomb squad laughed and pulled the pipe out of the box. Then, he pulled out the clock and batteries. He said, "Someone must have forgotten the stuff they bought at the hardware store he joked; there is nothing here that is dangerous." The amused soldier laughed. The principal was furious; the officers laughed as they resumed patrol. Inside the shoe box was an alarm clock a piece of pipe and some batteries, nothing more. Sara said to Vill, "Some kid must have really wanted the day off from school today!" They laughed as they road away.

The laughing was interrupted by the radio, "837 to all available units!" Sergeant Griffith yelled into the radio, "See the conductor of the train stopped at Fifth Avenue He says he needs the police; the train hit something, and it may have been a person; let me know what you got."

The call at Fifth Avenue was a terrible sight. A young man had just been hit by the train. People on the street who saw the incident said the boy just jumped in front of the train. There was nothing anyone could do the witnesses said, it happened so fast.

Sara and Vill had been the first car to the scene. They secured the scene around the body which was jammed half under the train. It had been dragged quite a ways before the engineer could bring the huge vehicle to a stop. Tony and Pete were next to arrive and took charge of securing the back end of the train and the surrounding area. Detectives Moose and Jones were on the way to conduct the investigation.

The crime scene was a grisly sight. There was the ruined body jammed under the train. There were body parts that had been ripped off and strewn all along the path of the train from the point of contact to where the train stopped. The engineer and conductor were in shock. Passengers were taken off the train and were waiting for a special train on the other track to take them to a neighboring station. Most stopped to take a look at the shredded corpse before they left.

The detectives found a wallet hanging out of the jeans of the corpse. They carefully picked it up and looked through it after pictures were taken of the area around the corpse. It had a student I.D. inside that said this was Robert Pile a senior at the local high school. He was nineteen years old. He was about to graduate this June. The question now was why would he jump in front of a train? He was doing well in school. He had received a basketball scholarship to a local college, and he was gainfully employed after school at a local fast food place. It seemed a strange case indeed.

After the crime scene examination was complete, the body was removed from under the train, the loose parts were collected, and the whole matter was sent to the coroners office for a post mortem.

Bonzoni and Big Geno were sent to Robert Pile's home to break the news to Robert's mother. Big Geno knew her well. He dreaded this chore, but he knew it had to be done. Leona Pile screamed, and she collapsed to the floor crying when she was told the news. Big Geno picked her up and sat her in a chair. The broken hearted woman just rocked back and fourth sobbing. Big Geno tried his best to comfort the poor young woman, but hearing about the death of your child is about the worst news a person can get. The young woman went into shock. Her mother and sister arrived. Big Geno broke the sad news to them, and they rushed to Leona. There was comfort in their company, and the officers slowly left the house. Big Geno told Leona's Uncle Bill that he could call police headquarters later, and they would give him instructions on how to retrieve the body. Big Geno suggested that the family contact an undertaker of their choice to make the funeral arrangements.

That afternoon, Patty Plummer called police headquarters. She wanted a cop to come so she could give them her sister Penny's baby. The baby had been left at her house yesterday by Penny's boyfriend, and Penny had never come to the house to pick the baby up. Now, Penny won't answer the phone or her door. Patty said she is tired of taking care of Penny's baby she has three of her own.

Big Geno and Bonzoni responded to the call. They put Patty and the baby in the police car. They drove to Penny's apartment. When they arrived the officers knocked at the door, while Patty waited in the car with the baby. There was no answer, but the lights were on and so was the television. It was still daylight, the lights did not need to be on. The officers became suspicious. They called the desk sergeant, and asked him to send the custodian to the apartment complex with a pass key so they could enter the apartment. The officers waited in the car, and played with the baby until the custodian arrived.

When the door was unlocked the smell hit them like a punch in the face. All three men fell back. There was no mistaking this smell. It was the smell of death. As the officers walked in, all seemed okay, but the putrid smell increased as they made their way to the bedroom.

On the bed was the naked body of Penny Plummer, she was lying in a puddle of dried blood, and it had several visible wounds in the center of her chest. The wounds were numerous, and appeared deep as well. It appeared that most of the blood had drained out through her back. There was very little on her chest. The handle of a knife protruded from the center of her chest; the knife appeared to be buried up to its hilt. The officers closed the door to the bedroom, secured the apartment, and called for a detective. They went to a neighbor's house and called the desk sergeant to advise him what they had. Sergeant Harriman laughed a dry laugh and said, "Moose and Jones just finished with the suicide, they will be real happy getting this." Detective Fowler heard the desk sergeant and he volunteered to take the call. He left for the scene with Detective Sergeant Berg

The two officers went back to the car and broke the news to Patty. She let out a wail and tried to run into the apartment. The officers restrained her and took her to the neighbor's apartment. They asked them to call Patty's mother.

When the two homicide detectives arrived, they looked haggard, but they realized that when duty calls you just have to suck it up, and do your best. They put some Vicks Vapo Rub under their noses put on rubber gloves, and entered the apartment. Arnold began to sketch the rooms. Sergeant Moose went over to the phone, called police headquarters, and asked Sgt. Harriman to call the county forensic squad to help them process the scene, and then, the two detectives began their investigation.

Detective Fowler found out that Patty had been the girlfriend of a real bad man Frank Grates. He was a stick up artist, and had shot several people during his last crime spree. However, he was still in jail and could not have done this. The baby was his, and could be turned over to his family if the Plummers did not want her. On the side of the bed, there was a picture frame face down in a pile of broken glass. When the detectives turned it over, to their surprise, it was a picture of Penny and Robert Pile. There was a stab hole in the picture through Penny's body. It had shattered the glass.

This was turning into a strange case. After the scene was processed, the two detectives returned to police headquarters to check the possessions of Robert Pile. In a knapsack they took off his back, were some books and a pad. The detectives slowly opened the pad, and on the first page was a letter to Robert's mother written by Robert. It said:

> Dear Mom:
> I love you very much, but I have just killed the only other thing in this world I will ever truly love. I will see you again in the next world. I hope you can forgive me for the shame I have brought to the family, I hope we will meet again in heaven
> Robert.

This letter had simply explained the tragic suicide and a brutal murder. The detectives could get some rest tomorrow. Now, they must tie up the loose ends and close both cases. The tragedy would devastated the two families and leave the neighborhood in shock fore a long time.

It was found out later that Penny had told Robert this was his child. She had done this to get Robert to help her out while her boyfriend was in jail. When Robert found out that the baby was not his he confronted her, and they argued. She broke up with him and refused to take him back.

He found that he loved her, and he did not want to live without her. He did not care whose kid she had had. What hurt him was that she no longer loved him. She refused his attempts to make up. Another argument ensued, and he stabbed her to death. In despair, he had written the note to his mother and walked in front of the train.

Arnold went home and sat down in his easy chair with a bottle of whisky and a tumbler. He had called Mary to cancel their date tonight, she did not answer so he left a message on her machine, she must not be home from school yet.

The exhausted detective was determined to finish the pile of paperwork from the tragedies earlier today. He was sad and shaken from the tragic event, but he wanted to get it done. He was almost finished with the reports and halfway through the bottle of whiskey when Mary walked into the room. He had not even heard her come in his house.

He smiled, he was always glad to see her. He tried to get up, but fell back into his chair. He found he was unsteady on his feet. Mary told him to stay seated. She glanced at the reports on his desk, and just shook her head. "What a shame two beautiful young people with their whole lives ahead of them, and now they are gone." Arnold answered, "It is such a shame, and I never get used to seeing young people dead. It is a terrible waste, and a total tragedy."

Mary said, "Here I brought you over some dinner." Arnold shook his head no and said, "I am not very hungry, but I could use a hand getting to bed." She looked over at the half empty bottle of whiskey and shook her head.

Mary helped him into the bedroom. Arnold kicked off his shoes and flopped onto the bed. Mary pulled off his clothes, but Arnold was asleep before she finished. She smiled at her man, set his alarm to go off a half hour earlier than usual to give him time to clear his head, and kissed him on the cheek. Then, she covered him with a blanket and left him to rest.

Richard loved the freedom Fizz gave him. He could go anywhere now that he could move around easily. He had spent so much of his youth in detention he had never learned to drive or gotten a driver's license. There was no place for him to drive to in prison. Now he could keep his lovers with him. He could put them where he could always be near them if the need arose.

The girl he met last night was a fine example. After he had done what a good lover should do, he had gutted her corpse. He carefully cut it into pieces. He wrapped the pieces in the girl's clothes, and put the pieces in a suit case he had in the trunk of the car. When Fizz opened the trunk and saw the suit case he wondered what was inside. When he saw it he was shocked. He began to have second thoughts about Richard. However, he had seen worse, and he did like playing with the parts. What a pair these two were.

To Richard, things were getting much better. He would care for her for a long time. He loved this new way to take care of his lovers.

He began to think; maybe he could lure some girls into the car, with the lure of a ride home? He would have to think on this. It would add a new dimension to his passion. He could not count on Fizz being careful about whom he picked up so he decided to take charge of getting the girls himself in the future. But this had been fine for a start.

The car and the mobility and privacy it gave added a new dimension to Richard's lovemaking. It gave him a new sense of adventure. Richard had been getting bored with the ease at which he could get his lovers and perform his diabolical deeds on their fine innocent bodies. He would prowl the beachfront with his new partner and look for potential lovers. The car would give him a much broader selection to choose from.

When he arrived at the house, he walked up the stairs and lay down in the bed. He reached under it and touched the skull. You will have much company soon he muttered as he fell

# CHAPTER TWENTY—TWO

## The Streaker

As Mary dressed for work, she was still upset that two of her students had died so brutally the other day. Robert Pile was one of her most promising students. He had been accepted on a full basketball scholarship to college. He was also a good student. He would have been very successful. Penny Plummer was a drop out. She had a young child. Mary was hoping she would return to school or at least get her G.E.D. It was all moot now.

The 0800/1600 shift started with the usual escorts for the city offices. Bank deposits of the tax monies and other revenues must be safely made, and interoffice mail had to be delivered for the politicians. It was boring, but it started most days. After this type of work, there was only one thing to do, get some coffee, and check out the beachfront. As Pete was coming out of the coffee shop with two coffees and a hard role, he was knocked to the ground by a naked young girl who ran into him. She bounced off him, blew him a kiss, and sped around the corner. By the time Pete recovered she had disappeared. Tony got out of the police car laughing, as Pete sat there in the parking lot with coffee dripping down his shirt and a surprised look on his face.

"Sh, sh, she was naked." Pete stammered in a high pitched surprised voice. "Boy if my daughter ever did that she would really get it!" Pete said. "You don't have a daughter." Tony reminded him. "Well, if I did." Pete replied. This was the time of the sexual revolution and morality was changing. Streaking became a national pass time and in the city down the shore, there was no exception. It was a pleasant manner of illegal display, but it could not be tolerated in this conservative religious city.

Just then, the police radio came alive. Sergeant Griffith called "837 to all available units, there is a report of a young woman running through the city park. They say she is n- n- naked! " He then added, "You guys better get her, the phone calls are killing me up here, I got the whole switchboard lit up." Tony and Pete laughed as they drove to the park. "That's your girlfriend." Tony joked at Pete. Pete just exhaled and blinked his eyes. He still hadn't recovered from the collision.

When the officers pulled into the park, people were laughing and pointing to the east end, the area where the girl disappeared. She was nowhere to be found. Frank and Davy radioed that the subject was G.O.A., and that the area was checked negative for the subject. They volunteered to stay in the area in case she returned. Big Gino asked over the air, "You guys got a description?" "Very funny, now cut it out, and get that girl." Sergeant Griffith barked over the air.

Lucky Mattie had caught her boyfriend Leophie with another woman. She had slashed the girl across the breasts with a straight razor, and she was chasing Leophie down Lake Avenue with a felonious intent. Big Geno and Bonzoni got the call. Pete and Tony were called as the back up.

When the officers arrived, Sissy Bates was in the ambulance crying. She was naked from the waist up, and had a large bandage across her chest. Two blocks away Leophie was up a tree, and Lucky was underneath yelling up at him. Leophie was fortunate that Lucky Mattie was not built for climbing at barely five feet tall she could not reach the first branch. She was swirling her razor like an artist using a paint brush yelling at Leophie to come down so she could cut off his balls and the rest of his private parts.

She yelled to Big Geno to get away, and as she turned to lunge at him with the razor in her hand, Bonzoni, who had worked his way behind her, hit her with one blow to the side of her head, and she dropped the razor, and collapsed to the ground. Before she could get her senses the officers had her turned over and handcuffed behind her back. It was done quickly, a very good job.

Pete said to Tony, "I thought it was supposed to be quiet on the day shift?" Tony said "I don't know this is the first time I ever worked day shift." The two young officers laughed and resumed patrol.

The short peace was interrupted by Sergeant Griffith's yell over the radio, "All cars get back to the park and get that mutha fucken girl! And I mean get her; the phones haven't stopped all morning." Tony and Pete laughed they knew the sergeant never cursed over the radio, so they knew he was very upset, they figured he had really lost it. All the other cars were laughing too, the two young officers laughed with amusement as they drove back to the park.

When they got to the park, Frankie and Davy were running on the east side. They were chasing something, but weren't doing too well. It was an amusing sight. Both were in their forties and had figures to match. In the distance, Pete and Tony saw the faint form of a naked woman, and they knew what Dave and Frank were chasing. They drove across the park, but were too late. The girl had disappeared, and Frank and Dave were winded. They got into the back of the patrol unit panting, and Pete and Tony drove the gasping officers back to their car.

"This girl is going to wear us out. If we don't get her soon, Sergeant Griffiths will have us for lunch. Did you hear what he said over the air?" Frankie said. Just then Sergeant Griffiths called Tony and Pete to report to police headquarters.

At headquarters, the two young officers were met by Captain Tallon. He said, "Who is the faster runner?" Pete answered, "Tony." Tony said. "What!" The captain said to Tony, "Go home, and change into something you can run in; then get back here as soon as possible, and see me in my office."

When Tony returned, he was wearing his police academy gym shorts, a tee shirt, and sneakers, Captain Tallon looked at him and nodded in approval. Then, he said, "Here is the deal, go to the east end of the park, sit on a bench, and wait for that girl, when she runs through get her, and I mean get her. Don't let her get away, is that clear. Pete you stand by near the park in the police car just out of sight, but keep an eye on Tony; when Tony catches her get her into the police car, and out of the area to police headquarters as soon as possible. Is that understood?" Both officers nodded as Captain Tallon walked away.

At the park, Tony laid on a blanket in the corner at the east end of the park. He could see the whole park from this spot. The naked girl had prowled here before, and he waited hoping she would return. He was there for several hours, and no sign of the young girl.

Then there was a call for all cars to go to J.J. Newberries an off duty officer was chasing a shoplifter down Munroe Avenue.

Piggy McDonald had walked into the store, and he was looking good. He was one of the cities premiere drag queens. He was wearing a black leather vest, over a pink bra, pink mini skirt and black fishnet panty hose with six inch high heels, and a blond wig. At six feet two, he was impressive. In six inch heels, he was awesome. He had gone into the store, picked up a small suit case, and filled it with cosmetics. He ran out of the building with the goods, and Sammy Zoza, an off duty special officer, gave chase. Sammy at five feet four inches, and over two hundred pounds had no chance of catching Piggy, who could run faster in high heels than Sammy in sneakers; Sammy was just trying to stay close until help came. And help did come. When Piggy saw he could not get away he stopped short turned around with his hands up. Then when Sammy arrived, he kissed the little man on the top of his bald head as the pudgy special officer stopped to grab him. "You know I was just funning with you, you sexy beast?" Piggy said to Sammy. "Shut up and get up on the wall." Sammy said to the drag queen. Piggy said "I love it when a strong man like you orders me to do something. Now, don't you get fresh with me, well I mean don't get too fresh, you know I just love a man in uniform!", and Piggy tried to kiss Sammy again.

When the other officers arrived, they laughed at the sight of Sammy frisking Piggy, and Piggy moaning with pleasure every time Sammy touched him. "Boy this job sucks!" Sammy said as he handcuffed Piggy and put him in the back of Big Geno's police unit. He got in with Piggy, and they headed to police headquarters. The radio barked, "All cars get to the park Tony is chasing that girl."

As the officers arrived from all over town to surround the park, Tony was walking across the park with a naked girl in his grasp. She was smiling, and Tony was blushing. The press was there taking pictures, and the people were making cat calls to Tony. Pete just looked and laughed as Tony put the naked girl into the back of the police car. "Did you search her for weapons?" Pete joked as Tony put her on the back seat of the police car. Tony then went to the trunk, got out an army blanket, and gave it to the girl, but she threw it back and said, "That itches, why don't you come and sit next to me to keep me warm?" Tony just blushed more, shut the door, opened the front door, and slid into the front of the police car as Pete laughed harder. "Nice catch partner you should get the Medal of Honor for this." The young girl in the back waved to all the onlookers as the police car sped away. Tony just slid down in the seat and ducked his head.

At police headquarters, the young girl was taken into the ladies room by two female specials, searched, and given some clothes, she was then brought before Sergeant Griffiths to be booked. Just then, the Chief walked in and said, "Sergeant, Have the officers bring the girl to my office; better yet, you and Tony bring her into my office, Pete can watch the desk until we are done. Tony, Sergeant Griffiths, and the girl walked into the chief's office.

"Hello Debbie", the chief said to the surprise of the officers. "Gentlemen, this is Debbie Howder Congressman Howder's daughter. Debbie say you are sorry to these good officers." Debbie got up and went to Sergeant Griffiths; she shook his hand and said, "I am sorry if I caused you any trouble today good sir." She then smiled sweetly, and walked over to Tony, she apologized to him, kissed him on the cheek, and whispered in his ear, "Meet me in the park after work today, okay?" The Chief said immediately, "Whatever she said forget it, she's going with me. Sergeant, There will be no complaints at this time , and no information is to be released to the press. It they have any questions direct them to me. Is that understood?" With that, the old chief took Debbie by the hand and left with her to take her home. As he left his office, he said to the officers, "Resume."

The sergeant was noticeably ticked off, but he said nothing. He just walked out and took his post behind the desk. He told Tony "You can't finish the tour dressed like that, and there is not enough time for you to go home change and come back, so you can take the rest of the shift off." He turned to Pete and sent him back out on patrol. Pete gave Tony a dirty look as he walked out to his car. Tony laughed, and ran to his car. He might just have time to take a swim in the ocean before it got too cool. In the heat of May in the late spring, the ocean was a blessing, but it did get cold in the evenings.

The late spring was a blessing for most, but for Richard it had become a nuisance. He had three lovers in Fizz's trunk. They were stinking badly. He had decided to visit his mother and do some gardening.

They drove all the way to her house with all the windows opened. Still it smelled horrible. They pulled up the driveway and deep into the back yard. Richard went in to the house, and said. "Hi mom." She nodded and said "Hello Richard how is my good little boy?" Richard ignored her greeting and told her to sit in her rocking chair. He taped her arms and legs to the chair; he did not need her hovering over him babbling while he buried his lovers.

Richard went to the mud room in the rear of the small house. He took a shovel, and went out the back door to the small plot of ground in the back of the house. Fizz had backed the car to the plot. When they opened the trunk, the stink was terrible. Richard took out the three suitcases and inside each was a large plastic bag. He had Fizz dig three deep holes and put each bag into a hole. He then told Fizz to fill them in. Fizz planted several small marijuana plants as he filled in the holes and planted some flowers around the marijuana plants. He admired his work for a moment then got into the car. Richard was already sitting in the passenger's seat, he told Fizz to drive home. Fizz said, "Aren't you going to say goodbye to your mom and let her out of the chair?" Richard just said, "No." and looked away. Fizz knew better than to press him so he just drove home.

On the way Richard thought of his lovers. He hated to leave them. He wondered how long it would take for the stink to go away. He could always go back and dig them up if he needed to see them again. No, he thought; he would just get new lovers. That would be much better, and it was easy because there were plenty of girls that would love to meet him. He would have his pick. Tonight, he would rest, and tomorrow he would find a new lover. He said to Fizz, "Stop at the next Stewart's, I need some supper." Fizz nodded.

The next night Richard was anxious. He would try to keep this next lover alive for as long as he could. He had a plan. He would try drilling a hole in her head and pour a small amount of battery acid into the hole in an attempt to blank out her brain, but hopefully not enough to kill her. Then, he could control her like a zombie. It had worked for the doctor in the movie he saw last week, he hoped it would work for him. He could not wait to try this.

Fawn was a young girl from Wisconsin. Sadie Gruppen was her real name her father was a dairy farmer. She was so happy to be by the shore. She had read about places like this but did not know if they really existed. She was in heaven.

Fawn was working at the amusements center on the boardwalk during the day, and hanging on the beach at night. She did not have I.D. yet so she could not go into the bars, but at fifteen she really did not want to. Instead, she hung with the boardwalk people that slept on the beach, and on the roof tops of the beach houses and amusement stalls. They slept on the beach in groups of about a dozen, they went under the boardwalk in bad weather, and slept on the flat roof tops when it was hot.

The kids cleaned up at the public showers in the beach bath houses off the beachfront or pool area. Fawn had only been here a month, but she knew she would stay because she loved it here.

She had met a man named Richard last week, and he had given her beer and hot dog. He was nice. She would work on him and maybe he would let her go home with him. She was to meet him tonight at one o'clock. She would offer him sex for the use of his bathroom. It would be glorious to take a real bath. This was her plan. Richard also had a plan.

Fawn, was true to her word, but a little late; she met Richard on the boardwalk about 0200. Richard said he had a friend he would like her to meet. He had a car. She agreed. The pair got into the Chevy and Richard passed the girl a beer. Fizz, Fawn, and Richard went to Richard's house to get better acquainted. This was too good to be true. Richard was so happy he almost wanted to scream. He controlled his urge to kill her on the spot. He would do it the new way later.

Fawn too was pleased. At the house she asked to use the bathroom to freshen up. Fizz said, "Only if I can freshen up with you!" Fawn readily agreed. She thought that this was just too easy. For three hours, Fizz and Fawn went at it in the bathroom. Richard listened to the sounds and he grew more and more excited. This could be the answer to his dreams. He had everything ready, duct tape, battery acid, and drugs. He would try to keep her alive for a month.

Fawn came out of the bathroom with a towel rapped around her. She walked over to Richard and asked for something to drink. As Richard handed her the drink she let the towel drop. "Woops" she squealed as the towel hit the floor revealing her slight young body. Richard just smiled and sat down. Fizz came in and giggled as he watched the naked young girl walk over and sit in Richard's lap. "This is good; what is it?" Fawn said as she drained the glass. "Just rum, coke, and a red" Richard answered. The girl did not know what a red was, but she did not care. She had these guys just where she wanted them she thought.

She was so proud of herself, and then she felt it. Her head spun, and she fell off Richards lap. The empty glass slipped from her hand, and she sprawled to the floor next to the sofa. She tried to get up but found she could not move. She felt warm, and smiled. It would be the last smile of her unhappy, pitiful, young life.

Richard took out a two by four and taped her arms to it. Then, he put duct tape over her mouth. He wound it around her head several times. He opened two holes for her nostrils so she could breathe. He liked what he saw. Fawn blinked her eyes in horror, but she soon passed out again. Fizz came over, and looked at the girl. He laughed. "Can I do her?" he said to Richard. Richard nodded and walked away. When Fizz was finished, Richard returned. He had a scalpel, a drill, a small hibachi filled with smoldering char coal, and a flat butter knife with black tape on the handle. He squatted next to the girl and removed her eyes. He put them in the jar on the T.V. with his other lover's teeth and the single eyeball. The alcohol turned pink.

Fizz became scared. He had never seen Richard like this before. He popped two reds into his mouth, and drank them down with a beer. He quickly fell asleep.

Richard took the drill and drilled into the side of the girl's forehead. Her lower body contorted in spasms as the drill made its way through her skull. He pressed too hard, and the drill bit went deep into her brain. Her body was still. Richard did not realize it at first, but the drill in her brain had killed her. The girl was dead before he could make the second violation of her body.

He poured some acid into the drill hole in the side of her head with an eye dropper. He stepped back to inspect his work. That's when it hit him, that Fawn was dead. Richard flew into a rage. He yelled, "You dirty horny bitch, don't you go away on me now." He kicked her over and over then jumped on her head crushing her skull. The insides splattered on the floor, the walls, and Richards clothes. He was out of breath. He fell to his knees and cried.

In a few minutes, Richard came out of it. He composed himself. He calmly went upstairs, changed his clothes, then returned and cleaned up the mess, and went to the car. He opened the trunk and took out one of the suit cases. He took the dead girl back into the bathroom and put her into the tub. He gutted her, and put her insides into a garbage bag. He turned on the water and let the ruined head and body drain. An hour later, he returned, cut the body up his usual way, and put it into the suit case. It seemed so light. He put the suit case back into the car trunk. He sat in the old car in a daze. What was he doing wrong, he thought to himself. He fell asleep shaking with anger. He could not dream.

# CHAPTER TWENTY—THREE

## The Hitman

On this rare night, you could stand on the corners in the dead silence, and the only sounds you might occasionally hear would be the braying of stray dogs, fighting over scraps found in the alleys, or cats screeching and fighting for a chance to mate with a female in heat. This night, the calmness was shattered momentarily by four gunshots that no one heard. Instantly, the quiet continued.

Eduardo Ricardo Gonzalez was a Cuban refugee. He was adopted by Doctor Phoebes Hedd and his wife Eleanor Hedd two displaced persons from World War II that were also refugee's from another era. They were allowed to come to the United States after the war. Eduardo was two when he was adopted. He was given the surname of his new parents, but was allowed to keep Ricardo as his given name. This was a mistake because children are cruel, and by twelve he was nicknamed Dick Hedd by all the children behind his back. Sometimes when someone wanted to be really mean, they would call him that to his face. This did not happen too often, because Ricardo would fight at the drop of a hat, and he was very good at ending most altercations in a painful and final manner. It was because of this talent he found his true passion in life.

When a bully, Oscar Brooks, a much older and larger boy, began taunting him in seventh grade, Ricardo decided it was time to stop this unbearable behavior. One night, he made his way to Oscar's house and tapped on his window. Oscar answered, and Ricardo told him to be quiet and follow him. He said he had found some money and wanted Oscar's advice on what to do with it.

Being greedy and thinking he could take all the money for himself, Oscar followed Ricardo. In the rear of an abandoned lumber yard, there was a deep dry well that was used to catch the drippings from the saws. It had not been used for over sixty years and was about fifty feet deep with a concrete base. It had been boarded over, but most of the boards had long ago rotted away, and those that remained were weak and weathered. No body ever came here anyway, so there was no real danger to the public.

Ricardo grabbed a shovel from his garage, and the two boys left to get their treasure. When they got to the old drywell, Ricardo told Oscar to look down and see all the money at the bottom. As Oscar bent to look down the deep well, Ricardo hit him hard in the back of the head with the shovel, and Oscar went quickly where many greedy bullies end up, to his death. He was barely conscious when the sudden stop at the bottom fractured his skull and broke his neck. His remains would not be found for over a year, and they would not be identified for many more.

The bully disappeared, and so did Ricardo's foul nickname. Ricardo found out who his real mother was. She had died in childbirth a Maria Gonzalez. He had been baptized Eduardo Ricardo Gonzalez. His adopted parents had called him Ricardo to give him an identity with his birth mother's culture, and gave the baby there surname name. They innocently chose the wrong given name to place with their surname.

At eighteen after he graduated high school, He changed his name back to Eduardo Gonzalez and left home to start a new life.

Because he enjoyed killing Oscar so much, and because he did it so well, Eduardo realized what he wanted to do for the rest of his life. He would become a professional killer. He loved to kill. The murder of Oscar would be the first of many murders Eduardo would commit throughout his lifetime. He would become an enforcer for the local organized crime lords; he did this by eliminating the current holders of the position. It was then he was able to achieve his dream, to become, a professional killer, a bone breaker, a hit man.

Santino and Pasquale Dentino were twin brothers. They were called Sonny and Patsy by their friends and relatives. They had grown up in the city. They left to fight in the Korean War in 1952 and came home two years later. They bought an old block long building called The Prospect Plaza.

It was a decrepit old three story building with a huge cellar that ran the length of the building. It had three full stories above ground.

The ground floor was large, and the brothers made it into a grocery store with three small stores on the south side. One was a dry cleaner's. The second was a barber shop, and the last was a small sandwich shop that only opened at night.

The second floor was the Prospect Plaza Bar, with a small package goods store on the side.

The third floor was divided into two rather large apartments. The two brothers each took an apartment. They both soon grew into the large dwellings as they both married within the year.

As with many people returning from the war, the brothers each began their own businesses with their severance pay and a G.I. Loan. Patsy took over the Liquor business and Sonny ran the grocery business. Soon, both were doing very well, and Sonny was creating a large family. Patsy and his wife were not blessed with children. Sonny decided to supplement his income with a little bookmaking, while Patsy stayed out of the rackets as he felt he needed to stay clean to keep his liquor license.

At about 4:30a.m., Ricardo entered the rear of the grocery store and confronted Sonny and Patsy. At 5:30, Bud the milkman was surprised when no one appeared to be in the store to take his delivery. He wheeled the dairy products to the rear storeroom and was shocked to see the two brothers lying in a pool of blood, face down with their arms over each others backs. He almost fainted. He left and called the police.

Tony and Pete received the call, "Car #5, See the man at the Prospect Plaza grocery store, suspicious situation, Car #2 back them up." Sergeant Harriman sounded distressed. He added "Let me know what you got right away." This meant that it could be a dicey call so the officers responded quickly and carefully.

The officers secured the scene right away when the saw the men in the pool of blood. There was no doubt they were dead. Pete called Sergeant Harriman from the pay phone at the front of the store. They preserved the scene until Doc Berg and Johnny Moose arrived. Then, the county forensics unit and the F.B.I were called in.

The detectives had been warned by an informer that there was trouble within the mob, however no one knew who were the principals of the threats. The investigation revealed that Sonny had been warned that he should stop loan sharking in this area. He could run a book but not loan money. He was making more on the loan shark than on the bookmaking so he tried to hide the business. He was found out and warned the first time, just his arm was broken. More severe penalty would have been meted out, but for the fact he was married to the old Don's daughter. But the big boss new that if Sonny kept it up he could not interfere with the punishment. That was the code he lived by.

Sonny continued. He tried to hide what he was doing but could not. For this he paid the ultimate price. Patsy was just there to have breakfast with his brother after he closed the bar. He ate with his brother most mornings, he was just in the wrong place at the wrong time.

They never were able to find out who the hitman or hitmen were, but most in the town figured it was Eduardo. About twenty years later, Eduardo was found dead in his home. He had no heirs or relatives that anyone knew. The police searched and indexed his home and sealed it for the tax man. In a safe the officers found four guns and because of his past record the police took them in and sent them to the F.B.I. to be checked out.

The four guns were a .22 cal. Ruger auto pistol with the barrel cut to one inch, a two inch barrel chief's special in .38 cal., a two and one half inch barrel .357 magnum colt python, and an old army .45 cal. Smith and Wesson Revolver that was made to fire .45 Auto rounds with half moon clips. All the pistols had the serial numbers removed, and the bores were machined smooth. They would be impossible to trace ballistically, and it would be hard to get a ballistics confirmation on rounds shot through them.

The Dentino brothers had been shot twice in the head with a .45 cal revolver with no rifling, and the marks the smooth barrel made on bullets fired from it would be very similar to those marks on the four bullets taken from the bodies of the Dentino brothers even though there were no engravings from the lands and groves to match up. It could be shown that a gun similar to this was used in the killings, but it could not be proved that this was exactly the same gun. Although the case remains listed as unsolved, all involved believe that Eduardo Gonzalez was surely the killer of the two men.

Richard sat on the bench and gazed out to sea. He saw Fawns face in the full moon. He cursed her. He needed a lover now more than ever. He found he was shaking. He hoped Fizz had overdosed and would die. In a trance like state he dreamed of his past lovers. He was brought back to reality by a sight that never failed to warm his heart. It was a young girl screaming at a boy on the beach, then slapping him and running away. The girl came up on the boardwalk and sat two benches away from him. The young boy yelled a curse at her as she ran away up onto the boardwalk, and he left the area without her. This may be a good night after all, Richard thought.

The girl sat down on the bench, put her head in her hands, and began to cry. Richard was drawn to the tears just as a vulture to carrion. He softly asked the girl, "Would you like me to call the police or a cab for you? You look like you have had a hard night." She looked up and replied, in a sarcastic scream, "Mind your own business mister, or I'll give you a reason to call the police." Richard slowly backed away, and went back to sitting on his bench. He knew she would come to him when she was ready. They always did.

In about fifteen minutes, the girl was at Richard's side. She laughed and said, "I hope I didn't scare you I was just pissed off at that little shit from the bar. He figured he could fuck me for two beers. What a jerk. So what's a nice man like you doing here?"

"If I told you my troubles you would break down and cry!" Richard replied. The young girl laughed and said, "What did your wife leave you for a women, or was it your son who told you he was a fag?" Richard just looked out to sea.

She stared at him for a while then said, "Come on what's the matter? It can't be that bad." Richard told her, "My best friend just died, he was twenty-five and just dropped dead." The girl felt bad. She said, "Gee I'm sorry mister, I'm a little drunk and still pissed off. Why don't we go down on the beach, and you can tell me all about it. I know I can make you feel better."

A little over an hour later, Richard was on his way home with a bag under his arm. He had a smile on his face and a song in his heart. He was actually happy. This girl had been just what he needed. She had offered him sex for one hundred dollars. Richard of course agreed gave her the money and took her under the boardwalk. For a half hour, he had tortured, raped, and sodomized this young girl. She had great stamina, he thought to himself. Even when he cut her throat, and pulled off the tape that covered her mouth so he could hear her death rattle, the girl was still strong enough to spit in his face. He loved the feisty ones. These were the ones with enough guts to live through the torture and become true lovers. He knew he shouldn't but he took her head. He had to; she had been such a great lover. He carried it home in his doctor's bag.

His good feelings waned as he approached home. There was still Fawn; she had really bummed him out. He put the doctor's bag with the head on the kitchen table. He carefully removed the dripping head, and stared into the lifeless eyes. It brought back memories of the fear and terror of the girls last moments. This pleased him.

He cleaned the new head, and wrapped it carefully. He put it in his freezer, it would not be alone because it would have plenty of company in the freezer. He went to bed and dreamed about his new lover. He relived the night, and this wonderful girl's suffering over and over in his dreams. Each time it was better. This was the kind of girl he needed to get to his home.

# CHAPTER TWENTY—FOUR

# The Car Thief

A s the sun set in the city, the need for police intervention increases tenfold throughout the town; bars fill up, and the tempers at home become short. Even in winter, peace is rare at night in the city down the shore.

Davy and Frank received a call from the squad room that there is a fight at Martino's Tavern, and they must leave the briefing for the 2400/0800 shift. Sergeant Bolton cuts the briefing short, and sends all the units to the bar for back up. As they are leaving, the sergeant pulls Pete and Tony aside and says to them, "Listen we have had two cars stolen every weekend for two weeks. I want you two to take an unmarked car and stake out the used car lots on Main Street. This will be a good place to start as many of the cars have been taken from this area. Take a walkie talkie with you, and check in with the desk every half hour."

As Davy and Frank pull up to Martino's, Patty "Fists" Burke comes flying out the door and across the sidewalk. He ends up against a parking meter pole passed out with a large wound on the top of his head pouring blood down his face. Patty Fitzpatrick follows him out the door and shouts, " Keep your little Irish ass out of this place, you little shit!" and he walks back inside. Frankie follows Patty back inside, Davy calls for first aid, and goes over to the bloody Fists.

Fists opens his eyes slowly, smiles at Davy as he is coming to, shakes his head, and he says, "I'm getting up mom stop shaking me." he gazes lovingly at Davy and tries to kiss him. Davy pushes him away and asks him what happened. Fists shakes his head again like a punch drunk boxer, blinks his eyes several times, and say's, "I think I fell off my bar stool." Then he burst out laughing.

The ambulance arrived, and the medical crew cleaned the cut on Fists bald bloody head; they wrapped it with a large gauze bandage, and walked the woozy pugilist to the ambulance. Once Fist's was safely inside they prepared to go to the emergency room. Fists yelled to Davy as the first aid men were closing the ambulance door, "Hey Dave, I go to the hospital so much they want to name the emergency room after me; they want to call it 'The Fists' Room', ha, ha, ha." The driver closed the door shook his head, he got in the ambulance, and they sped off to Fitkin Hospital.

Inside the bar, Frank found out that Fists did fall off the bar stool after his girl, Sheila O'Dell hit him over the head with a beer bottle for kissing Rhonda O'Connor, her worst enemy. Sheila was sitting in the corner crying. She asked Davy as he approached, "Oh please sir how is Fists?" "He is fine Sheila" came Davy's answer, "But you have to come with us until we know for sure." Davy walked the crying girl to the police car. Of course, it turned out fine. Fists was brought back by Big Geno and Bonzoni, when they returned with a stabbing victim they needed to interview.

At headquarters, Fists kissed Sheila and refused to press charges. Fists said to Sgt. Harriman, "She hit me because she loves me; if she didn't hit me, I would know she didn't love me any more." Sergeant Harriman said, "If she had a stronger love for you, you'd be dead." With that the sergeant Fist's and Sheila burst into laughter.

Sheila and Fists left police headquarters together; they were singing a popular Irish ballad as they walked home.

As Pete and Tony pulled into the car lot on Main Street, a black Caddy came flying out. It flew passed them and disappeared down the street. Pete turned the police car around, but it was too late. The car was gone. They called for Sergeant Bolton. The sergeant got out of his car, and walked over to the officers shaking his head. "What happened" he barked. "The car just flew out as we were pulling up."

Pete said frowning. Sergeant Bolton said, "Okay get out there, find that Caddy, and get the guy who took it." The sergeant left, and Pete and Tony began searching the town for the missing car.

David Lee was a child born with Downs Syndrome. He was a happy boy, but could not learn to read or write. What he could do is fix mechanical things, especially electrical things. He loved working on cars. He could be found every day at the high school in the auto shop working on the school teacher's cars that were broken down. At car repair, he was a genius. The teachers would drop off their cars for repairs, and the students in the auto shop class would work on them for nothing. This worked out well for the class; they always had different cars to work on, and the students became quite good at fixing cars. David Lee was the best of them all. Mr. Feeney the Instructor had promised David that when he graduated he would let him return and work at the school in the auto shop as his helper. This made David happy.

Tony and Pete searched all night, but the two young cops had no luck. The car seemed to disappear. The city just swallowed it up. At the end of the shift, they came in with their tails between their legs. They were beat; they had worked hard, but to no avail. They had nothing, no car, and no suspect; it became just another car stolen with no recovery, or arrest to clear it.

The next night Pete and Tony came in early. They had the owner of the used car lot meet them at his office, and had the cars positioned so only one a beautiful Lincoln Town Car would be able to be removed from the lot without moving all the other cars. The young officers returned to their unmarked police car, pulled across the street, and parked in the alley deep in the shadows and waited.

At 2355 during the change of shifts, a van pulled across from the used car lot, made a u-turn, and road toward the used car lot. Tony jotted down the plate number of the van as it pulled slowly to the edge of the lot. From inside the van, a shape emerged and slid across the street. The van slowly pulled away.

The dark shape entered the lot and got into the Lincoln that had been positioned at the entrance. The officers had drained the gas tank, and it just had enough gas to get started, and go a few blocks. They were ready. The van pulled away as the Lincoln sprung to life.

The engine revved a few times, the Lincoln pulled out, and followed the slow moving van. The officers radioed Police headquarters, pulled out of the alley, and gave chase. When they put on their grill lights, the Lincoln accelerated away, and turned left. The van sped up and turned right. It took off quickly down the street. The two officers gave all cars the description and plate number of the van as they pursued the Lincoln. They knew he did not have much gas and would not get far. In a few minutes, the Lincoln bucked and began to slow. Pete pulled along side so Tony could get a look at the driver and prepare to chase him if he ran. They recognized the smiling face waving to them. It was David Lee. As he turned to wave and smile again, he lost control of the big car and hit a telephone pole. Tony and Pete jumped out and they grabbed David. The boy was not hurt, he was smiling and laughing. He said to Pete, "Boy that was fun, I love cars." They took David Lee to police headquarters. Sergeant Bolton had spotted the van and stopped it. Jose Reynaldo was driving and Bombo Rivera was riding shotgun. They said to the sergeant, "What's up Bolton?" Both were known to the sergeant. They were members of a street gang "The Kings", and they were mixed up in numerous criminal activities. When back up arrived, the two men were frisked and arrested.

It turned out that the Kings had enlisted David to help provide material for their chop shop on City Avenue. After talking to David, the officers had all the particulars. They got a search warrant and executed it before a lawyer could arrive and get the gang members released. They had recovered all the stolen cars, most of which were already apart. It turned out to be a statewide enterprise, and led to many arrests in the city, and throughout the state.

David was given immunity for his help. The Kings would pay him with a bag of candy for every car he brought them, and they would let him drive the car all night. David loved this because he could not legally get a driver's license, but always wanted to drive. The smiling youth was released to his father. He resumed his position at the high school auto shop. He promised not to take any cars ever again, and he was good to his word.

The Kings suffered a great loss both financially and in perception by their community. Their chop shops in the city, and all over the state were shut down. This gang of criminals lost much face in their communities for using a handicapped youth to do their thieving work. And they soon faded as a major gang. They just became another small time group of bullies.

That morning when Arnold picked Mary up to drop her off at school he smiled and said, "Your going to have to find a new place to get your car fixed. They picked up David Lee last night, and it turns out he was a car thief working for the "Kings" His father is sending him to New York to live with his aunt for a while so he can get away from the influence of the Kings." Mary answered, "That stinks, he was the best mechanic in town and you couldn't beat his prices." "Yea free is pretty cheap." Arnold said as he kissed Mary, and stopped to let her out to go to work.

Richard was still in shock. It had been some time since Fawn. He did not call her his lover he had grown to hate her. He and Fizz had dropped her body in a vacant lot in a neighboring town and covered it with dirt. Richard did not want to leave the body in a lot but Fizz insisted. He said it would never be found. He also said even if it was they would never trace it back to them.

Richard was loosing his eagerness. He blamed it on Fizz. He and Fizz quarreled. Richard thought of getting rid of Fizz.

Richard had thrown out Fawn's eyes; the ones that he had put in the jar of vodka, and could not stand the thought of her. He asked himself, was he losing his desire? He did not know.

Fizz was becoming worried. He could no longer trust Richard. The man was just too unpredictable. He began dating a barmaid, Mary, from a local tavern. Three weeks later, he began sleeping at her place. They would end up getting married. He still hung at Richard's house, but was spending more and more time with Mary. Richard accepted her. She was always drunk, had a history of mental illness, and was an intervenus drug user. She was no threat. Richard believed he understood her; he kind of liked her in his own perverted way. She liked him too, but for some reason she could not understand why she could like him because deep down inside she feared him.

Fizz came to Richard one night with a proposition. He had been in touch with a local biker gang to see about purchasing some drugs and they asked him if he was interested in making some easy money. Of course, Fizz said yes. Buddy Moore, a member had been skimming money from the protection stops he collected for the gang. The gang's president Nails Iacadelli wanted him to disappear. The deal was that they make Buddy disappear, and they would get five thousand dollars no questions asked. It had been a slow winter so Richard accepted. He disliked Buddy, who had sold him some bad drugs once, and this was a good chance for Richard to even up the score.

Two days later, Buddy came to Richard's house with some drugs Richard wanted. It was LSD, Reds, and some marijuana. Richard paid him and offered Buddy a drink. It was the same stuff he used on Fawn. Buddy greedily gulped it down in two large swallows. Then, he staggered back. He said, "Phew what ya got in there horse piss?" he laughed as he passed out on the sofa. When he woke up, Buddy found he was taped to a kitchen chair. He had tape over his mouth, and he was naked. His feet were in a pail of water. Richard was sitting across from him smiling.

Buddy's eyes were wide with fear as Richard walked towards him with a pair of jumper cables. He clipped one to Buddy's calf, and touched the other to Buddy's chest. Buddy stiffened and grimaced with pain as the current jolted his body. The cables were part of an arc welder. Richard said, "The setting is on very low but it will get higher as we become friends." Then he laughed. For hours Richard and Buddy played together until Buddy's heart gave out. Richard continued to shock the corpse. He loved the way he could make it jerk and wiggle; it was almost like it was dancing, even though Buddy was long dead. He played with his new toy for hours until finally he got bored. He put the corpse in the bathtub, and removed Buddy's head, put it in a plastic bag, and then, he placed it in the freezer. Richard carefully gutted, and dismembered the rest of the corpse, put it in garbage bags, and put the bags in the car trunk. He wheeled the motor cycle to the rear of the house, and he called up Fizz. He said get Nails, and tell him to bring the money, and a rider to take the bike away, Then you come over we got some work to do. The pair dumped bags with pieces of Buddy in various dumpsters all over town that night.

When Nails arrived the next day he was smiling. He said to Richard, "I believe we have some business to finish." Richard nodded. Nails said, "That's Buddy's bike in the back, but how do I know he won't be back?" Richard smiled, and went down to the freezer. He returned with a box. He opened the box, and removed a plastic bag. He walked over to Nails and emptied the bag into Nail's lap.

Nails looked down to see Buddy staring blankly up at him. Nails laughed, "I like your work." How do you want your payment, cash or drugs? Richard said, "Cash." And Nails counted out fifty one hundred dollar bills. He walked outside with the keys to the bike and threw them to his girl Zero. He told her to drive the bike home.

192

The biker came back inside and said to Richard, "I like the way you work, if I need you again, can you and I do business?" Richard nodded, and smiled. Nails shook his hand and left. When he was gone, Richard went to the sink and washed his hands. He hated when someone touched his skin. Then, he went to Buddy's head, rubbed it, and cleaned it off. He wrapped it in butcher's paper and put it in a fresh plastic bag. He put the package back in the box, and then back into the freezer. This is a fine city to live in he thought as he walked to the bedroom. He picked up a favorite skull and rubbed it; he thought about all his lovers, and his new profession. Torturing Buddy had been as good as making love to the young girls. Life was getting better he thought as he curled up on his side, and soon he fell into a deep dream filled sleep.

# CHAPTER TWENTY—FIVE

## The Fire

It was a cold winter night. The moon was a golden sickle in the clear star filled sky. The city was quiet, and the officers working were having a rare easy night. Car 2 with Davy and J.W. was preparing to go to Davy's house and start to cook breakfast for the shift. The bars had closed without incident and after they checked their respective posts, the 2400/0800 shift would report to headquarters one car at a time to catch up on their reports. When they finished they would usually have something to eat before beginning their final nightly checks.

It had been an uneventful night on post one and two this shift. There had been two small bar fights, one at The Odyssey Bar and another at The Sands Bar, but both were settled without incident or arrest. They had to chase Herman Brown from a parking lot; he was directing traffic again, but in all it was a very quiet night.

As post 1& 2 Patrol Officers Ray Mansky and Frank Solomon were making their checks, they noticed a cloud rising in the area of the 500 block of Cook's Avenue. As they approached the corner, there could be no doubt; their noses told them that there was a fire somewhere on the block. When they entered the 500 block of Cook's Avenue, their worst fears were met when they saw flames spring from the roof of the Steinbach's Department Store Building.

This seven story gargantuan had been the anchor of the business district for over sixty years. It was a masterpiece of turn of the century architecture, but it was now in decline. It would be a challenge for any fire department to control a serious fire within this structure.

The officers called in the now blazing fire to police headquarters from the call box on the corner of Cook's Avenue and waited for the Fire Department to arrive. All police units of the 2400/0800 shift responded to the scene, and they took up positions of traffic control around the perimeter of the block long building. The desk sergeant called the county fire police for additional help, but knew it would be several hours before they could collect a force and respond.

In a few minutes, the fire department arrived, but by this time, the top of the building was completely ablaze. The fire moved fast along the roof of the building as the cold winter winds whipped it along. The Fire Captain recalled the whole fire department, and Sergeant Harriman notified the fire captain that he called the county fire police to relieve his patrol officers on traffic control, notified all neighboring fire departments in the county, and his men would stand by until the reinforcements arrived.

Soon, fire departments were responding from all over the county. This was a big one. They would need every available unit in the county to control the fire. Trying to save the landmark seven story block long building was going to test all their skill.

They had some near tragedies in the beginning when the concrete molding around the building's top story began to crumble and fall in large chunks to the ground. The debris shattered around the firemen scurrying to get water to the building, but no one was struck, and there was nothing more serious than several close calls.

The most important task would be to keep the streets clear so they could run the lines of hoses from the hydrants to the pumper trucks. They needed to pump water high to the top of the ladders of the aerial trucks. The cold weather made it necessary to keep the fire trucks from running over the hoses and shattering them because the outsides of the hoses were freezing over. They needed the most powerful pumper trucks as close as possible to the building so their stream could reach the high roof.

It was touch and go for hours, the firemen were barely holding their own; and then, three big pumper trucks came roaring up Cook's Avenue The were from Atlantic City and they came all the way up to help fight the fire. They would be just what were needed. The problem now was how would they get them close to the fire scene without running over the hoses? There was a maze of hoses blocking their way. It would take an expert to thread them through to the south side of the building.

A figure in a bright yellow and black oil cloth coat and big black leather fire helmet came out of the crowd of fire fighters. He signaled the lead truck, and began to direct him through the spider web of hoses, sometimes even onto the sidewalk, then safely to the side of the burning building. He did this twice more, and the trucks were in place. His training with the "Red Ball Express" during World War II was finally paying dividends.

With this new supply of water, and the power of the three large pumper trucks the fireman were able to get water to the hoses on the high aerial trucks and soon the roof was covered with a river of water.

The fire was under control. They would loose the top floor of the building but the remainder would be saved. No firemen were seriously injured, and no one lost their life. No body could find the Fireman in the bright yellow slicker.

Herman Brown finally made it back to his sister's house it was almost sunrise when he got there. He was tired and wet. He took off his bright yellow slicker, and fell into an easy chair. His sister Melvina asked, "What happened to you you're all wet?" He answered, "They needed me at the fire to direct the trucks through the maze of hoses, so they could save the Steinbach's building." Melvina just nodded, she mumbled to herself, and shook her head and walked away.

Melvina walked into the kitchen heated some water. She brought Herman a hot cup of tea and a soda cookie; she put them down on a napkin on the coffee table in front of the old warrior. Then she stepped back and shook her finger at him and said, "Your too old to be out late at night chasing cars and trucks like a misbehaving dog. Especially fire trucks! You leave that fire stuff for the young men, you here." She scolded as she covered the old man carefully with a thick down comforter She loved her older brother he had raised her since their parents had died. He had never been the same after he returned from the war. She kissed him on the forehead and went back to bed.

Herman sat in the warm chair sipped his tea , nibbled the soda cookie. He was pleased with the work he had done this night. When he finished his snack he closed his eyes, and fell asleep thinking of the great job he did at the fire. He was a happy man this night.

Richard heard the sirens from his bench, and he returned from his dream. The western sky was a glowing light, but it was still night. It must be a fire he thought, and a big one at that. He had thought about burning one of his lovers alive, he thought it would be great fun. He had burnt cats and dogs before, and he had enjoyed that very much, especially watching them squeal and squirm while they were still alive.

Nothing was as good as watching a lover suffer. Now, he really wanted to burn one alive. He just could not work out a way to do it yet. He got up and slowly walked toward the blaze. If he was lucky, maybe he could catch a glimpse of someone burning to death in the fire he thought. Maybe he would even see some police and firemen burning up trying to save someone burning in the building. The thought of seeing a police officer burning to death excited him.

When he arrived, the whole block seemed to be burning. People were running everywhere. Police, fireman, civilians it was pure chaos. He slowly walked over to a park bench about a block and a half away, pulled the collar of his coat up around his ears, and settled down for a night of entertainment, curtsey of the city's fire department.

He had loved fires; as a kid he had set many of them himself. He wished he had set this one it was really a fine fire. He really thought he would get to see someone burn to death when one of the aerial ladders collapsed, but the firemen escaped injury and were able to fix the problem quickly without any further incident. There was no one in the building it was empty at night. That was a shame Richard thought. He wished it had happened on a Friday night when the whole area was crowded. He smiled, maybe a fireman would fall into the fire while he was watching, or get burned, or catch fire from the heat; he closed his eyes and wished.

He gazed at the blaze, and slowly it put him in a trance. The dancing flames had put him under their spell. He was back in Staten Island, and he was very young. He had caught a neighbor's dog, a toy poodle, and had just gutted it. He had dug a shallow ditch and threw the squirming crying dog with it's insides dragging on the grass into it. He poured lighter fluid on the dying dog. Then he set it ablaze. He smiled; Richard remembered it even squealed a horrible yelp once before it succumbed to the caresses of the flames. He covered the smoldering pet with dirt and rocks.

Richard wondered if the dead dog was still where he had buried it. He smiled. He would have to check the next time he visited his mother. He almost fell asleep on the bench. The fire seemed to soothe him. He loved its warmth and was held captive by its glow. He thought about the flames at the prosecutor's house, his first killing.

The memories the fire brought back to him were so good. How he loved these memories, and he soon was off into his own dream world from the thrill he enjoyed from the inferno. He dreamed his own special dreams and enjoyed the trip. He came back to his body just as the fire was being extinguished and he smiled. He thought to himself how everyday he was in this fine town he found new ways to enjoy himself. He promised himself that he would find many more new and exciting pleasures here in this wonderful city. He slowly rose from the park bench and headed home.

# CHAPTER TWENTY—SIX

# The Ambushers

R ay Mansky and John Koolman were walking post 5 & 6. They were the new guys, and this was their breaking in period. The newest men got the toughest posts. Both were fresh out of the army; they just finished the State Police Academy, and now they were finally out in the action. Ray exclaimed, "This is not the way they drew it up in the academy." John just quietly smiled, and they walked into the projects.

As the two rookie officers came to the first building they were greeted by three rats running from the garbage in the hallway; John looked at Ray and nodded toward the scurrying rodents; Ray said, "The finest resort on the North Jersey Shore!" They laughed as they walked to the call box. John opened it and picked up the phone. Before he could say anything, Sergeant Griffith answered the phone, and he told them that there was a threat called in by an unknown woman that the Black Panthers and the Five Percenter's had come to town, and they were looking to kill some cops. She hung up before they could trace the call. "Be careful, and you call in right away if you come upon anything suspicious; we got plenty of manpower, don't get hurt." He admonished as he hung up. "This could be a fun summer." John said as he hung up the phone. He told Ray about the sergeant's warning, and the pair resumed their patrol.

Bonzoni and Big Geno called in they were stopping a car. Post 5&6 heard the location, and they were only about a block away. John and Ray decided to walk over to backup the car. As they turned the corner, they heard two loud shots then something like a machine gun. "I haven't heard anything like that since Nam." John shouted.

Suddenly, the radio erupted into a burst of frantic screams as Big Geno yelled over the air, "Send back-up right away were under fire." The radio went dead.

Post 5 & 6 drew their weapons and ran to the scene. As the turned the corner they were shocked to see a bullet riddled police car in the roadway behind an old Caddy with the trunk opened; Bonzoni and Big Geno were running into Castilucci's Alley. The windshield of the police car had a huge hole in it.

John and Ray followed their brother officers down the alley. When they got to the end, they met Big Geno who had a young man by the throat against the wall. He yelled to them, "Keep going Bonzoni is alone, and there are two more. I got this one, I'm okay."

Post five ran out of the alley and into the City Village Projects where they found Bonzoni. He was crouched behind a garbage can. He had his gun drawn and signaled them to be quiet and get down. He pointed to a shed at the end of a vacant lot against a fence. Bonzoni whispered their location into the portable radio, and the officers slowly made their way close to the shed. The officers sought cover in the rubble around the shed that was strewn throughout the vacant lot, and they now had it surrounded on three sides. They waited for reinforcements to arrive.

Sergeant Delbello arrived in the police van with ten officers in flack jackets with shotguns. Bonzoni pointed to the shed, and said, "I think there are two still in there, Sarge." Delbello nodded, and he made a motion to the officer next to him. The officer took out a tear gas gun and fired two canisters into the shed window.

Nothing, the officers waited for ten minutes, and then they stormed the shed. As the gas was clearing the officers entered and found two shotguns, an ammo box with fifty shotgun rounds, and two 9mm handguns in it on the dirt floor. They also found 1,000 rounds of 9mm ammo. There was a trap door in the center of the shed floor. It led to a narrow trench that ended on the other side of the fence. The two other men had made good their escape.

The rookies went back and helped Big Geno put his arrest in a police car. They then walked back to post 5 & 6 and resumed their patrol. "This is much better; at least I think it's much better?" John said to Ray as the pair walked back to the projects. "It is more exciting, but much more dangerous." Ray answered.

Big Geno went with his arrest to police Headquarters. Bonzoni told Sergeant Delbello that when he got out of the car to approach the driver, the trunk sprung open, and up popped the kid they had caught with a shotgun. The first shot misfired, as he ducked. The second went through the windshield of the police car. Then two men got out of the car, and opened fire with MAC 10 machine pistols. They did not hit anything, but the police car which they raked with several clips of ammo. When one of the guns jammed they fled. They recovered the shotgun in the car trunk, and the two jammed MAC 10 's were found in garbage cans in Castilucci's alley by officers searching the scene.

"You are a lucky pair of cops." Sergeant Delbello said and he took Bonzoni to police headquarters to help Big Geno finish the paperwork.

The information was put out to all cars, and the neighboring towns, then a state and national alarm was sent. The county sent a crime scene crew over to examine the scene, and the FBI and State Police also responded with their investigation units to question all the witnesses, all the officers involved, and to gather information with their forensic and analysis teams. The FBI investigators also interrogated the suspect that Big Geno had under arrest.

It would be a long hot summer in the city if this kept up, Ray thought. He said to John, "This is some first day hey buddy?" John smiled and nodded. They continued their patrol of post 5 & 6.

At police headquarters Detective Fowler tried to interrogate the captured assassin, while waiting for the F.B.I to arrive. The man arrested was identified as Cinque El, aka John Saunders. He was arrested for murder in Newark and was an escaped felon from a breakout of the Essex County Jail earlier this week. He asked for a lawyer, and he told Arnold nothing else. He asked for his lawyer every time he was given a question then just sat quietly and stared at the wall. His prints were on the shotgun. After the processing by Arnold the FBI took him away for their interrogation.

Big Geno and Bonzoni were lucky; this set up had been used successfully throughout the country to ambush and kill officers in six states. This was the first time it failed. Cinque El was the first suspect arrested in these attacks and was a very valuable person to the FBI. The guns and ammo recovered would put a dent in the local gangs, but would have little impact elsewhere. If they could get some information from Cinque El, maybe they might be able to stop these ambushes, and save some lives.

The rest of the tour was routine, but two cars were sent to every call and the officers were called in four hours early from the oncoming shift to bolster the manpower. This shift was held over for four hours into the next tour to give the oncoming shift some needed reinforcements. This practice was to continue all summer. The Federal Government came up with some emergency funds for the city to ease the budget crunch this dilemma was causing. It was much needed in this poor city.

At dinner that night, Mary said to Arnold, "I am glad you were not involved in that mess today; you have to be careful; today the criminals have no respect for the law or its officers." Arnold nodded as he put another bite of a very good meatloaf into his mouth and continued reading the sports page of the Press.

Richard awoke from a troubled sleep. He had been without a lover for almost a month. He needed one badly. Fizz had quarreled with Mary, and he had spent the last two nights at Richard's. They would go out tonight. Richard could hardly wait. He decided to play it by ear. It seemed every plan he made failed. The random ones had been the best in the past so he would just let it happen.

Dee Dee was a big girl. At just over six feet tall, she was bigger than most men. She was not fat but you could say she was a powerfully built farm girl type. She was not petite. She was a strong girl too. She had grown up a tom boy on a farm in the mid west, and did all the physical chores necessary to help work a farm. Her father died when she was fifteen, and she ran away soon after this tragic event; she hated her mother, the new boyfriend she had taken up with, and two older step sisters.

Dee Dee came to the city down the shore, and assumed the identity of Dorothy Banks a young girl of twenty one who had died of leukemia the day Dee Dee arrived in the city. She went to the town hall and got a copy of her birth certificate, then used that to get a social security card. She planned to get her drivers license during the summer. She had never driven a car; she was only sixteen, but could easily pass for twenty-one. She had in fact driven some of the tractors at home on the farm, and she felt driving a car would not be a problem.

She wanted very bad to just be a girl. She ran away from home when she was sixteen after her father died to start a new life. Her father had been her whole life. They did everything on the farm together. She never got over his death, and she could not get along with her step father, who treated her like a freak. Now, she was sixteen, and out in the world on her own. She seemed to be doing fine.

She had identification for twenty-one, and she looked every bit the age. She had no trouble getting a summer job on the beachfront tending bar in the beer garden in the beachfront on Fifth Avenue. She doubled as a short order cook, too. She was making good money and was thinking of going to California at the end of the summer. She loved this ocean and wanted to see the other one.

The night passed, and Richard could find no one to love. Fizz had made up with Mary and left with her. Richard expected him to return permanently to her soon. He fell into an uneasy sleep at about noon time. When he awoke at about nine that night the moon was nearly full, and the call was upon him. He showered, got dressed, and walked to the beachfront. He stopped at the beer garden to get a beer.

When Richard walked into the beer garden and saw Dee Dee at the counter, he knew this must be the girl for him. The devil had sent her to him and he would not let this gift pass. He ordered a beer, and hot dog. He politely thanked her, finished his meal, and left her a five dollar tip.

He went to his usual bench four blocks away and thought about this new girl. A big one he thought. Way bigger than any before, even bigger than Buddy Moore. He would have to study her. He wanted badly to make this girl one of his lovers. His urges subsided at the thought of stalking this new lover.

He ate at the Beer Garden for the rest of the week striking up small innocent conversations with this new big girl and always leaving her a five dollar tip. He became a regular. Dee Dee was working double shifts and rarely took a day off. Her boss loved her, and she was a favorite with the customers.

When Richard found out she was saving to go to California, he made a plan. He would use this plan to get to her. He told her his name was Brian, and he was from Los Angeles, California. He said he was going back to California at the end of the summer. They soon became friends.

Tonight was the night. It had been almost two weeks since he spotted her, his need was so great he thought he would burst. He had made a date with her; they would meet at four this morning, after the bar rush and go to breakfast. They would meet at his bench. Richard was so excited he could hardly wait. He would make up some tales about how beautiful it was in California. He knew this would keep her interested. He had to get her to go to his house. He would ask her to go to his place for breakfast. He would tell her he would make her breakfast instead of her doing the cooking. It could not fail.

This would be his best work. He would drug her, secure her to a chair, and keep her prisoner in his house for as long as she lasted. There, he could torture and mutilate her for as long as he could keep her alive. She was a big healthy girl; she should be able to last for a very long time. He vowed he would make sure she would last a long time.

Fizz had gone back to Mary, and so tonight he would have his house all to himself. If he could get Dee Dee to come home with him, all the rest would fall into place. He was prepared. He checked his old doctor's bag, and all was ready, duct tape, his tools, and the drugs. They were hidden, but close to hand. He could handle all possibilities; he felt so secure he could barely control his anticipation. He put the bag on the end table in the living room next to a book case and left to meet his new lover.

Dee Dee met him at his bench on the boardwalk just as they planned, and after some small talk about the wonders of California Dee Dee agreed to go to his house where he would cook a grand breakfast for them. All the way to Richard's house, the pair talked about California. Dee Dee was so excited. This was her first night with a guy since running away from home, in fact she had never really been on a date in her short life. She felt he was a little weird, but that could be because he was so much older than her. She had only gone to dances where she met her dates at the dance and went home with her father after the dance. She had worked hard all summer, this guy seemed harmless enough, and she thought she deserved this. She would finally have a real date, and who knows a real friend too maybe even a real boyfriend. No one deserved what was to come for poor Dee Dee.

Richard was beaming with confidence. He had a foolproof plan. He would drug her drink like he did with Fawn and Buddy, then he would tape her up, and have his way with her for days or as long as she lasted.

At his house, he continued the small talk. He made himself a drink, and asked Dee Dee if she wanted one. She said she was not used to drinking, but Richard convinced her by saying its just coke with a little rum. This would be his greatest lover he thought as he slipped the powder from a red in some rum and coke. He stirred the drink, added some ice cubes, and handed the drink to her. Dee Dee sipped it as Richard began to cook some eggs. Suddenly, she felt unsteady, and stopped drinking. She asked Richard what was in the drink. He turned, and punched her full in the face. She did not fall like the others, but hit him back reflexively, knocking him into the stove. Richard was surprised. As he pushed off the stove; he burnt his hand and arm. He screamed in pain.

This distracted him for a moment. Dee Dee's instincts told her to run, and the big girl fled with the speed of a gazelle. Dee Dee ran for the door with Richard following close behind her. She could run very fast for a big girl. Richard grabbed a butcher knife on the way out of the kitchen. This slowed him just a shade. He had the large knife in his hand, and he slashed at her, cutting her across the back as she ran out the door. But she had gotten away. He dared not chase her on the street with a knife in his hand. He stopped at the door and watched her through the window.

She was dazed from the drug, but made it out the door down the stairs and into the street, The big girl stopped, turned toward an oncoming car, and threw up her hands to try to flag it down; only to be struck by the car that was speeding down the road. The driver saw the girl too late and braked, but she could not stop in time. The car screeched into the big girl. Dee Dee rolled over the hood, and onto the pavement unconscious.

The poor girl that was driving the car got out of the car, and screamed at the sight of the big bloody girl lying unconscious next to her car. Soon there was a crowd. Richard had retreated from the doorway into the house. He locked the door, and went up to the bedroom. He watched intently from out of his bed room window.

Car five with Pete and Tony arrived to investigate the accident and sent the unconscious Dee Dee to the hospital. They did the accident report and went to the hospital to check on the girl. It was then the nurse reported to them that the girl was in a coma, and she had an unusual long deep slash across her back that took several staples to close. The major damage was because of her head injuries; that is what had rendered her comatose. There were no broken bones.

Pete thought the cut was suspicious, but checking that out would have to wait until the girl regained consciousness.

Richard went down to the kitchen after the girl was taken away. His face felt warm. He went to the bathroom. He saw in the mirror that his nose was bleeding and his lip was cut. His hand and arm ached where they were burned. Dee Dee had done what no lover had done before, she had injured a god. She had hurt him and caused him to bleed, worse she had gotten away. He did not like this, and he hated the pain. Richard flew into a rage. He punched the mirror then ran to the kitchen where he threw the frying pan against the door.

Richard went to the sink, stuck his head under the faucet, and turned on the cold water. He held his head under the cool running water. He washed his face and tended to his bloody lip. He would have to find a way to finish it with this girl. He was a god; she could not be allowed to get away with this blasphemous act he thought as he slipped into bed.

He could not sleep, so he took a red. This relaxed him, and he soon plunged into a deep but troubled sleep. That evening, he awoke in a deep sweat from a nightmare. He was in a room with the big girl; he was taped to a table. Dee Dee was cutting him all over, and she was laughing at him. He was crying like a baby when he awoke. This dream had shaken him up. He decided that he must carefully plot what to do next.

How much did she tell the police? Are they looking for him? How come they haven't come to his apartment? Something was wrong. Maybe he should go out to see what was going on? No, he could not risk that yet. He would wait and ask Fizz when he came in, He was sure Fizz would have heard about the car accident that happened outside last night. He might know something.

Richard would pretend that he knew nothing about the accident. He would check the papers every day for news. He must be very careful now because he might be forced to move from this paradise. He may really have to go to California.

He decided that he would deal with these problems as they came. He did not feel confident planning for the unexpected. He liked to feel in control. He should have known this one would be trouble, she worked too hard. She was much too big. Maybe she was a man dressed like a girl. No, she was a girl. A very large girl at that, but she was still just a girl. Still just a girl, it rattled through his brain. Still, she was just a girl, and she had done this to him, a GOD. How can that be he thought to himself.

Not only that, she had placed all he loved in jeopardy. Maybe she was the devil. No the devil was his friend, but maybe the devil was jealous of his great success.

Richard left the house he needed a walk to think and clear his head. He walked to his bench on the boardwalk and gazed out at the ocean trying to clear his brain and make sense of this whole problem. The thinking put him in pain; he thought his brain would explode. His head throbbed as he stared at the horizon. Then he heard the sobbing behind him. The sound relieved his throbbing. He came back to earth. The predator shook his head and cleared his brain.

# CHAPTER TWENTY—SEVEN

## The Cat

It was a clear cool morning in the city down the shore, but this would be a memorable day for the people on Fourth Avenue. The First Aid had responded to the Pontegrasso house, and Leticia was in bad shape. She was taken to the hospital with an oxygen mask strapped to her face. She was in shock.

Primavera Pontegrasso was a kind old lady, and her passing was mourned by all in the neighborhood especially her spinster daughter Leticia. But ninety-four is a good old age; life must go on; and Leticia would have to learn to cope with the loss.

Her mother had loved cats. Leticia hated them, but she decided to keep her mother's three big old cats to help ease the loss. During the next year, two of the old cats passed on, but one big old tomcat still hung on. It was a great furry creature with a dark brown mane like a lion with a deep gold and white hue to its fur. It was the top cat of the block, and it slept most days on the front porch, hissing at anyone who disturbed its slumber.

Eugene Delmonte a senior in high school lived next door to the Pontegrasso home. Their families were friends. He was the son of Sergeant Delmonte, Eugene was a good boy, but trouble seemed to follow him wherever he went. He had a dog Butch. He and Butch were inseparable. The dog was a big good natured mutt, and he followed Eugene everywhere. This great mutt loved to catch a ball or Frisbee and dig holes, but most of all he loved to chase cats. Eugene was told by his father that under no condition was Butch allowed to chase the Pontegrasso's cats. Eugene had done a great job in this for years, and there were no incidents at all this year.

On this fateful afternoon, Eugene had cut his last two classes to come home early to get some rest. He had been out all night at a local party and was exhausted as well as a little hung over. They were just a study hall and Physical education. He knew his mother would be down the block at her friend Madge's house, so he would be able to sneak home and sleep for a couple of hours until she returned. He knew his mother would not return until after four o'clock, when she would begin to prepare supper for the family, so Eugene figured he should get a good rest, and that was just what he needed.

When Eugene walked up the driveway to go into the house through the back door, his usual way into his house, he was surprised to see Butch running loose in the back yard. He was usually in the house and waiting by the kitchen door for Eugene to come home. He must have gotten out of the house when his mother left, Eugene thought as he approached the playful dog. Butch had a mop like bundle in his mouth it was covered in mud. Butch was shaking it and running around the yard in a happy frolic. As Eugene got closer, he saw Butch had a dead cat in his mouth. Worse yet, it was the Pontegrasso's cat.

Eugene grabbed Butch by the collar, and he dragged the happy dog and his prize into the house. In the house, Butch dropped the cat, sadly walked to his bed, and lied down. He sensed his master was mad. Eugene looked at the ruined cat and became frantic. He picked it up, shook it in the dog's face, and scolded the dog, "Look at this you dummy, dad is going to kill me if he finds out you killed Ms Pontegrasso's cat, and worse he might even send you to the pound, that is a big dog jail, and you will not like it there." The big mutt just licked Eugene on the face, and lifted his paw.

It was then Eugene got a great idea. He took the cat upstairs and washed it with his mother's special shampoo. Then, he took her blow drier, dried and fluffed up the cat's hair. Yes, he thought it looks real good. He knew Leticia would not be home from the senior center until after four o'clock, or sometime before dark, so he surreptitiously took the cat over to the house, and carefully put it on the porch. He fixed it so it looked like it was sleeping. Ms Pontegrasso would just think the cat died in its sleep when she found it, and all would be well.

As he walked back to his house, he looked back twice to admire his work. He took Butch up to his room with him to keep him out of any further trouble, and admonished the dog all the way up the stairs, then he closed the door. After a quick shower, he and Butch settled in for an afternoon nap. Boy that was a great idea he thought as he fell into a deep slumber.

It was two hours later, but it seemed like two minutes when Eugene was awakened by the ambulance siren. He glanced out the window and saw Leticia Pontegrasso on a gurney with an oxygen mask on her face. He got dressed and walked down stairs as the ambulance pulled away. His father and mother came into the house, and he asked them what happened. His father told him. "Leticia had fainted when she came home, and saw her dead cat." Eugene replied, "the cat was old she should have known it would not live forever." His father said, "Yea, but the cat died last week, and she had her cousin bury him behind the garage!" Eugene just said "whoa" then, he left the living room and went back to his bedroom.

After a short stay at the hospital, Leticia returned home. Sergeant Delmonte had her cousin take the cat's remains away; he knew that she would not be able to even look at it when she got back. He told her it was some other cat that just looked like her old cat, and someone was just playing a foul prank on her. His story was not convincing, but it was the best he could come up with to assuage her for the moment.

She would never come home up the front stairs when she was alone again. She would always pull in the driveway and use the back door unless someone was with her.

Mary said to Arnold when he came to pick her up late that day, "Did you here about the Pontegrasso cat. It is a cat from hell you know. " Arnold just laughed. Mary said "Really all the kids say Leticia is a witch, and the cat is her dead mother." "Well, if you believe that, there is no hope for you." Arnold replied. "Just the same,

I would appreciate it if you would keep an eye on me at night for a while. I'm not superstitious, but there is no use tempting fate." "That will be my pleasure." Arnold replied with a lascivious smile on his face. Mary just turned and punched him in the arm, Arnold replied, "Hey, I would love to keep my eyes on you at night, or any other time you want." Mary just shook her head as they arrived at her house.

"Did you know that Dee Dee our favorite waitress at the beer garden was hit by a car last night?" Arnold asked. Mary shook her head no; Arnold said "I think I will ask about her tomorrow at work. Tony and Pete are doing the accident investigation. They are very good."

Eugene became a special officer that summer, then, he went away to college. In the years to come, he would become a police officer. He never told a soul what he had done. The secret would always remain his.

The tale of Leticia Pontegrasso, and the cat that would not die became a local legend. The neighborhood kids always thought Leticia was a witch anyway, and there were many scary tales told in the neighborhood about Leticia Pontegrasso, and her mother's cat. For many years after that on Halloween night very few kids from the neighborhood would trick or treat at the Pontegrasso house after the sun set. Even on a regular night most kids felt it best to walk on the opposite side of the street when passing Leticia's house after dark.

Richard was in his bedroom sitting in a chair and looking out the window. He had been especially brutal with the crying girl. He had done some things that even surprised him. She had died hard and he did not take any trophies. The killing had merely satisfied his need for the night, but there was no satisfaction; he felt he still needed something. The something was to finish it with the big girl.

He gazed at nothing; he just looked out at the sky and daydreamed. He was thinking about his lovers, and how different they were. Then, he thought of the monster a few months ago; she looked worse every time he pictured her. This was a good reminder of the dangers he faced with the runaway girls. Now, he had to think about this big girl, Dee Dee.

He loved the fact that he never knew what kind of girl he would get. But these problem girls were a reminder that there were some dangers in this type of love, even for a God.

Richard was getting at least one girl a month, and when the pickings were good he could have as many as one per week. He was never in a hurry and always let the lover choose the time and place. He was the mountain lion of the city, a god among men, the maker of saints, and the servant of the devil. He liked these titles he had made for himself. He felt they gave him power. He also liked this new drug, this LSD. It was while he was high on this he had envisioned these titles. He thought he was really something special. Life was good. He did not want this big girl, Dee Dee, to mess it up.

Richard had begun to come out of his shell. He went to some of the beachfront bars, he had a beer or two, but never more than two. He ate dinner at the snack bars, and he had to admit they cooked much better than he did. He still said very little and made no friends; but he always listened and watched.

Tonight he thought he would hang at the Bootlegger Tavern until it closed then retire to his bench on the boardwalk for a quiet evening of contemplation and thought.

As he neared the bench, he was stopped by a query. A soft voice from behind him asked the question, "Do you mind if I sit up here with you for a while, I just don't want to be alone right now?" When he turned to look at the voice, he saw a young girl. She was clean cut and neatly dressed, not the usual runaway type he was used to. She interested him. He nodded yes and walked over to his bench and sat down. The girl followed him.

The girl sat on the bench next to him. She looked out to sea and sighed. She began to talk about her home life and how unhappy she was with the way her parents treated her. She was being forced to go to a large prestigious college in Massachusetts, and what she wanted to do was to go to New York City with her boyfriend, and be a painter in the village. Her parents would not hear of this and threatened to lock her away until they could send her north to a relative that lived near the Massachusetts school.

After her tale of woe, the pretty girl got up and walked down onto the sand, and out toward the water. As she reached the water's edge, a young man came running onto the boardwalk. He was yelling the name Jennifer. He approached Richard, and asked him if he had seen a girl. He gave a description of the pretty girl that Richard had been talking to. Richard nodded, and pointed to the girl now up to her waist in the dark night surf. The young man screamed, "Jennifer" and ran to the water's edge just as the pretty girl disappeared beneath the rolling waves about one hundred yards out to sea.

The young man ran back to Richard, and asked him to call the police for help; then he took off his sneakers and ran back into the water. Richard walked to the pay phone, dialed the operator, and told her what had happened. She connected him with police headquarters. He told them what had happened, and then he walked into a dark doorway. Richard waited in the shadows for the emergency people to arrive. He watched for a while from the dark doorway, and then he started for home.

In only a few minutes, the boardwalk was swarming with police, fireman, and emergency response people. A police line had been put up around the area, but it was way too early for there to be many people out at this time of morning.

Two of the police officers swam out to the frantic young man who was splashing around in the water; they pulled him out of the water and questioned him. Then, they launched three life saver boats with firemen and lifeguards into the ocean to try to see if they could find the girl, or her body. They searched for hours until after daybreak, and almost into the afternoon, but they had no luck. The girl was lost. Her body would wash up about twenty miles south in six months.

Her name was Jennifer Kalder and her father was the owner and President of The Bendax Corporation. They were one of the wealthiest families in the state. When The Kalder family got the news, it was as though they had both been shot. The greatest loss to parents is the death of their child. This was their only child, and the loss totally devastated them.

At home, Richard went upstairs and sat up in bed. He began to think over the events of the night. He thought to himself, did he will the girl to walk into the ocean and kill herself? Did his mind have that much power? He knew he had wanted her dead. In his heart, he knew that he did not will her to kill herself, yet with his mind could he do it? He knew that he wanted to kill the girl himself. He knew that killing herself was something she had wished to do. The girl had probably planned this for some time. She was obviously despondent. For some reason he felt the girls suicide quite satisfying.

Richard would think about the girl's suicide many times in the future. In his mind he would always wonder about one particular fact. He wondered if he really had this power, the power to will a person to destroy themselves. If he did have this power then he would truly be a god.

Richard rolled over in the bed shut his eyes. He reached under the bed touched his favorite skull. It relaxed him, and he fell into a calm and dream filled sleep. He dreamed wonderful dreams. Life was good for this monster of the beachfront in the City Down the Shore.

# CHAPTER TWENTY—EIGHT

## The S.L.A.

It was a sad time in the country. There were riots, fires, and random bombings throughout the country. There was a political upheaval throughout the nation. The east coast was not spared. There were ambushes and shootings of police officers in the cities and on the highways for the last ten years. The radicals were waging war against all government agencies, and the police were to be the major targets.

All this killing was done in the name of peace, of course. Three of the first S.L.A. members to be convicted of blowing up a government building were serving time in New York State's Attica Prison. Harry "Brain" Vogel could make a bomb out of toilet paper, one S.L.A. member was heard to say. He was once an engineering major, who dropped out of Columbia University in the rebellious sixties. He moved from radical group to radical group until he found a home in the S.L.A. Cosintino "Chico" Mendez was a young misguided youth, who was a tag along with Luke Johnson; it got him life in prison. Luke "Cold" Johnson was the worst of the bunch. He joined the S.L.A. because they killed people. He loved violence and really enjoyed killing.

Kiddo was a mutt. He was a mix of New Finland retriever, German Sheppard, and what ever else walked by his mom that day.

He was black, brown, and white in a pattern only a mother could love. He was a playful dog, he was not graceful, and he had a propensity toward being a lap dog, but at one hundred fifty pounds, that is probably why he ended up in the pound. He was a large dog too about thirty inches to the shoulder, and after a stay at the pound it was thought he would never be adopted. He had a great temperament, and was very good with children. It was his good fortune to be spared from euthanasia, this was mainly because he was just a year old, and very fit. He was chosen by the evaluators to be a police dog. Kiddo was a good learner, and soon became attached to his trainer Frank Solomon. Frank and Kiddo soon became a part of the cities new canine patrol.

Kiddo would walk the business districts at night with Frank. He would be used to check out open buildings, rout out any unwanted intruders, and hold them at bay until Frank could secure them. Frank and Kiddo turned out to be the best team in the area. However there was limited use for the pair in the winter.

Kiddo's primary job soon became community relations. He was great with kids, so Frank and Kiddo began to make the tour of all the city's schools to improve police community relations. The twosome soon became a hit with the kids, and all the teachers loved to have this shaggy mutt as a visitor because it meant for an easy day for all, and the children would be on their best behavior for days before the visit, so they could play with the loveable mutt.

When the school announced that Kiddo and his partner were coming to talk to the kids, the attendance for that day rose to almost perfect. None of the kids wanted to miss seeing the great dog. They new his visit would be a treat. Kiddo would romp in the playground with the kids, and the little ones in the early grades would be allowed to ride on his back, or he would pull a cart with them in it. As for Kiddo the kids would give him treats, have him sit, roll over, and do every trick he could perform. Kiddo was a born showoff. You couldn't tell if the kids or the dog was enjoying this the most. Everyone always had a fun day.

After Easter, the pair went back into patrol. Kiddo suffered through the summer because most of the time, even the nights were hot. There was always a breeze on the north end of the beachfront, and that was where Kiddo and Frank could be found between post checks, Kiddo also loved to take a dip in the cool ocean. This he did every night in the summer heat; he would be dry by the time they were back on post.

The shaggy police dog was a favorite at the Beer Garden. There was always a hot dog and a pan of water waiting for Kiddo when he got there. Carmine the owner, loved the big mutt, and he was Frank's uncle.

Frank and Kiddo had just completed a refresher course, and learned how to approach, and hold at bay a barricaded armed suspect in a building; the dog learned to run low to the ground, and attack in a zig zag approach to make him as small a target as possible. Of course, Kiddo's great size and the flack jacket he was taught to wear would make it seem like a barn door was rushing you, but the big dog learned these lessons well; he was surprisingly agile and determined.

One could never perceive Kiddo as anything other than huge. Kiddo could never be a small target. He was trained to wear the special flack jacket for his own protection, and to give cover for the hostage, or police officer if needed. This great dog was hardly slowed by its thirty pound weight. He was taught how to rescue hostages, stay between them and the bad guys, lead them to safety; he learned how find and protect wounded officers or civilians by covering them with his great bulk until he was called off by his trainer.

This training was because of the increased actions by the Black Panthers, Weathermen, S.L.A. and other violent subversive groups, who had stooped to taking and killing hostages during their escapades. The summer had gone by quickly, and soon Labor Day would mark the beginning of the cool weather and the end of the good times for the kids; they would have to go back to school. Kiddo and Frank would go back to the schools, too, and it would mark the good times for this police team.

Frank and Kiddo had just gotten off duty. It had been a humid rainy night, and they were glad to be home in the comfort of their air conditioned residence. Frank had just settled down for some rest when the phone rang. He looked at Kiddo, shook his head. He answered it, but knew before he picked up the receiver that they were being called in. He was told by the Desk Sergeant to report to the squad room as soon as possible with Kiddo. Nothing else was said, but he could tell by Sergeant Harriman's voice that it was urgent. He took a quick shower dressed, then he and Kiddo reported for duty.

In the squad room, there were Chief Tillman, a squad from the county tactical unit, the midnight shift, and the oncoming 0800/1600 shift. Sergeant Bolton was in charge of the group. When Frank and Kiddo entered, they were told to sit down and the briefing began.

At the briefing, the officers were advised that Ray Mansky and John Koolman were in the abandon north end train station barricaded in the baggage room. Inside the station on the second floor were three SLA members that had escaped from Attica Prison in New York State. It was confirmed they had already killed at least one person. John was shot in the leg, and the wound was bleeding heavily. Ray had managed to slow the bleeding, but the wound was severe. John could not walk, and Ray refused to try to leave without him.

Ray had radioed police headquarters about their plight. The criminals had them pinned down and were threatening to kill them if their terms were not met. The terms Brain stated when he talked to the negotiator were one million dollars in small bills and a truck.

The two rookie officers were safe for now, but they had limited ammo, and John was doing poorly, his wound was deep and painful. They would not be able to stand off a pressed attack. The criminals had robbed a sporting goods store in Pennsylvania on the way to New Jersey and were armed with shotguns and semi-automatic weapons. Ray and John were simply outgunned.

Brain gave the city four hours to meet the terms; he asked for something to drink. Chico suggested some beer and junk food to help pass the time. Brain refused saying the cops could poison the food, but accepted the beer, but only in cans.

The captain felt that the police must act quickly. The fact that John's wounds were serious, and Ray could only slow the bleeding was a determining factor. John was barely conscious and unable to stand for long, or walk very much. He needed medical treatment as soon as possible. He may not last four hours.

Harry "Brain" Vogel, Cosintino "Chico" Mendez, and Luke "Cold" Johnson had been doing life in Attica for blowing up an unemployment building in New York City in which eleven innocent people were killed. They had escaped when a female jail guard, who was in love with Luke, smuggled them a gun. They took her hostage and made good their escape. Cold shot her twice in the head when they were clear of the prison and safely in the woods. He left her as she fell, and the three fled in her car down the mountain roads into Pennsylvania. There they ditched the car, robbed a sporting goods store, shooting the owner, and fled into New Jersey with a new car compliments of a Cadillac Dealer who left one running in the sales lot.

They made their way to the city down the shore just as the big Cadillac ran out of gas. They loaded their weapons and ammo into duffle bags and walked into a nearby diner to get something to eat. A waitress thought she saw one of the strangers had a gun, and she told Ray and John when they came in for coffee. The young officers looked out the diner window to see the three walk behind the abandoned train station and disappear. The rookies decided to check the trio out. They called headquarters and advised them, then walked to where they last saw the men. When the officers walked in to the empty station, the three convicts opened fire. Ray and John ducked into the baggage room, but John was a little too slow, and he was shot in the legs by a blast from Cold's shotgun.

It was now three hours later and things were getting worse by the minute. The plan would be to try to get Ray and John out of the baggage room and arrest the escapees with as little loss of life as possible. The tactical unit would climb to the roof and blow a hole in it as the ground forces shot gas into the second floor. Frank and Kiddo would enter the rear door, and make their way to the baggage room to try to get Ray and John out. This would all be done at the same time to confuse the convicts.

When the charge went off on the roof the ground officers shot six canisters of pepper gas into the upper windows. At the same time, Frank and Kiddo entered the rear of the building as planned. They were wearing flack jackets and Kiddo was dragging a Kevlar blanket for John with another flack jacket lying on it for Ray. The pair made it into the baggage room as the shooting began. Brain was shot right away, and he was killed by the tactical officers, but Chico and Cold had slipped behind a barricade they made from old benches and returned fire. Cold heard the officers enter below, and he went down to see if he could finish them off as Chico held off the tactical team with fierce fire from his assault weapons.

Cold had a semi-automatic shotgun in one hand, and an AR-15 in the other. He poured shots into the baggage room as he charged down the stairs. Frank and Ray ducked back into the room, but John was left exposed on the blanket in the doorway. Bullets ricocheted all around him. He looked like a dead duck.

Suddenly, Kiddo jumped up. He charged Cold weaving from side to side, drawing the convicts fire, and blocking the maniac's view of the doorway. Cold was enraged; he screamed a curse at the dog, turned his attention to trying to shoot the charging monster. Shotgun pellets bounced off the heavy flack jacket, and Kiddo just kept coming. While Kiddo charged, Frank and Ray got John to cover. As Kiddo jumped to pin Cold two bullets entered the dogs shoulder just below the flack jacket, but Kiddo did not stop. He knocked Cold to the floor and pinned him there with his great bulk, his huge jaws clamped tightly around Cold's head and face.

Frank and Ray ran to the great dog, disarmed Cold, and cuffed him. Kiddo looked bad. There was a large puddle of blood under the big shaggy hero, and it was getting bigger. Chico had been wounded, and he had surrendered. It was over as quickly as it started. John was put in an ambulance; the paramedic said he would be alright as the ambulance took off for the hospital. No other officers were hurt. No officers except for Kiddo.

In the end, Brain was dead, Chico agreed to testify against Cold in order to avoid the death penalty. Cold would be convicted of the murder in Pennsylvania, and the jail guard in New York State. He was given two more death penalties.

All the officers from the shoot out would heal well and return to work with a great war story. None had been seriously wounded. Even John was lucky that no major arteries were hit and no bones were broken in his leg. The officers were all treated and released from the hospital that day except for John. John was admitted to the hospital where after a few hours of surgery the shotgun pellets were removed from his leg.

John was young, and the doctor was skilled. It was touch and go whether John would have permanent damage to the tendons in his legs, but all worked out well, and John would return to duty as good as new in a month.

Only one officer did not return to duty. Kiddo was seriously injured his right front leg had been shattered at the shoulder by the two bullets. The vets tried, but could not save the leg. They recommended he be put down, the city agreed, but Frank would not hear of it. He said he would take care of his wounded buddy, and assume all the costs it took to get him well. He asked the vet to do what he could to save the great dog. A couple of weeks later, Kiddo was home. The vet had saved him, but it took three operations. The veterinary bills were huge.

Mary had organized the high school kids, and they did car washes on the weekends to raise money to help Frank pay for the veterinarian bills for their pal Kiddo. The younger kids from the middle school did the interior work on the cars. Even the little ones in the grammar school raised money by doing special chores around the house and giving the extra allowance to help pay the dog's veterinarian bills.

Some of the merchants in town had, "Save the dog" canisters on their counters in their stores, because of this the veterinarian's bills were paid in no time. The great dog lost his right leg but soon learned to walk with only three. He was as frisky as ever within six months. He had been retired from the police department and was now a permanent part of Frank's family. Frank and Kiddo still made the rounds to the schools in the winter, Frank was now the juvenile officer, and Kiddo was his assistant. The kids just loved him more. Having three legs made no difference to the kids, and the big shaggy mutt really loved playing with them.

It had been several weeks since Dee Dee had gotten away from him. Richard was sitting in the Beer Garden trying to hear news about Dee Dee. This was not to be. The suicide of the rich girl, and the shoot out with the S.L.A. had overshadowed the news about Dee Dee.

Carmine, the owner, was happy and bragging to all the customers about his nephew Frank, and how he and his dog Kiddo saved two rookie cops from being killed by three ruthless escaped criminals from New York. All the customers listened as Carmine told his exciting tale. Richard was upset. He wanted to storm out of the Beer Garden rather than listen to this boring tale about a stupid dog, but stopped to put a dollar into a cup for Kiddo to help defray the veterinarian expenses incurred to save the hero dog. He had to be careful now, he might be wanted. Somehow he had to get news about Dee Dee; even more than that, he had to take her down. She had injured him, and she must pay.

Fizz had been no help he was drunk everyday now, and had gone back to using heroin. He barely knew there was an accident that fateful night. Richard went to his bench so he could think this out. He gazed out to sea and began to think of what he should do. The obvious thing was just to forget it and leave town for a while. He could not even consider this. This was his town and his playground. He would be hard pressed to find a place so perfect. No, that would not do. He would have to think of something else.

As the good lord provides for his flock, the devil takes care of his own. While Richard was staring out to sea in deep thought, he was brought back by the sound of a young innocent voice. "Do you mind if I sit here for a while Mr.?" came the weak question. Richard turned to see this nervous little girl about fifteen standing behind him. His mind cleared of past thoughts. He must concentrate on this tempting toy that had been tossed at him by fate. "That's fine with me." Richard heard himself say. It was like he was out of his body looking at the scene.

As the young girl sat down, she began to sob. Richard could not believe his luck, he did not hesitate; he gently took the young girls hand, and said to her, "It can never be that bad. What is the problem young lady?" It was said like the spider asking the fly into her parlor. This poor naive girl would regret this moment for the remainder of her short troubled life. "It's my boyfriend. He took that old barmaid Sindee home last night, and he never came back. I just know she seduced him, and I will never get him back. I feel so alone." The little girl broke into raking sobs. As Richard re-entered his body, he returned from his journey, and he was whole again. Now, every fiber of his consciousness tingled. He was again like the mountain lion with his fangs around the neck of an elk. He could sense the kill, and there was no need to rush, just hold on to the throat, and let nature do the rest. It would all be over soon. He knew this was too good to pass up.

Would he get his prisoner? Should he be careful, someone may see him with this girl. He had to make a plan. He would fall back on the tried and true. He said to the girl, "I have to go to work in a few minutes. I get off at 10:00 P.M. if you meet me here after that, we can get something to eat; and then, we can talk." The young girl nodded. Richard stood up and reached into his pocket. He gave the girl ten dollars and said, "Take this in case you need something until then." She shook her head no, but she took the money anyway, and slowly walked away, "I will meet you here tonight around midnight." she yelled back as she disappeared into the throng of people coming up onto the boardwalk.

Richard turned and walked away. He could not believe his luck. He walked home in a daze of anticipation. He fell into his bed and was immediately in a deep slumber. He was smiling in his dreams. No innocent young girl is safe when Richard smiles.

When Richard awoke, he was refreshed. The short nap sharpened his thoughts. He realized it would be much too dangerous to bring her to his house. That would have to wait for a better time. This would have to be under the boardwalk in his usual manner. He did not mind. He always did well in the old days. He seemed to have problems when he tried new things. He decided it would be a quick brutal kill, and then a long enjoyable night with the remains. It would be just what he needed to get him back on track he thought.

He would arrive early and prepare his usual spot under the boardwalk with his doctor's bag and all its wonderful treasures. Then, he would go to the upper walkway, watch for her, and make sure her boyfriend was not with her, or following her. He would then go to his usual bench, and just let it play out from there if all was clear, then, he could do what he wanted when he wanted to. It was a safe plan that had always worked in the past. He was full of anticipation, as the moon was full, and the need was coming upon him. Tonight, he would have a lover. He may have acted rashly with the big girl, but this kind of lover he knew well.

As Richard stood over the gutted corpse, he thought how wonderful it was to see, and taste the young girl's tears as she painfully succumbed to his mutilations of her innocent body.

The sad girl had arrived alone in tears about ten after twelve. She told Richard she had thrown her boyfriend out of their apartment after he had told her she was not enough woman for him, and that he needed more. She had sobbed that she was told by her mother, that if she gave the cream away free, who would need the cow? This caused her to be very cautious about loving men freely. Her mother had been right; the young girl thought. Richard told her she had done the right thing. This made the little girl feel better.

The unsuspecting girl stopped crying, she looked at him and said, "You are so kind, do you really mean it?" He nodded yes and got up. He walked down the steps to the sand, and the girl followed without being called. Richard said, "I like to watch the stars through the cracks in the boardwalk and think about things. Under the boardwalk, it's quiet and peaceful; come I'll show you." The young girl followed blindly. When she bent to enter the woodwork, Richard hit her hard on the back of the neck and kicked her brutally inside to his killing grounds; here he would make her his lover.

He taped her to the support beams. She looked like Jesus on the cross he thought as he cut her clothes off her body. He was just finishing as she started regain consciousness. He put two pieces of tape over her mouth in an ex so he could hear her wining and whimpering; then he backed away. He surveyed his work and was pleased.

As the young girl came too, she shook the moths out of her aching head. When she realized she was taped to the supports and could not move she screamed, but only a squeaky moan escaped her taped mouth. When she tried to open her mouth, she found it was taped shut and tears welled in her eyes and rolled down her cheeks. Richard licked them from her face as he lasciviously rubbed her young, slight, pale body.

He took a box cutter from his pocket and cut around her nipples, lightly at first barely drawing blood. Then, he went crazy. The blood was too much. He viciously removed one nipple. He put it into his pants pocket. The girl shut her eyes and mercifully passed out.

Richard then cut a line across the poor girl's stomach and her bowels began to spill out. He had cut too deeply. In frustration, he then gutted her from the crotch to her breastbone. Her insides spilled onto the sand. Richard cut the bonds around her wrists, and she fell face first to the sand over her steaming entrails. He cut the bonds on her ankles, and she tipped backwards, and she landed on her back spread eagled as if to beckon him.

Richard did terrible things to the corpse, then, fell asleep next to it. When he awoke, he was refreshed. He had no worries. He covered the gut pile with sand. He then dismembered the corpse, wrapping each part of the girl in a piece of the clothing he had cut from her body. Then, he took them far back under the boardwalk, and buried them as deep as he could dig. He retrieved the entrails and put them in a plastic bag. He took them out on the jetty for his deep dwelling friends to feast on.

He wanted to keep the head. He put it in a plastic bag when he returned from the jetty, then, into a paper bag that had contained some beer. He buried the beer and took the bag with the head inside home with him. He found that he whistled a favorite tune as he walked home, he felt good again. This had been just what he needed.

At home, he scalped the head, and put the scalp in borax salt. He took the eyes, and pulled the teeth from the bloody skull, washed them, and put them in a jar of vodka. He crushed the skull with a hammer, flushed the brains down the toilet and put the shattered ruined skull in the trash. He would put the whole thing out for trash pickup the next day.

Richard went upstairs, showered, and went to bed. He picked up his favorite skull from under the bed and stroked it. He thought of the girl he loved this night and felt satisfied. As the sun rose over the city, Richard fell into a deep dreamless sleep with a smile on his face. The fear and worry were gone. He was back.

# CHAPTER TWENTY—NINE

## The Dog and the Ducks

The sun rose quickly in the clear summer sky. Labor Day weekend had passed without any major incidents, and the town was due for a breather. But breath comes hard in a city down the shore. There is just too much in too small a place.

At Fitkin Hospital, the day was started with a scream in the intensive care unit that was heard throughout the floor. Dorothy Banks sat up in her hospital bed with her eyes wide open, and she screamed again. The floor nurses rushed in to see the unconscious girl had returned to the real world.

Dorothy blinked and asked the young nurse, "Where am I?" The young nurse smiled; she told Dorothy, "Lay down, you are safe, and in the intensive care unit of Fitkin Hospital." The young girl lay back down and asked, "Why am I here? What happened to me?" The nurse answered, "You were hit by a car. and were seriously hurt; now you are here safe, and we hope to make you better." She tucked Dorothy in, and soothed her by wiping the sweat from her forehead as Doctor Brown entered the room. "Well hello young lady, and how are you feeling this morning?" the old doctor asked. "You gave us quite a scare here for the last few weeks. You have been in a coma." Dorothy's mind was a blank. She said, "Who am I?" The doctor answered, "It says here you are Dorothy Banks from Third Avenue in the city, and you work at the Beer Garden on the beachfront. Carmine your boss has been here every day to see how you were doing. He asked us to let him know if you need anything. He is really worried about you. He says you have no relatives in the area."

Dorothy looked at the doctor and said, "How come I don't know who I am?" The kind old doctor walked over to the young girl, and took her hand in his; he patted it in a gentle fatherly way. He said, "You have serious head injuries from a very bad car accident, and you have been unconscious for a week. You seem to have lost your memory. It is not unusual in cases like this. Hopefully it will return in time, and all will be fine. For now, you need to rest and relax. Let us at the hospital take care of you, you are safe here, and in time all should be back to normal in your life." Doctor Brown smiled and patted Dorothy's hand as he released it, and the young girl relaxed, closed her eyes, and fell asleep. The kind old doctor had reminded her of someone she loved from her past, and she knew that when she was with him she was safe. It comforted her.

In a few days, Dee Dee was up and walking around. Carmine had brought her snacks every day. He came to visit her before he opened the Beer Garden every morning. When she started to improve, the kind old man told her that she liked to be called Dee Dee. He came every day without fail, and Dee Dee was glad to see him. Last time he came, Carmine told her about his nephew Frank the cop and Kiddo his dog. She liked the story, but could not remember Frank. She did remember the big shaggy dog.

Mary and Arnold came to visit her. Mary brought her some things she knew a girl would need and made a list of things the young girl wanted. She folded the list, put it in her purse, and took it with her when her and Arnold left.

Dee Dee really appreciated the help she was getting from the people that visited. She felt lucky to have such good friends. She felt she belonged, but she still could not remember exactly who she was, or who they were.

Dee Dee felt fine physically, but sometimes she awoke from sleep in a frenzy. There was this face, this horrible face that always seemed to be there watching her when she was sleeping. It made her want to stay awake all the time. There seemed to be something sinister about this apparition, but she did not remember what it was.

Pete was just finishing telling Tony about the girl from the accident, and how she had lost her memory when the voice of Sergeant Griffith broke in. He shouted Car Five give me a 10-2. The officers knew that this meant he wanted to tell them something, but he did not want to put the information over the air. This call meant to give him a phone call. Pete stopped at the nearest pay phone, and Tony got out and dialed "O". He asked the operator to connect him to police headquarters, and he waited. Sergeant Griffith answered, "Yeah, this is police headquarters." Tony said, "What's up Sarge?" Sergeant Griffith answered, "You guys go over to West Lake Avenue, and meet Phoebe Yates. She is having some trouble with a dog. See if you can help her." He hung up.

Tony went back to the car, and told Pete to drive over to West Lake, and look for Phoebe Yates. She was having trouble or something with a dog. The two officers sped off to the lake.

When they arrived, the officers were treated to a rare sight. Old Ms. Yates was knee deep in the muddy water yelling at a big black dog. The black dog was chasing the ducks around in the water. The spry old lady was covered in mud and swinging her cane in the air yelling at the dog. The dog was ignoring her, and having the time of his life chasing the ducks, which he could not catch as they would simply fly away if he got too close. This was not good enough for Ms. Yates, these ducks were her babies. She fed them every day, she had even given them names, and she just would not stand for anything upsetting them. What a sight this was. When the elderly woman saw the two officers, the upset old woman pointed her cane at the dog and ordered them to arrest him.

Pete went over to the edge of the lake and offered Ms. Yates his hand. He said, "Here let me help you out, and then we will go and get the dog." She tried to turn to the officer, and she found she could not move her feet. She said, "Oh my gosh I am stuck in the mud!" and she started to cry. Tony said to Pete, "We have to do something." And Pete answered, "Let's just wait for the Fire Department to come." But this would not do for Tony he noticed that Ms. Yates was starting to shiver. So, Tony decided to go into the water and rescue her. He put his gun belt and cuffs in the police car trunk, took off his shoes and socks, and entered the lake.

He put his arms around Ms. Yates, and as gently as he could, he lifted her from the muddy bottom. The smell of the released gas was terrible, but she was free. Then, he helped her to Pete who was waiting on the shore with a blanket. Pete helped the old woman out, and wrapped her in the blanket. A local merchant who was watching the event brought over some hot coffee to help warm up the old woman who was now shivering, and she gratefully sipped it as she sat down in the back of the police car; Tony climbed out of the lake, and they all waited for the First Aid to arrive.

Bonzoni and Big Geno had arrived just as Tony was pulling himself out of the Lake. Bonzoni joked, "Hey your prisoner is escaping; you better swim across the lake, and catch him before he gets away." During the confusion, the dog had swam across the lake and was now running along the opposite shore sniffing and doing what dogs like to do. He had gotten away. Tony just laughed, and he helped Ms. Yates into the ambulance. When he walked over to the police car, Pete said to him, "You don't smell too good why don't you walk to police headquarters, the sun will help you dry off; the fresh air will do you good." Then Pete, Bonzoni, and Big Geno broke out in laughter as the soggy, smelly, young cop opened the police car door, and got in. "Lets go." Tony said, and Pete just grinned as he drove away towards police headquarters to get his partner some fresh pants.

This had been a bad time for Richard. Just after Labor Day, the police had found the body he and Fizz had dumped in a neighboring town and were now alerted that there might be a serial killer in the county. The police had no idea who it was, or where the body had come from, but the fact someone found the body annoyed Richard. All police departments had been alerted. This had never happened before, added to that the big girl that got away could spell trouble for him. The big girl would certainly know him if she saw him again, and worse she would know where he lived. This would not do. It could become troublesome.

Added to this misfortune was the news that Fizz brought around this morning. The police had stopped him and towed his car to the city impound. They would index it, and store it if he did not come in this morning with a good registration, and proof of insurance. Two of Richard's suitcases were in the trunk; they had lovers in them. This was surely the worst news of the day.

Late that night, Richard took many of his trophies down to the jetty in a suitcase. The beach was desolate. The late summer chill was in the night air. He sat on the edge of the rocks and slowly threw the contents into the ocean. Fish and other denizens of the deep began to rise to the surface and greedily grabbed at the tasty debris. This gave Richard an idea. He quickly discarded the contents of eyes, teeth, and chopped up scalps into the water; he went under the boardwalk. He laid down over one of the mounds and began to collect his thoughts. He would come here on the weekdays like today late at night and saw the remains he could locate into pieces. He would put them in paper lunch bags and throw them off the jetty little by little. The undertow would take them out to sea and the creatures would eat much of it. The pieces would never return in any recognizable form. Most would be eaten. This would get rid of them in no time. He knew this was a good plan, and it could not fail. He would begin immediately.

It was a close call this afternoon. Richard had dipped into his hideaway stash of money and he took two thousand dollars out. He told Fizz he had some money for him; he gave it to him with strict orders to fix the problem right away. Fizz thanked him, and he said Richard was a savior.

Fizz went right out and bought some insurance, and new plates for the car, then, he rushed over to the impound and got the car out just two hours before the city offices closed. That was a very close call. In another two hours, the police officers would have been over to index the contents of the vehicle and prepare it for storage deep in the lot.

Richard took the suitcases out of the trunk as soon as Fizz got to his house. He would dump their contents at night over the next few weeks. Until then, he would store the suitcases in the basement. He hated to have to part with his lovers like this, but they had to go. He would work on them today; he began sawing the limbs and chopping them up. All would be well if he could just find that big girl and finish her off too. He wanted her in his hands, under his power, and at his mercy. He wanted to make passionate and complete love to her. One thing at a time, he thought to himself, as he made for the basement with his tools.

Richard fell into bed exhausted late that afternoon; this had been a hectic day, but he could not sleep. When he closed his eyes, he had that dream again. This time he was chained to two trees, and the big girl was hitting him with a bat. Then, she heated up a frying pan and pressed it against his chest. He sat up in a cold sweat his body shaking. He actually felt the burn on his chest. Why was this happening to him? He reached under the bed for the skull, pulled it to his chest, and curled up into a fetal position in the center of the bed. He pulled the covers over his head and closed his eyes. "I will never let you go my love." he said as he stroked the skull. Soon, he fell into an uneasy sleep.

# CHAPTER THIRTY

## The Artist

There was a new moon in this lonely sky over the city down the shore. There was a thick fog; it seemed that no stars existed this night. In the darkness crept a shadowy figure. He skulked along the alleyways and made his way to the freshly white washed wall on the west side of the abandoned warehouse just off the railroad tracks. When he left, the wall was alive. Yellows, greens, bright reds, purples, and jet black adorned the wall in a wild pattern; in the center was a celebration of colors that spelled in the most garish way "KLASCH." It was an act of vandalism; it was a political statement; and it was a work of art.

This young man would adorn the walls of many vacant buildings throughout the city for many years. Everyone knew who he was, but no one could ever catch him in the act of producing one of his masterpieces. They just seemed to appear. It was like magic.

Abraham Ruiz was the son of a Puerto Rican father and a Jewish mother. He was a happy young man and a gifted artist. The legend goes that when he was born, he painted KLASCH on the back of the doctor as he turned to walk out of the delivery room, and he hasn't stopped yet.

Frank and Davy had gotten a call to respond to the alley between First and Second Streets just off the railroad tracks. There was a report of a prowler in the area of the large electrical warehouse in the far end of the alley. Frank dropped Davy off at the north end of the alley, and then, he pulled the police car around to the south side end; he got out and waited. On the signal over the walkie talkie, Davy would walk to the south side, and Frank would walk to the north side. They would meet somewhere close to the middle.

The officers met and Davy said, "It looks clear. I saw no broken glass." Frank answered, "My end was secure also." As they were preparing to call in the disposition, Davy leaned against the west wall, and as he touched it with his hand it felt moist. He looked at his hand, and it was covered with paint. He stepped back and shined his light at the wall to find a full size colorful mural of abstract art with the word " KLASCH" colorfully printed in the center. Davy said, "How does this kid do this? He must carry a ladder with him."

They called in to headquarters and advised the desk sergeant about the vandalism. Sergeant Harriman barked angrily, "Well you guys just stay in the area, and catch that son of a gun, and don't leave until you get it done; you get me!" Frank answered, "Yea." And the two veteran cops said good-by to breakfast and took up a position hidden in the darkest corner of the ally to watch for the return of the painter.

After years of petty vandalism, the town fathers decided that something had to be done with Abraham Ruiz. They pressured the chief for a solution to this problem. The chief decided to arrest the young man, and charge him with the vandalisms.

Abraham was picked up that afternoon at the high school; the kids booed the police as they took him away. Abraham raised his hands in fists high over his head, and shook it as he was walked to the awaiting police car. The whole school yard cheered him.

Abraham was sent to juvenile hall while his case was being prepared for trial, for his own safety, and in his best interests according to Judge Cole. After six months, he was convicted and given an indeterminate term in The Jamesburg Juvenile Correctional Center. His lawyer would appeal the conviction.

J.W. and Big Geno received a call, "837 to Car Three see the man at the Odyssey Lounge, report of a suspicious man in the parking lot." When Car three arrived, they saw a sight to behold. There was

Brown, the town drunk, in the lot directing traffic. He was leaning back almost parallel with the ground, and he was waving his arms at the valet parkers directing them into parking spaces. A good size crowd had gathered amused by Brown's antics, and he loved the attention. Dayton Loveday the head doorman came over to the officers. He said, "Guy's you gotta get him outta here, no one is going inside they are all out here watching him; he could put us out of business in one night!" J.W. just laughed. He and Big Geno went over and got Brown. The crowd threw cat calls at the officers as they escorted the inebriated Brown out of the parking lot. They put Brown in the back of the police car and took him to Big Jim's Diner.

Big Geno gave Brown a dollar; he told him to get some coffee and stay away from the parking lot at the bar. Brown handed J.W. back the dollar, and he smiled. He pulled a handful of change and small bills out of his pocket. He said to the surprised officers, "I got plenty of money J.W.; those nice people were throwing it at me for helping them park their cars. I was working there," Brown smiled and walked into the diner. Big Geno gave J.W. an angry glare as the old cop began to put the dollar in his pocket. J.W. smiled and handed Big Geno back the dollar and said, "Oops."

Abraham won his appeal and his lawyer also filed a civil rights suit against the judge and the city. After a ten year struggle, Abraham received a three million dollar settlement from the City. It seems the Supreme Court agree that since he was never caught in the act, the State had failed to prove that he actually was the one who painted the walls.

It was a dream come true for Abraham. He opened a school of art. He specialized in teaching kids from the, ghetto, and he even got State funding for poor kids to go to the school. But still every now and then you can walk one of the back alley's of the city, and see bleeding through the white wash covering one of the warehouse walls a faint mural and the word KLASCH blazing through in the center, people will always remember Abraham Ruiz the artist.

Mary and Arnold had just left the hospital, and Mary was happy that Dee Dee was doing so well. The doctors said that once she was out of the hospital and back with her friends, she would begin to remember everything. There did not appear to be any permanent damage done to her brain. Mary looked at Arnold and said, "Lets go out for dinner and a movie. After all the trouble and heartache this summer, I finally feel happy." Arnold answered, "That sounds fine with me. Maybe, we can even have some fun after the movie?" Mary grabbed his arm, and nestled against his shoulder and said, "That sounds fine with me big boy!"

Richard was not in a good mood this day. He just found out that Fizz had married Mary. He decided to confront Fizz. He said to him, "Are you nuts, did you marry that crazy psycho junkie broad?" Fizz just smiled, and he answered, "Yea, I did it a month ago, but she really loves me, she's rich, and I'm a junkie too." Richard just turned and walked away. He could not believe how stupid Fizz was, but he figured all those years of drugs and alcohol had dulled Fizz's brain, and besides he had more important things on his mind. He must do something about the big girl. She should have never gotten away. There was surely a lesson to be learned from that one, he surmised.

The pressure was on. He knew if the big girl ever talked to the police the hunt would be on for him. He needed to get rid of any evidence he had around that would cause him trouble. What could she accuse him of anyway cutting her with a knife? He really did not do anything else to her. She ran in front of the car on her own.

He wished he could get the body he and Fizz dumped in the next town the other night. Dumping the body was a mistake; he should never take advice from Fizz. This would be the second body the police would find in this area. A contractor had started clearing the area for a new housing development. It would be just a matter of time before they would find the body. He should never take Fizz's advice on anything he thought to himself again, especially dumping the bodies of his lovers. He should have planted it in his mother's garden or put it in the sea like the rest.

No use crying over spilt milk. It was only two, and the police got nowhere with the first one. They should have just as tough a time with the second one. She was a run away and had no true identification. No one would be able to identify the mutilated corpse, or what was left of it, and no one would be able to link it to him. The only risk he had was the big girl, and he knew he could fix that; he just needed to get his hands on her. It was time to think on the problem

He went to his bed and lay down. He found his favorite skull, put it on his chest, stroked it with his hand, and as he stroked it; he began to formulate a plan.

239

He would dispose of what ever he could find of his lovers in the house, and under the boardwalk in the ocean; then, from now on, the new lovers would go to his mother's garden when they ripened.

He would be safe then. He would still keep his important trophies; he would just display them less. They were very important to him. No body, no murder; that is what he was taught in prison. They can't charge you with killing someone if they couldn't show the person was dead. If you don't have a name, how do you know what you have, they need a body and a name to put on it.

He knew he would come up with a plan, after all he was a genius, and he was a god. The only weak link that he could see was Fizz and that link could be fixed very easily. He smiled as he stroked the skull; he pictured different ways to deal with Fizz, each one pleased him. He remembered Buddy Moore and the fun he had with him, and he soon fell into a thought filled but peaceful sleep.

# CHAPTER THIRTY—ONE

## The Little Girl

It was the Fall, and as Winter approached, the city wrestled with its local troubles. It was, however, a chance for the officers to get back to addressing community problems and improving neighborhood patrols. The city was quiet most of the week, but was still busy on the weekends. The days were quiet now, and the cities children were back in school.

Arnold and Mary were in full swing with their relationship. They remained living apart, but both spent much time at each others home, they may as well have married and moved in together.

Davy and J.W. were on patrol. They were the veterans of the Department, and a better pair of officers could not be found anywhere. They had both joined the city police department after they returned from Korea and had stayed in patrol for well over twenty years. Both were fast approaching twenty-five years completed service and were considering retirement. They were just deciding who would go to lunch first when the call came in. It was to go to DeWitt Street, and see the lady about her missing child.

Leona Crosby was distraught. Her six year old daughter Ophelia had just come home from school. She went outside to show off her book and brag about being in first grade to the kindergarten kids in the area. Ophelia was so proud to be in school. She thought she was almost grown up. When Leona called her for afternoon snack, she did not come home. When Leona went out to look for her, she could not find her. All she could locate was the child's book on the porch. Leona was worried because she knew Ophelia would never leave her precious book like that. Davy took the report while J.W. talked to the neighbors.

Leona's mom Amelia Potts came over to comfort her daughter and help if she could. After the police left, the mother and grandmother scoured the neighborhood looking for any trace of the child.

Davy said to J.W., "She is just a baby only six years old; we have to find her fast. The two veteran officers new if she was gone overnight she was probably dead, and if she was missing more than two days, she would likely never be found. They called in the information to police headquarters. The desk sergeant put it out to all cars. The necessary state and federal alarms were sent. The two veteran officers went back to Dewitt Street and walked the neighborhood hoping to find a lead. They talked to everyone they saw on the street.

Brandon Blades was the fastest kid in the city high school; they called him the Buzz because that's all you heard when he went by you in a race. That was fifteen years ago before years of drinking and doing drugs.

He even had a tryout for the Dallas Cowboys. He never made it. He showed up high and could not pass the drug test, and his football career was over before it started. The Buzz now survived by his wits. He shoplifted, did petty burglaries, but his strong point was purse snatches. He had truly mastered the grab and run.

Pete and Tony were looking for the little girl when a call came in 10-39 purse snatch in progress on Cookson Avenue. All cars respond to the Plaza. Pete turned the police car around and headed to the business district. Tony yelled there he goes across Main Street. It's The Buzz. As soon as he said it, a young girl flew across the street right on the Buzz's tail. Pete stopped the car; Tony got out and ran after the pair, as Pete turned the car to continue after the group. He radioed headquarters and all cars about the pursuit, and finished just in time to see the young girl fly through the air, and tackle The Buzz. The pair fell to the ground, and the girl quickly jumped on The Buzz's back and began to bite, punch, and kick the surprised junkie. Tony arrived and carefully pulled the girl off The Buzz. The Buzz got up and handed a pay envelop to Tony, put out his hands in the air and said, "Take me away, lock me up, just get me away from this crazy broad." The young girl Nadine Russell was crying. She took the pay envelop from the surprised cop's hand, checked it, folded it in half, and put it in her jean pocket. She looked at Tony and blushed. She said, "I just couldn't let him take that, it's my first paycheck." Tony laughed. He said, "Come with us to police headquarters, we'll do a report, and you can have your money back, and go on your way. You must learn to be careful. A young girl could easily get hurt chasing junkies." "She could get hurt" The Buzz said, "What about us junkies?" Tony laughed as he put the bruised junkie into the back seat of the police car, then, the girl got into the front seat. Tony sat in the back next to The Buzz, and Pete drove them all to headquarters.

As J.W. and Davy were going off, they ran into Benny "Ogre" Potts the uncle of the missing girl. Benny was called Ogre because of his looks. He was Five feet two inches tall and two hundred fifty pounds. His teeth were splayed from twenty years of thumb sucking. He was a nasty and aggressive young man. He was marginally mentally handicapped as he had an I.Q. of about seventy. This had kept him out of jail. His abnormal strength had kept him alive. He was particularly nasty to the kids in the neighborhood, who teased him whenever they had the chance. He rarely washed and was especially aggressive when he was drunk. He was drunk most of the time. The years of ridicule from his peers and most of the neighborhood had left him bitter. He lived with his mother Amelia Potts, but it was not unusual for him to be on the street for days at a time.

Ogre was drunk, but he stood up and greeted the officers as they approached him. Good afternoon Mr. Davy and Mr. J.W., he slurred as the officers stopped to talk to him. They asked him if he saw his niece Ophelia, and Ogre just turned away, and he sat back down on the curb. Then, he said without looking at the officers, "Why do you think I saw her?" J.W. replied, "Listen you drunken bum she is just a baby, and she is missing; you make sure if you see her you tell your mom or your sister." As the two officers walked away, Davy said to J.W., "Don't you think you were a little rough on him?"

J.W. answered, "I don't know I just got a funny feeling he knows something that he isn't telling us." Then, the two veteran officers continued on with the investigation.

As they headed to police headquarters to sign off for the day, a call came over for Car #2 to go to DeWitt Street and see Amelia Potts. When they arrived, Ms. Potts was frantic. She told Davy, "They think they saw my baby under that porch." She pointed to the abandon hotel next to her house. "The junkies and wino's live in there, if she is under there, she could be hurt. She won't come out when I call. That's not like my granddaughter."

J.W. crawled under the trim, into the dark damp pit that was under the porch, and shined his flashlight around. There in a shallow ditch almost in the center of the dark area under the porch, and J.W. could make out a small shape in the crevice. It looked like the shape of a little child. As he got closer he could see that the body was naked except for a tee shirt and her arms and legs were spread wide, like a child making an angel in the snow. Her head was turned to the side; her eyes were open and staring at J.W. in a peaceful but lifeless stare; they could no longer see. The officer crawled under the porch, and he reached over and felt the baby's wrist. She had no pulse. His instinct was to drag her out and try to revive her, but his training told him not to ruin the crime scene. He could not risk it he would go with his instincts. . She still felt warm, and she deserved to have a chance to live. J.W. grabbed her arm, and carefully but quickly, dragged the poor child out to the sidewalk. He began Mouth to mouth in an attempt to revive her.

Leona Crosby arrived and screamed when she saw the condition of her baby. Amelia hugged her daughter, restrained her, and tried to comfort her. She told her all would be alright, but there was no fervor in her voice. The First aid arrived, and put a respirator on the child; they picked her up and put her on a gurney. When the paramedics lifted the small lifeless girl, it revealed a small brown purse under her frail body. The purse had the name Benjamin written on it in cheap beads. When Leona saw it she screamed, "Ogre, you bastard" and ran to her house.

Amelia's eyes were wide. J.W. asked her, "What was going on?" She replied softly, almost in a whisper, "That's her brother's purse.

He made it in school when he was a kid. It was his most treasured possession. He was never without it." The officers looked at each other, and then they ran down the alley to Leona's house.

Ogre had gone to Leona's house. He had entered to get some food when he saw her run out. Leona had returned too soon and was able to catch him as he was putting some groceries into a brown paper bag. She cursed him and screamed at him. He pushed her away roughly. When she turned around again to face him, she had a kitchen knife in her hand. She punched him in the chest with all her might, and drove the knife deeply in to his cold heart. She pulled it out, and punched it in again and again yelling "Why? Why Ogre? Why?", and even when the blade broke off in Ogre's chest she continued to punch him with the handle.

J.W. was the first to arrive; he grabbed Leona around her body and put the frantic sobbing woman into a chair. Ogre just stared at his sister, then, dropped to his knees. He said, "I've been bad, and now, I'm dead." and collapsed face down on the floor. Amelia screamed as she entered the house. Davy caught her as she fainted.

At the hospital, the baby was pronounced D.O.A. The officers took Leona into custody. J.W. sat in the back seat with her. The distraught mother never spoke a word she just gazed out the window, stared away blankly, and sobbed. Davy drove them to police headquarters.

Amelia was taken to the hospital, but was released soon. She rushed to police headquarters with the family lawyer and Reverend Meeks her pastor, who had met her at the hospital. They worked out an arrangement with the judge to release Leona to her mother on a $100,000.00 recognizance bail.

The family and the neighborhood would never be the same. It seemed the joy had been ripped out of their lives. It is the worst thing in life to have to burry your child. It's like burying a little piece of you. You can never get over it.

Leona would not be sent to jail. She was found not guilty of murder at her trial almost a year later. She would remain under the care of a doctor for the rest of her life.

The town condemned and tore down the old junkie hotel, and turned the empty lot into a playground for the neighborhood children. They called it the Ophelia Crosby Play Center. There was a small stone monument in the corner dedicating the lot to the memory of the child with a bronze likeness of Ophelia on it donated by the owner of the local newspaper. There was a small carefully tended plot of flowers around it. Leona could usually be found at the monument, every day she would visit her daughter there, clean the plot, tend the flowers, and think of what might have been. She remembered Ophelia like this every day for the rest of her life.

The tragedy left its scars on Mary, too. When Arnold came to the High School and gave her the bad news, she was shocked. Leona was one of her favorite students ever, and a good friend. When she graduated, Mary helped her go to night school, and Leona was close to becoming a nurse. Mary considered her the little sister she never had. Mary was devastated. She was hurt so badly by Leona's heartache that the loss felt like her own. She had spent many a night with sweet little Ophelia while Leona went to school. The little girl was so bright, and so full of energy and curiosity; she could not wait to start school this fall. Her grief became so bad Mary called the school and took an extended sick leave to get herself together. Arnold did his best to pick Mary up, but it seemed the spark had gone out in this woman. He needed to find a way to relight it.

Richard had been very busy these past weeks. He and Fizz had taken four suitcases of lovers to his mother's place in Staten Island. He had buried them in the back yard under the pretext he was working in her garden. She knew that she did not have a garden, but just smiled and nodded. While they were outside, she cooked them some food. It was inedible so Richard taped her to a chair again and left. The nurse's aid that visits her three times a week found her badly dehydrated but otherwise fine. She had saved the old woman the last time and was amazed when she saw the old woman in the same pitiful condition. She had come shortly after Richard left. The old woman couldn't remember who did this to her she just smiled and said "Yes." She could not remember many current things it seemed these days. She remembered the old days like it was yesterday, and Richard was still her baby.

Mrs. Bergerwasser was getting very forgetful as she got older. She was over eighty. Wasn't it nice of those young boys to plant a nice garden for me, she thought as she gazed out the back window of the house. Being taped to the chair was uncomfortable though, she thought to herself. Fizz took the five dollars he found in a jar on the counter, and twenty dollars the old woman had on her dining room hutch.

Richard had found and dumped the parts of ten or twelve other lovers in the ocean. The crabs and vermin had done a great job over the years under the boardwalk. Even most of the bones had been chewed up by rodents or washed away by the annual hurricanes and the violent storms. The undertow kept them away. The only things he had left were the skulls he loved, and the heads in his freezer. He polished the skulls and lacquered them. He made the skulls into lamps. Making lamps out of ordinary household items was a skill he learned in prison. It served him well. They worked too. He put two of the lamps in the bedroom on the end tables. He loved it. It was a nice touch he thought. He could play with them when he needed them. Two others were in the living room, and a fifth was in the den. His favorite remained under his bed.

The two special heads, his favorites, he left in the freezer down the cellar. He could not bring himself to alter them. After all, they were his best work. No one would ever find them he hoped.

Richard went to the Beer Garden, ordered some coffee, took it to a corner booth, and listened. There was no talk about the big girl. Carmine was only telling the tale of his nephew and that mangy dog Richard thought, and he had to sit through the story. He hated this place. After Carmine finished, Richard got up, put a dollar in the jar for the dog, and left.

The harvest full moon was coming, and it was tugging at Richard's soul. He would need a lover soon. He was sitting in his usual seat when he heard the young girl squeal with delight walking with an older man. He watched them talk, and as they walked away, he saw three plain clothes officers converge on the old man. They arrested him. He heard one of the officers advise the man of his rights, then cuff him. Richard watched as the officers took the man away. The two others joked about the "John" as they walked back to their concealment. The girl officer resumed her long walk back down to the other end of the boardwalk. He would have to be careful as long as the police were running a "Pussy Posse" he thought to himself.

As he observed the officers throughout the night, a thought entered his warped and twisted mind. He began to desire the young police woman as a lover. How could he work that? He did not know now. He would definitely give it some thought. It could become his greatest work. It definitely would be a great challenge.

Richard came out of his dreams as the moon fell in the western sky. The sun would soon make its appearance. He had better get along home. A crimson ridge had already appeared across the ocean. He did not enjoy the mornings. He walked home in a daze. The call of the full moon was still pulling him, and his need was great; as he came to his house, he found he was frowning.

# CHAPTER THIRTY—TWO

## The Contempt of Court

R ichard was up early this morning. He had spent the night in a troubled sleep He got no rest; he had much on his mind, his need was great, and he needed to find peace. He would go to his bench so he could think about his dilemma.

Richard was walking past the coffee shop, and saw one of the officers from the accident inside having coffee. He entered, and he sat down next to Sara and Tony. Richard said hello to the officers and ordered coffee.

He began some small talk with the two officers, then, got to the accident. He asked if they had seen it. Tony said, "Yea, I was working that night, but my partner Pete did the accident report. That girl was lucky to be alive." "She is still alive?" Richard said. "Yea", said Tony, "In fact, she may even be getting out of the hospital soon; gee's, it's been over a month." Richard looked at the officers, and replied, "That's great, it looked pretty bad to me, but I just rode by. She certainly looked dead." "No, she wasn't" Tony answered, "But she can't remember anything. Do you know her?" "No, I don't think so." Richard lied to Tony, "I did not even get a good look at her. Was she from this area?" Richard asked. Tony remarked, "She is from the other side of town. She worked at the Beer Garden. We think she was coming here for coffee, but we may never know." "Oh, that is terrible.

I hope all turns out well for the poor girl." Richard replied, "Well, I have to go. I have important things to do. Have a good morning gentlemen and here the coffee is on me." Richard put five dollars on the counter and left. The officers protested, but Richard waved them off as he walked out of the coffee shop. Richard began humming as he walked to his house. When he walked through the doorway, he noticed in the reflection in the door glass there was a grin on his face. Richard found that he was happy. Things were getting better.

Big Geno answered the call with a 10-4. He and Bonzoni were to go to Borden Street and see Lucius Dray. He claims he was robbed. When they arrived Lucius Dray, Mafrikee Dawson's boyfriend, was waiting by the curb and he was covered with blood. The officers noticed a large gash over his left eye. Big Geno called for first aid as the two officers arrived, and he and Bonzoni got out and walked over to Lucius. "I wuz robbed!" Lucius yelled at the officers as they approached him. Mafrikee Dawson did this to me upstairs. Lucius pointed to the motel across the street in the area of the second floor. First aid arrived, and they treated and cleaned the cut. Then, they closed it with some butterfly tape and covered it with a gauze bandage. They suggested that Lucius should to go to the hospital for stitches; Lucius refused to go to the hospital. The officers walked with Lucius across the street, and Bonzoni stayed down stairs with Lucius while Big Geno went up to speak with Mafrikee.

Upstairs, Big Geno found Mafrikee with her three kids watching television. She said, "Come on in Big Geno you know you're always welcome here. I know why you are here anyway. That dummy Lucius thinks because he made two of my babies, he can come up here anytime he wants and sex me. Well as far as I'm concerned even if the law says we are common law, we're not common law no more. You go tell him I said that, and I mean it."

"He says you robbed him?" Big Geno asked. "You tell him the babies need food and diapers, and he needs to get that before he puts his hands on me again. He took five dollars from my dresser, then he tried to have his way with me so, I hit him with the frying pan to make him leave, and I took back my five dollars before I kicked him down the stairs. If that means I tried to rob him, then, he tried to rape me," Big Geno could see this was getting nowhere fast. He went back down to talk with Lucius.

"Okay Lucius, what happened; Mafrikee say's you tried to rape her?" Big Geno barked as he came down the stairs. Lucius looked at the ground, and said, "Well you boys can go I can take this matter from now on. I don't want to report nuthin no mo." "Oh, no you don't", Bonzoni said as he grabbed Lucius' arm with a vise like grip. "You called us to report a crime, and we will settle this matter before we leave. We are not spending the day coming back here for this nonsense. Let's go, upstairs. We are going to end this right now."

Upstairs, they found that Mafrikee had gotten mad because Lucius lost his job. He had come to see if he could get some money to go gamble with the guys. He took five dollars he saw on the dresser and slid it into his pocket, but Mafrikee caught him. When he tried to run out with the money she grabbed him as he was leaving, and hit him in the head with the frying pan. Then, she took back the money and pushed his dazed body out the door. He rolled down the stairs and into the street a bloody mess.

"Okay, what can we do to end this?" Big Geno asked. Lucius said "Well she's my woman We been together seven years. The judge says we're common law. I don't want her to go to jail, I just want my five dollars."

Mafrikee grabbed for the frying pan as she said, "I'll settle this, I'll just hit him a little harder." Big Geno grabbed the big girl, and she dropped the pan. "That's it I'm through with you girl." Lucius yelled. "I thought you wuz my wife." "I wuz, but I ain't no more" Mafrikee screamed back. "You can't just do that girl the law has to end that; we're common law." Lucius said. "I got just as much right here as you and I ain't leaving." Big Geno said, "Alright I'm the law, and I will end this right now. If we have to come back again after this, I'll take you both to see the Judge Bianco and you will really be poorer."

"Mafrikee put your hand on my badge. Lucius you put your hand on Bonzoni's badge. Now, by the powers invested in me, I now pronounce you unmarried." Big Geno turned to Lucius and said, "Now, Lucius you go to your brother's house and don't come back for the rest of the day." Lucius slowly turned and began a slow walk down the stairs, when he got to the bottom, he yelled up." Hey girl, maybe we can go to the club tomorrow now we ain't married no more." Mafrikee replied, "You'll just have to call on me tomorrow, and see if I'm free." The two officers turned to each other, and they just shook their heads, then, they put Lucius in the police car and dropped him off at his brother's house. As the two officers pulled away to resume patrol, Bonzoni said, "Good work judge Geno."

Vill drove to the courthouse and dropped off Sara who had to report for a case. He had arrested a vagrant called Pockets, who had vandalized a store this morning.

Pockets Gressom was the local bum. He was usually mild mannered but liked to spend time in the county jail from time to time. He was an out patient from one of the now defunct mental hospitals that had been closed by the state. He decided that living on the street here in this beautiful shore town was as good as it gets. He could always go to the county jail when he needed a change, or when he wanted some "Home Cook'n" as he called jail chow.

At well over three hundred pounds and with an unpredictable personality he had few enemies and fewer friends, but he usually lived well on what he could beg. He was having trouble getting arrested lately, and missed his usual week at the county jail this month. So this morning he took a cement block from the gutter and threw it into a window of a store in the business district. Then, he sat down in front of the store and waited for the police to arrive. Sara arrested him at the scene.

Court was in session this morning, and Pockets case was called first because he entered a guilty plea. Judge Papper came in from a neighboring town and was helping out by having an overflow court today to help Judge Bianco clear up the backlog in the court docket. The court clerk, Nancy Mauro, called Pockets case and the large, smelly vagrant cool walked up to the bench. She asked him how he pled and he said guilty, but instead of sending him to jail Judge Papper sentenced him to six months community service, and a two hundred dollar fine.

This brought Pockets to a ranting rage. The judge warned Pockets to calm down, or he would hold him in contempt. Pockets didn't want to do community service, he wanted to go to county jail. He couldn't pay any fines; if he had two hundred dollars, he would be drunk somewhere.

He yelled at the judge, "I hold you in contempt you skinny, old, bald headed, stupid, mother fucker! If I had two hundred dollars, do you think I'd be here? If you do, you're crazier than I am." Pockets continued to curse him up and down. Suddenly, he stopped, stared at the judge, and screamed a banshee like scream. The courtroom emptied, as the people waiting for their cases to be called, ran out in terror at the outburst. They fled into the lobby.

Then, Pockets did the unthinkable, he charged the bench. The judge fled for his chambers as the angry Pockets knocked down Smoky the elderly court bailiff who had stepped in front of him to try to stop him. It was like trying to stop a train with a piece of paper. Pockets climbed up the front of the bench. Nancy stood her ground between Pockets and the judge allowing Judge Papper just enough time to flee to safety through a door behind the bench. It delayed Pockets long enough for the police to grab him. Tony and Sara were in court, and they grabbed the crazed vagrant, pulled him to the floor, and subdued him firmly and quickly.

Smoky got up dazed, but none the worse for wear. The judge peeked out of the door of his chamber's, and when he saw the officers taken control of Pockets, he prepared to return to his bench in the courtroom. Nancy helped the old judge back to the bench

Pockets was cuffed, shackled and secured to the pole in the barred area on the side of the courtroom. When the judge returned to the bench, he thanked the officers and found Pockets in contempt. Judge Papper ordered that Pockets be remanded to the Mental Ward of the State Hospital for sixty days observation and then to mental health wing of the county jail for diagnosis and stabilization for the next six months. Then, he adjourned court for the session, as he was visibly shaken from the event. In his fifty years as a judge, he had never been attacked by a criminal before. All pending cases had to be rescheduled. Nancy sat down with the lawyers and others and worked out a schedule for the new court dates; Judge Papper returned to his chambers and fell into his desk chair. Then, he and Smokey had a good stiff drink of bourbon, for medicinal purposes of course.

Richard had dinner with Fizz, and they decided to see what they could come up with tonight. Mary was on a heroin binge, and Fizz just left her on the grass in the park where she passed out. He told Richard, "I hope she falls in the lake and drowns." And Richard laughed and answered, "Who will support your ugly ass then, the good fairy?" Richard went up to his room, Fizz fell out on the sofa. They both went to sleep. When Richard awoke, it was dark and time for work. The moon was full, and Richard found the call was still upon him.

They got into the old Chevy, and the pair headed for the beachfront bar area. They parked near the Bootlegger Bar. Fizz went in to have a couple of drinks, and Richard walked to his usual bench on the boardwalk. It was a Thursday in late September and the boardwalk was deserted. There was a cool breeze blowing off the ocean, and you could see the lights on the horizon of the scallop boats returning from their ten day run.

Richard seemed hypnotized by the lights and he began to dream. He was awakened by a gruff, "Whatcha' doin' pal." It was Fizz, and he was totally drunk. He had a young girl with him, and she could hardly stand. "Dis is Billy." Fizz slurred, " but she ain't no boy." he finished. Billy opened her shirt and flashed her naked breasts at Richard and smiled. Fizz sat down next to Richard, and Billy fell into his lap. She winked at Richard as she fell against him. Richard got up and wiped his sleeve.

"You been up here for hours, the bars are closed, and it's almost four in the morning. Let's go get something to eat partner." "Buy me something and Ill treat you both real good." The drunk girl purred. Richard just smiled, got up, and slowly walked towards the car. It was the only one left on the street.

Before they went out, Richard had put a doctor's bag with his tools on the front seat. This would force whoever they stumbled upon to sit in the back with him. Richard and Billy got into the back of the Chevy. The seats were already covered with plastic garbage bags. Billy giggled as she slid across them. Richard sat next to her, and her head fell into his lap. She looked up at him and smiled. She began to loosen his pants. Fizz pulled out of the parking space and began to drive away.

As soon as they reached a dark spot, Richard grabbed the girl by the hair, lifted her head, pulled the .22 cal revolver from his jacket, and shot her once in the side of the head just behind the ear. He looked into the girl's face. He had shot her on the right side and her left eye had popped out onto her cheek. Amazingly, she was still breathing. "Gees', Richard" Fizz said, "I was going to nail her, why did you have to do her so quick?" Richard laughed and said, "She's still breathing, come and get some."

As Fizz looked for a dark quiet place, Richard began to torture the girl. He cut her with a box cutter, but she hardly moved. She made a soft moan, but then no other sound, nor did she cry out. Richard became angry. Fizz had found a dark alley and pulled the car deep into it. He shut off his lights and climbed into the back seat. As he undressed the dying girl he released a putrid smell. The poor girl had urinated and defecated from her ordeal. It was her last living act. She had died as she voided herself.

Richard hated this. He told Fizz, "I'll wait outside when you are done get rid of her then, call me." Richard picked up the doctor's bag with his tools, tucked the gun in his belt, and walked across the lot into the shadows and disappeared. Fizz checked the girl to make sure she had stopped breathing then, wrapped her tightly in the garbage bags and dragged her into the far corner of the alley. He stopped at the end by an old building, threw her onto other bags and urinated.

When he finished he fixed his pants, and walked back to the car. He opened the car door to get in, and just before he was ready to call Richard, the alley lit up. He heard someone say, "Alright freeze and put your hands in the air." It was the John Koolman and Ray Mansky on their walking beat.

The police officers checked the lot, and it was empty. They saw the garbage bags in the corner by the fence, and smelled the putrid smell. They asked, "What do you got in that bag?" Fizz said, Those are not my bags I just stopped in the alley to take a piss. They were already here. I don't know what's in them" When Ray looked into the top bag, he froze. He told John to call for backup as he handcuffed Fizz and read him his rights.

After John called for backup, he walked over and looked into the bag. He threw up. They put Fizz into the back of the first police car that arrived. Then, they advised Sergeant Bolton, and he had the officers secure the scene. He walked to a pay phone at the end of the alley; he called police headquarters and asked that the detectives be called in.

Richard was panting as he entered the doorway of his house. He had jogged all the way home along the railroad tracks then, up his street to the house. He knew he had to act fast. He took his tools out of his pockets, put them back in the doctor's bag, and hid the bag and everything incriminating he had in a hidden closet behind the wall on the side of the staircase that was there from prohibition days. Then, he closed the wall over it, hiding it. If you did not know it was there, you would never find it.

It was a good thing he had been destroying all the evidence he thought as he stripped off his clothes. He took a quick shower and changed into fresh clothes, and left for the train station. He caught the first train northbound and headed for Newark. There, he would take a train to Staten Island. It was time to visit Mom. He got on the northbound train just minutes before Detective Fowler arrived to secure the train station. The detective dropped off two officers to check the identification of everyone leaving town.

On the ride to his mothers, Richard closed his eyes, but he saw the girls that were his lovers running towards him laughing and screaming. He opened his eyes, and he was alone on a train. He decided to stay awake. It might not be safe to sleep he thought.

# CHAPTER THIRTY—THREE

## The End

The morning found Dee Dee sitting on the bench staring out at the sea. She was released from the hospital earlier this morning and for some reason she was drawn to this bench on the south end of the boardwalk. She sat and stared at the ocean for several hours. She found it relaxed her; she felt completely at peace.

She kept visioning a farm and a big bear of a man. She walked with him in the morning, and they drank fresh milk from the cow. She could not remember his name and could not see his face, but she knew he loved her, and she was safe with him. Why were these thoughts in her mind? She did not know, but she felt they were the key to her memory. There was something else back there too. It hid in the darkness, but it could not reach her when she was with the big man. Still, she dreaded this black, ominous thing. It came after her when she slept. It never went away, and it hid in the back of her mind when she was awake. Still, it always seemed to be there.

Richard walked into his mother's house, and it was empty. When he checked out the house, there was no one home. He went into the parlor and turned on the television. There was just static. He got up and went to the kitchen. He could find little to eat. All there was to drink was water and tea. It was better in prison he thought as he drank two glasses of water. He was very thirsty. He could not get the dryness out of his mouth. He sat in the doily covered rocking chair and fell asleep. His dreams were troubled. Girls danced around him. They were singing; some had no heads some were mutilated without eyes and broken teeth. They had carvings over their bodies. Most were bleeding. There were over a hundred of them. He could not move; he was duct taped to a cross. As each girl passed in front of him, they cut him, or prodded and poked him. He knew he was dreaming, but he could not wake up.

Suddenly, Richard awoke with a start. Across from him, sitting in an overstuffed arm chair, was his mother. She was staring at him and knitting. She said, "Good Morning Richard, did my baby get a good night sleep?" Richard looked at the mantel clock. He had been sleeping for sixteen hours. He had lost a day. He screamed to his mother, "I need some money, now" She smiled and said, "Yes dear." Then, she said, "Do you want me to sit in a chair so you can tape me to it again?" The kind old woman smiled. Richard stared at her and pushed her aside; he just shook his head and began to search the house.

In the upstairs bedroom, he found about a hundred small pocketbooks stacked in a closet. When he looked inside one he found an envelope, inside the envelop was two hundred dollars. As he checked he found each pocketbook contained the same an envelop, and each envelope contained two hundred dollars in ones and fives. Richard could not believe his luck. When he was done emptying the pocket books, he had two large piles of money. One pile was of new five dollar bills and the other was of new one dollar bills. He only had one problem. He had nothing to put the money into. He would need a box. He counted the money. There was just over ten thousand one dollar bills. The smaller pile contained a little over two thousand five dollar bills. There was twenty two thousand dollars all in ones and fives. Every month since his mother retired, she put away two hundred dollars from her social security check. She had asked for ones and fives, put the money in an envelope, and then the envelop into a small plastic pocket book. What a dumb old broad Richard thought.

He found a small suitcase in the hall closet and put the money in it. He filled it up and still had two thousand dollars in five dollar bills left over. He closed the valise and put it on the top shelf of the closet. Then, he took the five dollar bills that were left over and put them in four piles of five hundred dollars. He folded them and put one wad in each of his jean pockets. This was too much. He took the money out. In her dresser he found a large wallet, and he put fifteen hundred dollars in it. Then, he divided the last five hundred dollars into four stacks, folded them, and put them in his pockets. He put the wallet in his jacket pocket. That was much better.

When he went down stairs, his mother was waiting for him with a crisp new one hundred dollar bill. She held it out to him and said, "You are such a good boy, take this and get yourself some candy." Richard grabbed the money, pushed the old woman to the wall, and pinned her there. He said to her in a shrill yell, "Do you have more?" His mother smiled and said, "Yes" He shook her, and screamed "Where?" She smiled and replied "Yes"

Richards rage was unbearable, he wanted to slit her throat and rip the heart still beating from her chest. He felt deep hatred for her, but he also felt deep love. He could not kill this old woman. She was the only person in his whole life that really loved him, and that is what he really hated. He threw her brutally to the floor and stormed out of the house.

Richard had enough cash money with him now to stay anywhere he wanted without returning to his stash at home. He would wait until it was safe before returning to his house. This way if Fizz had cracked, he would just move away for a while.

He had his savings hidden at home buried in the basement. He could retrieve this at his leisure at night when it was safe. Now with his mother's money, he had some ready cash, and he had more in the closet in the valise for a reserve, and he still had his income from the trust. The money at home if it was absolutely necessary was a nice bonus. He was in good shape.

He would not go to his house until he felt it was safe. He took a bus back to the city down the shore and booked a room in a motel on the beachfront. He paid for a week. He bought the local news paper, Fizz' face stared at him from the front page. He took the newspaper to his room to read it. Then, he checked the gun. It was loaded only one shot was fired. He tucked it in his waist band and covered it with

259

his shirt. When he put on his jacket, no one could see anything was there. He went out.

At police headquarters, Detective Sergeant Doc Berg and Detective Johnnie Moose went to the interrogation room where Detective Fowler was finishing his interrogation of Fizz. He was questioning him about the body in the alley. The detective had been at it for two days. Fizz said that he was drunk, and stopped to pee in the ally, but he insisted he knew nothing about any dead body. He never changed his story. He kept asking for a lawyer; he was a pro.

Yesterday afternoon, his wife Mary had come in asking about Fizz's bail. The detectives did not want to charge him with murder because they could not prove the body had been in his car, and they would have to provide him with a lawyer right away. Fizz had no blood on his clothes, and there was nothing to link him to the mutilated corpse. An added fact was the victim had been shot, and they could not locate a gun. They searched Fizz, the car the lot and the area around the alley. They could not find a gun anywhere, and without the gun how could they prove he shot the girl.

The forensic team had found blood residue in the car. In fact, the car was full of blood residue in the back seat area, and in the trunk, but none of it matched the victim's blood. They decided to go with the charges of DWI and Criminal Trespass then, release Fizz on bail. They would shadow him around the clock. They felt that he would stay around. They could keep the car under the DWI laws so, they did. They did not want to charge him with the murder yet because they did not have a strong enough case, but both detectives knew he was at least involved in the murder. They all sensed it.

The detectives would keep him on a tight leash. They informed Fizz that he was charged with DWI and Criminal Trespass and stopped the questioning to delay him getting a lawyer. They booked him, printed him, checked N.C.I.C and S.C.I.C for wants and warrants, then, released him when everything came back negative. He was a felon on parole, and he was a three time looser. This would give them leverage in the next round of interrogation.

Dee Dee stopped off at the Beer Garden. Carmine was so glad to see her that he gave her a big hug and told her she could have her job back anytime she wanted. He told her not to rush back, but he hoped she would come back soon. He really liked this hard working girl. He gave her a beer mug with money in it. There was about two hundred dollars. He said it was from the regulars and the guys in the back, they really missed her. He said, "Take it and have a night out on the town. It's on us." Carmine always made her happy. She really loved this place. She went in the back and thanked the guys then, returned to the counter, and finished her coffee. She continued her talk with Carmine.

Detective Fowler along with Doc and Johnnie met with the street crimes unit and advised them about the case. They brought the officers into the detective's office and briefed them. The street crime unit consisted of Sgt. Mont, who headed the unit, Mike Lam, Pete Kowalsky , Mark Kingman, Buddy Lane, and Jeff Johnson. They also brought in post 5&6 which was Ray Mansky and John Koolman. An extra pair of young eyes could always come in handy. This would give them four two man teams to use for the surveillance, and the two detectives in reserve. The watch teams would take twelve hour shifts every other day and keep this schedule until the investigation was complete.

As soon as Fizz got out, he went to Richard's house. He knocked on the front door, but there was no answer. He opened the door with his key, went inside, and he fell asleep on the couch in the den.

Richard went to his house as soon as it got dark. He walked the shadowed alleys and made it to the back door unseen by the stake out that had been following Fizz. He went in the back door. He was surprised when he saw Fizz sleeping on the couch in the den. He woke him carefully, and the two began to talk in a low whisper. Fizz asked him why he left him in the alley with the cops. Richard responded, "I was covered in blood and carrying a gun did you want me to stay?" Fizz answered "No." "Where's the car?" Richard asked. Fizz told him, "The cops kept it they really tore it apart looking for evidence." Richard smiled, and said, "It's a good thing I was smart enough to clean it out and destroy our things. I took all my tools with me. We would really be up shit's creek if they found our lovers." Fizz thought to himself what does he mean O U R things, and OUR lovers, but he just said, "Yes." Fizz decided to go home to Mary. He left through the front door; he knew he was being watched. The watchers followed him. When he thought it was clear, Richard went upstairs to lie down and think.

First thing in the morning Dee Dee awoke and decided to go to work. She did not know what to do with herself home alone. Carmine and the guys were glad to see her. With almost two months of Carmine's cooking, the customers would be glad to see Dee Dee, too.

Ray and John had been watching Fizz and followed him when he left the house. They never saw Richard. They followed Fizz around the block to Mary's home and saw Mary welcome him happily. John said to Ray, "My leg is a little stiff from the wound, I got to get out and walk. I am going to walk around the block. I will walk clockwise if you need me." Ray smiled and said "Go ahead I'll be okay."

When John returned, he was nervous. He said. "Call headquarters; ask them to send Doc, Arnold, and Johnny down here." "Okay." Ray said, and made the call. Then, he asked John, "What's up partner?" John looked at Ray swallowed then, he said, "I walked by the house Fizz went to, and there was the shadowy guy upstairs in the window, and he was holding a skull." "What?" Ray exclaimed. "You heard me right he was holding a skull, I am sure of what I saw. I barely glanced up and did not stop, but he was standing by the window, and he was holding a skull, I am sure of it."

Richard had seen the man glance up at him as he stroked his favorite skull. When the man passed, Richard put the skull away, and shut off the dim light. He took a shower, gathered his tools, cleaned and reloaded the pistol, and put it in the doctor's bag with his tools. He took the rest of the small box of ammunition and put it in his front pants pocket. Richard left the house surreptitiously through the rear. He decided to spend the night in the motel room. One could never be too careful he thought to himself.

When the detectives arrived Doc questioned John. Then they left without comment and rode by the house around the corner. It appeared dark and empty. The detectives returned to police headquarters. The two young officers resumed their lonely vigil. Doc had brought them some fresh coffee and some donuts, a staple of the police stakeout. The two young officers chatted about the matter as they devoured their repast. They had told Doc about the man with the skull, but

Doc had made no comment. Both believed Doc was surprised, but neither could guess what he had in mind.

Dee Dee felt good behind the counter of the Beer Garden. It was a slow night, but most of the regulars showed up to give their regards and have the usual. The time was flying, and the big girl felt better than she had felt in months; and she liked it. She had a great job in a great town, she thought as she worked the grill.

When Richard arrived back at the motel, he was greeted by a young girl. She said, "I can give a lonely man company if he wants." "I'll remember that." Richard replied as he closed the door in the young girl's face. He flopped into the bed and gazed at the ceiling. His mind was a riot of thought.

Why had that bum Fizz gone to his house after he was released from city jail? Could he trust him not to give him up for a good deal when he went to court? Who was that man that saw him in the window with the skull? Did he notice it was a skull? Finally was he being watched? Richard could stand it no more. He looked out the window, but he saw nothing suspicious.

He decided to go to his bench where he could think more clearly and see everyone that was around him. It was a full moon, and the call was upon him.

As Richard walked out of the room, the young girl came over to him again. She looked at his bag and asked, "Are you a doctor mister?" Richard answered, "No, I am an artist. Some day, I might show you my work." He laughed as the girl followed. "If you show me your work, I might show you some of mine." She said. Richard could not believe his luck. He was surely one of the chosen. He thought, why would these lovers always arrive when he needed them the most? He was truly a god. He walked with the girl to his favorite bench. On the way the girl kept up a whirl of conversation, Richard hardly heard it. She asked if they could get some food, and Richard suggested the Beer Garden. He would listen for news about the big girl.

As he crossed the street to go to the entrance he froze. He saw Dee Dee at the grill. He turned around and went back up to the boardwalk. The young girl followed. She said, "Wow mister you look like you saw a ghost." Richard reached into his pocket and pulled out the wad of bills. The girl's eyes opened wide when she saw the money.

He gave her twenty dollars, and he told her, "Here go inside and get us some food and a couple of soda's. My leg hurts. I won't be able to sit in those small chairs. It's an old war wound. Bring the food to the last bench at the end of the boardwalk, and we can continue our date." The girl nodded, and left for the Beer Garden thinking how lucky she was to grab this man before the other girls got to him. She was tempted to take the twenty dollars and run away, but she felt the lure of the wad of bills the man had put back in his jeans. The money seemed to call to her.

When Doc got back to police headquarters, he called in the rest of the team. He decided to bring in Fizz and his wife and sweat them; he needed to find out about the house, and the mysterious man in the window. Even though it was almost ten at night, he had a gut feeling that something was up.

Why did Fizz go to this house instead of his apartment? Did he know the man holding the skull? Was the man with the skull his partner? They needed the answers to these questions. Johnny Moose agreed. Detective Fowler said, "Separate them; leave Mary with me, and you guys work on Fizz. I will get the whole story in an hour."

When the team united at police headquarters, they split into teams, and one team went to the house Fizz lived at and picked him up. The other team picked up Mary and the pair was brought to police headquarters separately. They kept them apart, and took them to police headquarters in separate cars. They put them in separate rooms on different floors, and the sweating began.

Fizz was drunk and Mary was high on heroin. This could be a great break, if in fact Fizz was lying, and he did know about the murder.

Sgt Mont and Mike took Mary upstairs to the juvenile office for questioning by Detective Fowler, and Johnny Moose and Doc Berg concentrated on Fizz downstairs in the detective bureau. Ray and John went off to get something to eat and catch some Z's. It could be a long night and next day if they did get a break. Pete and Mark took over a surveillance of Richard's house, Buddy and Jeff stayed at police headquarters in case back-up was needed and to help with the paper work.

Fizz held fast and would not break down under questioning, but Arnold was doing better with Mary. He had gotten the first name of the man in the house Fizz went to, it was Richard, and found that Mary was very afraid of him; she said he was a very dangerous person. Mary did not know that there had been a murder. When the two officers showed her pictures of the mutilated girl Mary broke into tears. She sobbed, "That's the kind of thing Richard would do. Fizz would never do something like that." Then, she caught herself, but it was too late.

Downstairs, Fizz was told his wife had said Richard killed the girl, and Fizz only helped hide the body. They told Fizz he could get thirty to fifty years for his part, and that if Richard gave evidence first, and he said Fizz killed the girl Fizz might even get the death penalty. This broke Fizz down, he thought he was too young to die, and he decided to make a deal.

After a two hour statement, the team prepared warrants for Richard Bergerwasser and prepared to execute them, immediately.

Richard was at his bench waiting, the young girl was late. About two hours later she arrived with two soft drinks. "What kept you?" Richard softly asked. The girl answered, "They closed the Beer Garden it was too late to order food so I brought you something to drink." The young girl was thinking dangerous thoughts. She would take Richard under the boardwalk for sex and then, rob him. Then, she would tie him up and ransack his room. That wad of bills looked like several hundred dollars. It would last her for over a week. She was making the worst mistake she could make. She would surely be the one surprised, and the surprise would end her life.

The raid team hit Richard's house, and it was empty. They prepared to search the premises, Doc called in Ray and John to come to the house. When they arrived, he filled them in and sent them to the boardwalk where Fizz said Richard hung out. He gave them a description of Richard and an old picture from the state prison. "Don't do anything if you spot him unless you have to." Doc admonished, "Just call headquarters, wait until we all get there, and we will do it the right way and together. We don't want to lose any evidence."

Dee Dee had gotten off work and did not feel sleepy. For some reason, she wanted to go for a walk on the boardwalk; something drew her to the bench on the south end of the boardwalk. She slowly began her walk to the spot.

The young girl had convinced Richard to go under the boardwalk with her. She had her straight razor hidden in her sleeve. She could drop it into her hand in a flash. Richard could not wait he would enjoy this one very much. He would love her all night if he could.

When the girl entered, she swung quickly to her left and pulled out the razor. She was left handed, and Richard swung the hammer he had retrieved from the sand as he crouched to enter the bowels of the boardwalk, but missed her with the hammer expecting her to turn right. The young girl launched the razor and cut deeply into Richard's left arm as he raised it to block the assault; this caused her to only graze his neck. If Richard had not lifted his left arm quickly she would have slit his throat from ear to ear. Richard opened the doctor's bag, pulled the revolver out, and fired twice, hitting the young girl in the center of her chest. She dropped the razor, looked down at the two small holes in her shirt, and fell to her knees. She stared at Richard as the life drained from her body. She crumpled to the sand dead before she ended her fall.

Richard looked at his arm. The pain was sharp. He took the razor and cut up the young girl's thin jacket. He wrapped the fabric around the cut and duct taped it to hold it together; he taped the home made bandage in place. He tucked the gun in his waist band and closed the doctors bag. He buried it in its usual spot.

Richard felt faint. He needed some air. He walked out on the beach; he took several deep breaths, and began to climb the stairs back up to the boardwalk.

Dee Dee was about a half block from the bench when she saw the bloody figure climb the stairway and walk onto the boardwalk. She froze; it was the face.

Ray and John were just coming on the boardwalk from the street, when they spotted Richard covered with blood coming up from the beach. They were about one hundred feet behind Dee Dee. As Richard recognized the big girl, he smiled and slowly pulled the pistol from his waist band and began to aim at Dee Dee. Ray saw the gun and yelled, "Police, freeze!" he pulled out his gun and took aim at Richard. Dee Dee ducked for cover as she saw the gun in Richard's hand, and Richard turned to aim at the cop. The two men exchanged shots. Both missed. Richard ran for the beach with John and Ray in hard pursuit.

On the beach, Richard made for a fog bank hiding the jetty. The two officers lost him for a moment, but picked him up as he climbed onto the jetty. Richard turned and fired two more shots. John and Ray returned fire and John hit Richard high in the leg. The shot spun Richard around, but he regained his balance. Richard made his way to the end of the jetty, but he slipped on the seaweed covered rocks. He fell down and slipped off the jagged rocky edge into the stormy water. There, he was soon greeted by the creatures that had helped to destroy the remains of his victims for the last several weeks.

They were waiting for there nightly feeding. The creatures gathered around Richard biting at the blood coming from his body then following the trail to dine on his flesh. Richard screamed. The animals that so fiercely helped destroy his lovers were now destroying him. Their onslaught was relentless driven by the blood in the water, and their need to feed quickly whenever food was available. Richard was barely able to cling to the last rock, as he writhed in pain from the creature's attempts to devour him. Their nips and bumps stung him like a swarm of bees. He began to weaken from the loss of blood, and he was losing his grip on the rocks. He began to slip into the depths of the sea.

John jumped into the water and grabbed Richard by the collar just as he was going down. Ray joined them, and the two young cops pulled the torn and bleeding Richard onto the jetty.

Dee Dee ran to a phone booth and called police headquarters for help. She told the desk sergeant that two officers needed help, and there was shooting. The police and first aid arrived within minutes. The paramedics helped Ray and John stop the bleeding from Richard's wounds. His clothes were in tatters, and he had sustained bites all over his lower body. Some were very deep and severe. Richard was cuffed then, put on a gurney and he, John, and Ray were transported to the hospital.

At the hospital, the full extent of Richard's injuries were visible. He would loose part of one leg, it was so badly bitten and the bones were broken from the shot that the doctors were unable to save it. One of the fingers on his left hand had been chewed to a stub as well as his groin area on the left side because of the bloody wound in his left leg, he was severely mutilated. His testicles and his penis had been mangled. The doctors and nurses were able to close the wounds and stabilize his condition. Beth, the head nurse, commented to Ray, "This one will probably live but he will never rape again." Richard had bites over most of the left leg and lower left side. He would be in severe pain for a long time, but he would live to go to trial.

Ray and John were cold and bruised but were treated and released from the hospital that night. Mark and Pete were sent to guard Richard who was given a special room.

Doc Berg and Sergeant Mont came to get Ray and John. They were debriefed at police headquarters by detective Fowler, and the proper reports were filed. The team was congratulated for their hard work. Chief Tillman was pleased. The Mayor and the community were much relieved, and the people in the community felt much safer. They were happy to have solved the brutal murder of the alley girl, but could not believe what was to come from the investigation.

Dee Dee stopped seeing the face at night when she slept. She had formed a friendship with Frank Solomon and loved his dog Kiddo. They would even live together for a while, but would eventually they would go their own ways.

The runaways in the city would find it a little safer for a time.

# THE EPILOGUE

O f the items recovered in the raid on Richard's house, there were five skulls. Four of them had been made into lamps and one had been polished, varnished and stored under Richard's bed. They were taken and sent to the F.B.I. lab in Virginia to be fleshed out by Facial Reconstructionist from Georgetown University.

The first two to come back were identified by Tony and Mike as "Pizza Face Gina" a particularly unpleasant young hooker believed to have been a rejected Biker Girl. No further identification could be made. The second was positively identified by the two officers as a girl known to them as Johanna Stevens. The problem was that Johanna Stevens had lived in a neighboring town and had died many years before Richard came to town at six years old.

The second pair of skulls came back. No officers could Identify them for sure, but Mary Beeman could. They belonged to Darla and Dina Christianson, the two sisters who disappeared before they could pick up their High School Equivalency Diploma's. It upset Mary to see them like this. She left the building very sad. She went home and cried herself to sleep.

Mary was called in to view the last skull when it came back. She was hesitant, but knew that she must. She went with Arnold. When the box was opened, it shocked everyone in the room. Staring at the people with a look of innocence was the face they had all been looking at for many years. It belonged to Janet Morrow the lost niece of Horace Gamboll the billionaire. It was Mary's missing young friend. Mary looked into the girls eyes and froze, as her knees buckled, and she burst into tears. Arnold ran to her, and caught her as she fell into his arms. She cried on his shoulder. In a few minutes, she composed herself and stopped her sobbing. She looked up into Arnolds eyes and softly said, "I hope that monster burns in the hottest corner of hell for all eternity!" Arnold hugged her and the pair left the building together.

Arnold had proposed to Mary, and they had set an informal date to get married. The old zest for life and its adventures was returning to the young woman. The pair just realized that they were made for each other. They enjoyed being together so much that it was only natural for them to get married, but they both agreed it was best to wait.

Even if the searing sterilizing sun could cleanse the shore town of the brutal past, the memory of this troubled time would never go away.

The reign of terror, for the runaways who come to the city down the shore to try and start a new and better life, has been brought to an end. The city appears safer, but can it ever be safe for the many potential victims, who come to the shore city with wide eyed enthusiasm, only to find that it is the same as the struggle they left; the only difference being the faces are new, and the area is changed.

The lives and adventures of the men and women who protect the people who live in the city will continue forever. The interaction between the protectors, the victims, and the predators is what makes the city alive. Every era will have its monsters, and every story will define the city, its people, and the era in which it took place. They become the memories that we carry in our hearts until we perish, and are they become the tales our friends and relatives tell about us in our memory.

Fizz started talking after Richard was arrested, and he didn't stop. He was so afraid he would get the death penalty that he gave everything up. He made a deal for the promise that the prosecutor would not go for the death penalty. He was more than co-operative.

The state called in a Clinical Psychologist, Dr. Craig Kourham, to examine Richard. After an extensive examination, he ruled that Richard was in fact sane and fit for trial. He also stated that he believed Richard knew right from wrong when he committed his atrocities. He asked to be allowed to go along with the investigators to Richard's grandmother's house so he could talk to her about Richard. This request was granted, and the doctor followed the parade of people to Mrs. Bergerwasser's home in Staten Island.

The investigators found the remains of seventy-eight different victims in Richard's mother's garden along with several marijuana plants Fizz had planted on several of his visits.

After talking to Mrs. Bergerwasser for an hour and getting nowhere, Dr. Kourham asked her if he could hypnotize her. He sensed she was hiding something. When she agreed, with the promise that he would never reveal to anyone what she might tell him while she was under hypnosis, he was overjoyed; he agreed to her terms and the necessary paperwork was filled out and signed. After his interview with the old woman, the Doctor walked out of the house in a daze; he was stunned. He could never have been prepared for the story that Mrs. Bergerwasser was to convey to him while under hypnosis.

It seemed that Mr. Bergerwasser was a serious child molester. He had sexually abused Richard's real mother, his daughter, since she was five years old. When he found out she was pregnant at thirteen, he ordered Mrs. Bergerwasser to take their daughter to get an abortion. Mrs. Bergerwasser was a good Catholic and refused to have her daughter do such a thing. Mr. Bergerwasser flew into a rage, and beat both his wife and daughter severely then, he went out and got drunk for three days. He returned drunk and told the women that the abortion was set up, and he would take the pair of them to Pennsylvania this weekend to take care of the matter. He then went to bed. He fell into a heavy drunken slumber.

That night, Mrs. Bergerwasser carefully took her husbands .38 special out of the safe and loaded it. She calmly went upstairs, put the gun in her husbands hand, cocked it, then placed the barrel against the drunken man's ear, and pulled the trigger. After the shot, she let the hand with the gun fall where it may, went to the bathroom, and took a shower. Afterwards, she got dressed and called the police.

The death was declared a suicide. The old woman never told anyone not even Richard or her daughter.

She let her daughter have the child, and after the baby was born she sent her daughter to live with her sister in California. Mrs. Bergerwasser then, formally adopted Richard and raised him as her own. Her daughter died several years after moving to California of a drug overdose, and the only other person who knew the story of Richard's parentage died with her. True to his word, Dr. Kourham would never tell another soul. The secret of Richard's grandmother's act, and his true parentage would remain hidden.

The city was again safer for its young residents, but only for a time. Runaways continued to arrive and this time, most passed along safely as they wandered through. These ingenuous young people can never be safe for they are forever the victims of their own enthusiasm.

Dee Dee stayed another year. She did not find what she was missing with Frank, they parted as friends, and finally, she left for California. She corresponded continually with Mary Beeman, and in one of her letters, she asked her to tell Frank Solomon that she had fallen in love with a farmer in New Mexico, and she never made it to California. The big girl had settled down on the farm and was pregnant with her first of hopefully many children.

Richard was convicted of thirteen murders and got thirteen death penalties. He was still appealing when the governor commuted all death penalties in the state to life in prison without provision for parole. Fizz got sixty years for his part in the crimes, and his wife, Mary, got ten years.

Most of the victims could not be positively identified. The remains of the few that were would be turned over to their relatives for proper burial.

Richard was crippled and will live in constant pain. He has since contracted cancer, and is gradually being eaten away by the disease. Hopefully he will rot to death slowly and painfully in prison. If so then there is a God.

Arnold and Mary set a date to be married, but keep postponing it. They still have not married. They really love each other and may eventually marry, but they figure why rush.

The City Down the Shore just took this in stride. It just ended one era and started another. Every day starts new in every city, and the saga that is the history of the city is never-ending. Things will get better, and things will get worse, but the people always find a way to carry on. Nature will always prevail.

Five years after Richard was sent to prison he was diagnosed with a slow acting painful cancer. The state was required by law to provide him with some treatment. The State Supreme Court ordered after a long and heated court battle that the state to provide him with radiation and chemo therapy.

A short time lafter the treatments began a prisoner transport van seemed to be abandoned in the Hackensack Medical Center out patient parking lot next to the Cancer Treatment Center. It was near where the cancer outpatients came for chemo therapy treatments. The van and its occupants had been the subject of a statewide search for two days. It had remained there in the parking lot over night. The next day the out patients began to complain about it. One of the patients complained about the vehicle taking up two parking spaces, another patient complained it had been that way since yesterday, and a third complained it stunk badly all around the van. The patient was worried it might contain toxic waste. Dr. Stoner called in his secretary, and asked her to send a memo to security to have the van checked out. She nodded and returned to her desk. She sat down, and she began to finish the Jumble game in the local newspaper. She put the note in a folder; she put it inside the top drawer of her desk. It would be several weeks before she remembered to send the information to the security department.

Printed in the United States
101252LV00003B/190/A